# Knowledge Leadership: The Art and Science of the Knowledge-Based Organization

**KNOWLEDGE
MANAGEMENT
CONSORTIUM
INTERNATIONAL**

About KMCI Press
Powerful Knowledge for Knowledge Professionals

KMCI Press is an exciting publishing partnership that unites the Knowledge Management Consortium International (KMCI), the leading organization for knowledge management professionals, and Butterworth-Heinemann's Business group and Digital Press imprints, one of the premier publishers of knowledge management books.

KMCI Press publishes authoritative and innovative books that educate all knowledge management communities, from students and beginning professionals to chief knowledge officers. KMCI Press books present definitive and leading-edge ideas of the KMCI itself, and bring clarity and authoritative information to a dynamic and emerging profession.

KMCI Press books explore the opportunities, demands, and benefits knowledge management brings to organizations and defines important and emerging knowledge management disciplines and topics, including:

- Professional roles and functions
- Vertical industry best practices and applications
- Technologies, including knowledge portals and data and document management
- Strategies, methodologies, and decision-making frameworks

The Knowledge Management Consortium International (KMCI) is the only major not for profit member organization specifically for knowledge management professionals, with thousands of worldwide members including individuals in the professional and academic fields as well as leading companies, institutions, and other organizations concerned with knowledge management, organizational change, and intellectual capital.

For information about submitting book proposals, please see our website at http://www.kmci.org

# KNOWLEDGE LEADERSHIP

## The Art and Science of the Knowledge-Based Organization

STEVEN CAVALERI AND SHARON SEIVERT

WITH

LEE W. LEE

ELSEVIER
BUTTERWORTH
HEINEMANN

AMSTERDAM • BOSTON • HEIDELBERG
LONDON • NEW YORK • OXFORD
PARIS • SAN DIEGO • SAN FRANCISCO
SINGAPORE • SYDNEY • TOKYO
Butterworth Heinemann is an imprint of Elsevier

KNOWLEDGE
MANAGEMENT
CONSORTIUM
INTERNATIONAL

Project Manager: Carl M. Soares
Cover Art: "Daybreak" by Salvadorean painter Jose Mario España (www.marioespana.com)

Elsevier Butterworth–Heinemann
30 Corporate Drive, Suite 400, Burlington, MA 01803, USA
Linacre House, Jordan Hill, Oxford OX2 8DP, UK

**Library of Congress Cataloging-in-Publication Data**
Cavaleri, Steven.
  Knowledge leadership / Steven Cavaleri, Sharon Seivert, Lee W. Lee.
    p. cm.
  Includes bibliographical references.
  1. Knowledge management. I. Seivert, Sharon. II. Lee, Lee W. III. Title.
  HD30.2.C43 2005
  658.4'038—dc22
                          2004028098


**British Library Cataloguing-in-Publication Data**
A catalogue record for this book is available from the British Library.

ISBN: 0-7506-7840-2

For information on all Elsevier Butterworth–Heinemann publications
visit our Web site at www.books.elsevier.com

Printed in the United States of America
05 06 07 08 09 10   10 9 8 7 6 5 4 3 2 1

# DEDICATION

We dedicate this book to the memories of Arthur Koestler
and Charles Sanders Peirce in grateful appreciation
for their inspiration.

# Table of Contents

# Part IV

## DEVELOPING PRAGMATIC KNOWLEDGE          155

# Part V

## LEADING *FAST* KNOWLEDGE-BASED
## ORGANIZATIONS (KBOs)          221

# Part VI

## PUTTING IT ALL TOGETHER          303

# FOREWORD

BY GEORGE ROTH, LEAN AEROSPACE INITIATIVE,
MIT SLOAN SCHOOL OF MANAGEMENT

This book takes the reader on a journey into a new territory. It was not long ago that most firms focused exclusively on behaviors and attitudes of managers and employees as the lever for improving organizational effectiveness. The role of knowledge—creating, deploying, transferring, depositing and retrieving know-how—is inextricably tied to organizational effectiveness. Leadership sets direction, manages change and establishes capabilities for organizational performance and improvement. *Knowledge Leadership: The Art and Science of the Knowledge-based Organization* brings together philosophy, theory and literature on knowledge management and experience with leadership styles to chart a new course of thinking and action.

In J.R.R. Tolkien's Trilogy, *The Lord of the Rings*, Frodo takes on the responsibility of destroying the ring before it falls into the wrong hands—a quest necessary to save Middle Earth from certain rule by evil. Having set themselves to the heroic task of assisting Frodo, the nine companions that make up the Fellowship of the Ring strike out from idyllic Rivendell only to find themselves filled with doubt. They doubt themselves, each other, and their ability to survive this treacherous journey. During their passage over the mountains, the heroes are constantly attacked by their watchful enemies and exposed to fierce winds, blizzards, and avalanches. They turn back, thinking of returning to the safety of Rivendell. The alternative, to go through the mountains, is fraught with unknown dangers in the dark confines of the Mines of Moria. They come to the entrance of a vast underground cave, the Doors of Durin. As they puzzle them open, the black water of the nearby lake seethes. A hideous stench overtakes them, and a long sinuous tentacle grabs Frodo, the ringbearer. His dedicated friend, Sam, jumps into the dark water to slash him free, and the Fellowship retreats through the doors and into the mountain. A crashing rockslide seals off the entrance—and their way back.

Now they *must* now go forward and face un-heard of terrors. There is no room for doubt; they have to depend upon themselves and each other.

As Tolkien's classic story illustrates, accomplishing a heroic leadership task often requires having no choice. Once Cavaleri and Seivert have brought knowledge and leadership together, the power of their combination sets forth a path from which there can be no turning back for managers. As co-authors, Steven Cavaleri and Sharon Seivert are fitting guides for this journey. Together they embody a complete action learning cycle. Cavaleri's university teaching, research experience, editorial leadership for *The Learning Organization: An International Journal*, editorial service for *The Journal of Knowledge Management*, and past Presidency of The Knowledge Management Consortium International provide a depth and breadth of knowledge about knowledge. Seivert's experience as CEO, entrepreneur, and business advisor gives an action-orientation that is grounded in first-hand understanding of managerial challenges and performance demands. In addition, her books on leadership archetypes provide a strong foundation for the analytic examination and development of principles for the leadership of knowledge.

The co-authors take a unique approach—turning to philosopher Arthur Koestler's 1945 book *The Yogi and the Commissar*—to examine leadership. The Yogi and Commissar represent contrasting, but potentially complementary mental models that result in different leadership styles that are particularly applicable for knowledge leadership. What we learn from their examination of leaders is that each archetypical style has strengths as well as weaknesses; they need to be combined to create a more robust whole.

As philosopher James Carse (1986) reminds us, there are two different possible visions of life. One vision is that of a finite game, played for the purpose of wining. Life, play, business and all activities approached from the perspective of a finite game comes to a definite and conclusive end. A winner is declared and the activity is over until a new one begins. The contrasting vision is that of an infinite game. An infinite game is played for the purpose of continuing the play. To keep the activity going, and participants involved, people with a vision of an infinite game change rules, adjust the boundaries, develop strength, generate time, and aim to create something eternal. The vision of an infinite game is particularly appropriate to the concepts of leadership and knowledge set in organizations. Leaders need to develop their own and others' strengths so that the organization continually learns, develops and applies its knowledge. The notion of integrating the divergent worldviews of the Yogi and Commissar is about changing the rules and boundaries for which we think about leadership and knowledge based on the vision of an infinite game.

Replete with explanations, self-diagnosic tests, frameworks, and ways of explaining knowledge and its integration into practice, with anchors in philosophy and management research, *Knowledge Leadership* makes a thoughtful companion to organizational programs and activities for improving effectiveness. The basis for that improvement is a knowledge strategy and capability that executives lead. These leaders can benefit from diagnosis of their learning, perceptual, and leadership style using *The Knowledge Bias Profile*. These leaders are then better able to change their firms into organizations that are *functional, adaptable, sustainable,* and *timely (FAST)*. FAST firms organize around their knowledge to drive performance and achieve results that competitors cannot replicate. This book helps managers make that link between leadership and the development of knowledge-based initiatives.

While investigating cultural factors that undergird knowledge-producing systems, I studied the rapid developments in radar at MIT prior to and during World War II. I sought to learn more about the culture of MIT at that time by interviewing Jay Forrester, founder of the field of system dynamics and pioneer in computing. He had arrived at MIT in 1940 to work as a research assistant in developing servomechanisms for radar antennas. In interviewing Forrester, I explained my interests and asked him to recall his experience when he came to MIT. I was particularly interested in, using my framing, the culture at MIT—how the institution supported what you could do and relationships among people working on the development of radar. Professor Forrester quickly corrected me. That environment allows people to develop great visions, he said, but these visions do not come from a group. A faculty and staff member could do essentially anything that was honorable and for which he could raise the money. Individual people did what they felt necessary within an environment of free enterprise and no inhibitions about dealing with the outside world. Theory and new ideas were only as good as the working results.

To illustrate, Forrester described the SAGE (Semi-Automatic Ground Environment) air defense system. Developed in the 1950's, it operated until decommissioned in 1983. The SAGE system had 35 control centers, each 160 feet square containing 60,000 vacuum tubes, all contained in identical four story buildings. People criticized the concept as too complex to operate reliably (vacuum tubes had a

500 hour life). However, engineers addressed these issues, made changes to vacuum tubes, and designed the system for reliability. In 25 years of operation, the centers were operational 99.8% of the time (a center was out of operation only about 20 hours per year).

How was this performance possible? Forrester explained that organizations run based on stories. If you go into a corporation that is uniquely different in some way and ask why it is so, the answer that invariably comes back is, "let me tell you a story." That story illustrates the culture. Where do the stories come from? They usually come from the top. For example, here was a man named Bertram who was head of the Power Equipment division of Raytheon. He had been a submarine man; it gave him a keen appreciation for why you wanted your equipment to work. He absolutely, without any compromises, insisted that he was only going to turn out equipment that he would be willing to receive.

In this example, the new radar set had met its design specifications. The Navy had approved it; the production prototype was complete and tested. It was exactly what the Navy wanted. There was nothing left to do before releasing it to the factory except to get together with the dozen people who had led the development. People assembled around the conference table. The production prototype was in the corner of the conference room. It was a big piece of equipment, six feet high and six feet wide. Bertram came in and took his place at the head of the table. He looked over at the prototype, scanned around the people in the room, looked at the radar set, and did not say a word. Then he got up out of his chair, used some things on the front of the device for a ladder, and climbed up on top of the device. He climbed back down, reached over and broke off two pieces of the front. He said, "Take it away. You may think it's ready to manufacture. The Navy may have approved it, it may have passed all its specs, but you don't make that junk in my factory." Right at the last minute before production Bertram declared: It is not up to our standards, we are not going to make it, even if the Navy wants it next week. He had been in the Navy. He knew that in the field an engineer would end up climbing on the machine, just as he had done.

Forrester made his point, "Bertram's action at this meeting resulted in reliable radar sets for the next twenty years." That action alone spoke loudly; nothing else would have done. Carelessness and the influx of other people's standards had begun to show up. Bertram's standards had to be reinforced. People told this story over and over again as they developed new radar sets. If Bertram had said: "We shouldn't have built it this way, but the Navy wants it and they have approved it and let's not do it again this way, but go ahead," he would have destroyed the culture. It takes years to build culture up, but you can tear it down in a week.

Was Bertram's leadership style that of a Yogi or a Commissar? My opinion is that it embodies both—taking bold action and being reflective about that action and its consequences. These are the kinds of considerations that Cavaleri and Seivert describe as being necessary to lead the sustainable, effective, knowledge-based organizations of the future. *Knowledge Leadership* provides practical tools for diagnosis and new frameworks for thinking that will help leaders chart a heroic path forward that brings together balanced leadership and pragmatic knowledge to build *FAST*, competitive organizations.

## REFERENCES

Carse, J. (1986) *Finite and Infinite Games* Ballantine Books: New York.

Forrester, J. (1992) "From the Ranch to System Dynamics: An Autobiography," in Bedeian, A. (ed) *Management Laureates: A Collection of Autobiographical Essays*, Vol. 1. JAI Press.

Tolkien, J.J.R. (1954) *The Fellowship of the Ring* Houghton Mifflin Company: New York.

# ACKNOWLEDGEMENTS

We would like to thank the many people who contributed significantly over the years to the development of *Knowledge Leadership*.

Lee W. Lee, for working with us to develop the *Knowledge Leadership Profile*, overseeing its testing and development, and contributing to the writing of Chapter Six.

Blake Zhang, not only for administering the KBP questionnaire in China, but also for securing the two Chinese business groups who participated in our study.

Joseph Firestone, of KMCI Press, for his support and helpful editorial recommendations on the manuscript.

Mark McElroy, for his collaboration in developing the patent-pending Policy Synchronization Method and for his innovative work in the field of KM.

A. Russell Fanelli, for his encouragement and belief in the importance of our work.

Fred Reed, Howard Seidel, and Anne Gilman, for reading earlier versions of this book and making such excellent suggestions for improving its content and readability.

Mario España, for permission to use his original oil painting, "Daybreak," as the cover art for *Knowledge Leadership*.

All of the more than five hundred business people and management students in the United States and China, for participating in the KBP research.

And finally, from Elsevier we would like to thank Karen Maloney, Carl Soares, and Dennis McGonagle for their consummate professionalism and enthusiastic support in making this book a reality.

# Part I

# Why Should You Care about Knowledge?

# 1

# The Knowledge Leadership Challenge

Although the vast majority of knowledge management experts stress the importance of knowledge processes and investing in people's capacity for creating new knowledge, most corporate leaders have instead chosen to invest heavily in the information technology (IT) aspects of knowledge management (KM) and virtually ignore the advice of these experts. This tendency reflects the fact that *information* has become increasingly viewed in the business world as being synonymous with *knowledge*. However, as we demonstrate in this book, there is often a high cost to be paid when companies blur the lines between information and knowledge. We suggest that leaders who fail to see the important distinctions between knowledge and information will be unable to effectively help their organizations capitalize on the power of knowledge for sustaining high performance.

How did knowledge become a synonym for information? What is going on? Some critics might argue that KM has taken a wrong turn along the way. We propose in this book that this is not exactly the case. Rather, many versions of KM are being practiced in the world today because KM has evolved in a self-organizing way. As a result, many interesting KM variations have developed, ranging from the simplest to the most complex strategies. Some organizations have made knowledge the focus of their business strategy, whereas other companies view knowledge as being simply a tool for improving profits.

What is most important to note is that a new and very exciting kind of knowledge-based strategy has evolved in elite companies— one that is providing them with increasing competitive advantage. This is not to say that other forms of KM are useless; that is hardly the case. However, we contend that companies that limit their use of knowledge to low-impact forms of KM will be progressively less able to remain viable when locked in head-to-head competition with companies that have mastered a more "pragmatic" knowledge strategy.

3

*Pragmatic* knowledge is situation-specific knowledge, developed over time, that helps leaders understand what actually works in practice—and also why it works, and under what circumstances. One of the major theses of this book is that leaders must use both "science" and "art" to develop and improve the pragmatic knowledge that will enable them to become well-balanced knowledge leaders who can build *knowledge-based organizations* (KBOs). Unfortunately, although many leaders try to manage their companies scientifically, they have been taught so-called "scientific" management theories that are often based in ideas long abandoned by modern scientists. Indeed, most leaders today still manage their organizations based on the 19th century "scientific management" principles of Frederick Taylor (1865–1915) who was a mechanical engineer, not a scientist. In *Knowledge Leadership* we present a more contemporary scientific knowledge-based approach to managing that is founded upon the principles of *pragmatism*. Pragmatic knowledge is the product of a scientific approach to learning from experience, employing various methods of reasoning, and interpreting the meaning of situations. Using this knowledge-based way of making business decisions transforms managing into an ongoing experiment of discovering the underlying patterns of cause and effect that reveal what is likely to work best in practice. This is the foundation of developing pragmatic knowledge in organizations. By developing this kind of high-quality knowledge, over time and through experience, leaders are able to give their companies a significant competitive edge—in other words, a knowledge advantage.

In this book we also provide several ways to develop the *art* of knowledge leadership. In particular, we help leaders to assess their current *knowledge leadership style* so that they can attain the balance they will need to both develop and manage knowledge in their organizations. To this end, we introduce readers to two colorful, distinctly different leadership styles that are personified by two memorable characters: the action-oriented "infrared" Commissar (who prefers to design systems for *managing* knowledge in organizations) and the introspective "ultraviolet" Yogi (who prefers to help others *develop* new knowledge). We will also provide leaders with a new way of interpreting problem symptoms. Pragmatists believe that this is the most essential part of problem solving, and that it is vital to understand what the problem really is before taking actions to improve any kind of performance.

In 1990, Peter Senge published the book *The Fifth Discipline: The Art and Practice of the Learning Organization*. This best-selling book significantly increased interest worldwide in the topics of organizational learning, business dynamics, and systems thinking. The book deftly integrated the scientific method of policy analysis (through the use of the system dynamics method) with the art of learning from experience.

It is no accident that this book provided a major breakthrough in both leadership and managerial thinking. In *Knowledge Leadership*, it is our intention to provide a framework for an even deeper analysis that will fuel further improvements in personal and organizational performance. We call this next level of leadership development *the art and science of the knowledge-based organization*. We will approach this challenge by "standing on the shoulders of giants"—by building on the work of the intellectual leaders who have preceded us in the fields of management, philosophy, and science. We will draw on the insights gained over the past century in diverse fields, such as philosophical pragmatism, Total Quality Management (TQM), knowledge management (KM), systems theory, organizational learning, science, history, political theory, and the social sciences. In the upcoming pages, we will provide you, the reader, with a guide that will take you forward into what is likely to be an exciting, unexplored territory. However, the decision to take this learning journey will require some degree of "heroism" on your part. It requires you to depart from the well-beaten paths of accepted management practices so that you can step into less-well charted leadership territory. We invite you to join us on this journey. We believe you will be well rewarded with new insights and ways of thinking about what it means to lead a business.

## ENTERING THE SECOND DECADE OF THE KM MOVEMENT

It has been more than a decade since Karl Wiig's (1993) pioneering book, *Knowledge Management Foundations*, was first published. Over the past dozen years, KM has become a critical strategy used by many companies to improve their performance and adaptability. KM's rise to prominence reflects the leading edge of a major shift in the way leaders view organizations. Leaders are much less likely to regard their workforce as being simply a collection of individuals charged with executing a set of management directives. Rather, employees are increasingly being seen as *knowledge workers* and potential problem solvers. In companies where problem solving is considered to be the most valuable kind of work, knowledge is the coin of the realm.

Astutely, many leaders have also discerned that it is not sufficient to simply provide employees with just any knowledge. They have realized that there is a need to provide workers with easy access to as many kinds of knowledge as possible. In many organizations, there has been a rush to acquire technologies that will assist employees of all sorts in gaining access to knowledge as well as in sharing it. This new worldview mirrors a sea change in conventional managerial wisdom that is no less significant to organizations than was the adoption of electricity and machinery in the industrial factories of Western Europe and America at the start of the 19th century.

Corporate leaders of household names such as 3M, Best Buy, BMW, BP Amoco, Canon, Fuji-Xerox, Hewlett Packard, Intel, Nokia, Siemens, Royal Dutch Shell, Sony, Toyota, UniLever, and Xerox routinely speak of the importance of knowledge to their long-term success. Some of these businesses, such as 3M, Toyota, and Xerox, have become much more than companies that use KM. They have transformed themselves into elite knowledge-based organizations (KBOs). Leaders of KBOs do not seek to *manage knowledge* within their companies; rather, they seek to *knowledgeably manage* for competitive advantage. This is a critical distinction for knowledge leaders of KM's second decade to understand if they are to transform their organizations into KBOs that use knowledge to achieve performance than cannot easily be duplicated by their competitors.

This distinction may seem subtle at first. However, the consequences of making this shift of mind are critical for success. Now that we are entering "daybreak" of the new *knowledge era*, the rules for using knowledge in business are changing. KM initially became popular because it was seen as being a useful tool for leveraging existing assets and increasing profits. Leaders who recognized the potential of this strategy to boost profits invested heavily in KM technologies because the return on investment seemed compelling to them. Other leaders, however, saw the potential role of knowledge in their companies more broadly—for example, as the basis for a comprehensive strategic approach to managing that could be integrated with TQM, lean manufacturing, innovation, and organizational learning initiatives to form the foundation of a powerfully distinctive business strategy.

Companies that employed this more comprehensive strategy used knowledge differently than the way it was being used in most companies that had jumped on the KM bandwagon. Instead, they embraced philosophies, practices, and strategies that would be considered heresy among their competitors. However, as a result of taking this alternative knowledge path, they are now achieving performance results that their rivals can only dream about. The chief example of this new breed of knowledge-based organization is the Japanese automobile manufacturer Toyota. Toyota has achieved mind-boggling performance results that are, in part, attributable to the way the company uses organizational learning and pragmatic knowledge.

Although the pragmatic knowledge strategy is a powerful one, we estimate that it is being used by less than 5% of all major corporations. However, without exception, these are elite businesses whose leaders understand the value of knowledge in a profound way, and who therefore have made long-term commitments to mastering the use of knowledge for gaining strategic competitive advantage. Though it can be argued that these companies are elite in many respects (such as customer relationship management, product and process innovation, managing quality, and strategy analysis), we propose that what differentiates these companies from their rivals is their proven capacity for knowledge leadership.

Knowledge leadership extends well beyond KM. Knowledge leaders integrate KM with *knowledge development* (KD) and make certain that knowledge is woven into the very fabric of an organization—its operations, management systems, and infrastructures. Because knowledge can significantly improve a company's performance and viability, we ask: Why have so few leaders chosen the path of knowledge leadership?

## CAN'T GET THERE FROM HERE

The simple answer to this question is that most leaders are not fully aware of the potential of knowledge for transforming organizations. Another answer is that new KM strategies often require greater capacity or a higher level of sophistication than is found in many companies. Yet another answer, probably the most important one, lies in the way the field of KM has developed.

The word *knowledge* often conjures up images of the ivy-covered walls of academe and esoteric theories of long-forgotten philosophers. Not surprisingly then, the gut reaction of many managers upon hearing proposals for knowledge-based initiatives is to raise a yellow flag of caution. Fortunately for the field of KM, computers, software, and support technologies (such as optical scanning devices, the Internet, and telecommunications technologies) had evolved by the end of the 20th century. These sophisticated tools facilitated a brand of KM that was very structured, easy to implement, and low risk. In conjunction with process-oriented approaches that evolved out of the TQM and project management movements (such as sharing best practices and post-project review sessions), the necessary infrastructure had emerged to make KM an attractive method for tapping into a company's intangible assets in a way that made sense to executives. That is, it appeared to give them more bang for the buck. The idea of drilling for intellectual oil or prospecting for knowledge gold was made even more palatable as computer and software companies developed full lines of products to fulfill this need.

Why was all this so fortunate for the field of KM? We believe that without these developments, KM would not exist today on such a wide scale, because many companies would have found knowledge-oriented pursuits to be too esoteric and risky to pursue. The problem that most leaders have faced since the beginning of the KM movement is that the most popular KM strategies are self-limiting and rarely confer benefits of sustainable competitive advantage on companies. The relative simplicity and low risk of conventional KM make it a double-edge sword. It is simultaneously attractive to companies because it is low risk, but it also is something that virtually any company can do.

However, sustainable competitive advantage usually comes from being able to execute strategies that are exceedingly difficult for business rivals to successfully duplicate. Unfortunately, most corporate leaders do not view KM from a strategic perspective; therefore, they do not think of the self-limiting tendencies we have described as being a problem. For these companies, KM is accomplished by using a "Cheez Whiz" strategy.

## CHEEZ WHIZ, YOU SAY?

Did you know that the myth of Earth's moon being made of aged cheese is more than 400 years old? This belief, first popularized in the mid-16th century among European peasants, held that the moon was made of aged cheese similar to French bleu cheese or the Italian gorgonzola cheese–because sometimes the lines that crisscross the moon's surface look similar to the bluish green veins found in these cheeses. Clearly, this was an illusion, but the aged cheese explanation enabled the peasants to make sense of the moon they watched in their night sky. While KM has nothing to do with aged cheese per se, you will learn as you read ahead that it has much to do with myth and illusion.

The success of Kraft Food's popular Cheez Whiz can reveal much about how knowledge is often viewed by managers in many organizations. In the 1950s, Kraft Foods was well known for its production of cheeses such as Cracker Barrel and Kraft Deluxe sliced American cheese. At the time, cheese processing focused on producing the harder, whiter types of cheeses because they represented the vast majority of the market demand. The soft, formless yellow cheese that was a by-product of the production process was disposed of after the harder cheeses were processed. There was no apparent use for this leftover cheese—and it was difficult to package due to its softness.

All this changed when a Kraft employee had the brilliant idea of selling the cheese by-product in jars under the brand name *Cheez Whiz*. Because the soft yellow cheese was heavier, it tended to sink to the bottom of the cheese-processing vats, whereas the harder, whiter cheeses stayed at the top of the vat and were the first to be removed. This allowed the remaining cheese to be easily harvested without any further effort. The new product was successfully marketed in a way that emphasized its potential usefulness both for cooking and as a spread. This innovation was a brilliant breakthrough for Kraft, because it enabled the company to utilize and profit from what had previously been waste. In economic terms, this innovation enabled Kraft to achieve greater *asset utilization*. Through innovative packaging and marketing, Kraft was able to transform an unused asset into a high-performing asset.

What does all of this have to do with KM? The central strategy in both cases is the same. KM is often practiced in a way that is based on the idea expressed by managers that "We have all of this unused knowledge, we might as well tap into it, find an application for it, and recycle it."

## GREEN KM STRATEGIES

When it comes to preserving the natural environment, there are various initiatives worldwide that are designed to recycle consumer disposables and use them in the manufacture of new products. This enables greater conservation of scarce natural resources, such as wood, and may also limit damage to the environment caused by landfills. In general, recycling is a component of what is often referred to as a *Green* strategy for environmental husbandry and conservation.

The concept of recycling plays a critical role in maintaining much of the myth that supports conventional approaches to KM. We will refer to this as the Green KM strategy. The Green KM strategy is to conserve the knowledge that exists within an organization and not waste what has already been created through investments in people. The Green KM strategy relies on such conventional methods as sharing best practices, collect-and-connect systems, and knowledge warehouses. The Green KM strategy is to achieve greater economic utilization of existing intangible assets by *leveraging* them. To leverage intangible KM assets means to get the greatest possible benefit out of what is already in the heads of an organization's employees. The essence of the Green KM strategy is to share existing knowledge within a company over the widest possible audience of employees.

However, such strategies are not truly "green" because the emphasis is placed almost solely on the recycling aspects—without really creating anything new. By contrast, in green environmental strategies, recycled newspapers are used to create other paper products, and recycled plastic is reformed to make new plastic containers. Green KM strategies focus on sharing existing knowledge, but not in using that knowledge to create new, higher-quality knowledge. Still, the economics of KM recycling are attractive to managers due to the low marginal cost of sharing the knowledge. The cost that goes into creating the existing *installed base* of knowledge within a company is essentially a sunk cost. The only variable cost is that related to the cost of extracting and sharing the knowledge. As the rate of recycling knowledge rises, the marginal costs associated with sharing and leveraging intangible assets declines.

Clearly, the economic and financial justification for using the Green KM strategy is compelling to most managers. Relying on the Green KM strategy does not usually pose a problem as long as a company competes within an industry where all other rivals also practice KM in a non strategic way. More to the point, if you are competing against one of the elite companies that employs KM in a more strategic way, either your company is close to going out of business or you are reading this book because you are seeking a miracle cure for your firm's chronically poor performance.

## DRILLING FOR OIL

Now, let us go to the final myth in our knowledge challenge story. We call this the *KM oil well myth*. For many managers, the greatest breakthrough offered by many so-called KM gurus is to help them see that their companies are literally sitting on top of a "knowledge oil well" that has yet to be tapped. Once a manager accepts this knowledge paradigm, the greatest challenge is to decide which extractive KM technology would be most efficient for getting the most knowledge out of this well at the lowest cost.

The proliferation of KM technologies and consulting firms that specialize in providing extractive processes offers clear evidence to the popularity of this drilling-for-oil approach. The good news for managers employing the KM oil well approach is that these strategies are all potentially supportive of improving profits by leveraging a firm's unused intangible assets. The bad news is that these strategies are self-limiting, superficial, and incapable of conferring long-term strategic competitive advantage.

Although there are many limitations to this approach, the major one is that it is unsustainable. All oil wells eventually go dry. Successful oil companies are adept at finding new places to drill for oil, but eventually those new wells will run dry too. The strategy of drilling endlessly for *knowledge oil* in an organization rarely accomplishes more than making employees aware of knowledge that has been previously hidden from their view. This does not mean that these employees will consider this knowledge relevant to their concerns, or that it will make sense to them, or that the knowledge is useful or of high quality.

Not all knowledge is created equal. Nor is knowledge the same as truth. Moreover, the reliability of most knowledge for producing expected results, for improving performance, is unknown. In other words, not all knowledge is good knowledge. The oil well KM notion of discovering unused knowledge in organizations, tapping it, and sharing it is not only overly simplistic, it is potentially confusing to many employees.

In most companies, managers have accepted KM, believing the conventional wisdom that corporate performance can be improved with the prudent use of technology and sharing best practices to get the right knowledge to the right people at the right time. We propose that this is a myth. Even though conventional KM approaches have the potential to improve performance, they usually do so indirectly and coincidently rather than through more pragmatic strategies.

Though some advocates of mythological conventional KM approaches argue that such strategies are benign and do no harm, we take issue with this myopia. We propose that the hyper competition most businesses face demands a more innovative, performance-driven approach to KM. Focusing an organization's scarce resources and attention on conventional "benign" KM approaches merely diverts leaders from addressing the true challenge of developing a sustainable knowledge-based approach for competing.

What does all of this have to do with knowledge leadership? In our view, making the transformation from using knowledge as a tool to *making knowledge the foundation for an enterprise-wide competitive strategy* is a decision that must be made and implemented by knowledge leaders.

## THE KNOWLEDGE LEADERSHIP CHALLENGE

Although knowledge leadership is not yet a well-known term, we assert that it will become increasingly important as corporations start to see how vital knowledge is to their survival. The new knowledge leaders will bridge the role of managers and leaders by overseeing KM systems and creating supportive workplace environments for *knowledge development* (KD). Knowledge leaders are needed at all levels in their organizations. Knowledge leaders hold the key to improving future business performance. To achieve this goal, knowledge leaders will need to be well balanced: they will create and use knowledge to improve both their own professional effectiveness and the effectiveness of the organizations they lead.

Knowledge leaders will foster the development of high-quality knowledge, which we define here as performance-driven, pragmatic knowledge that has been created from the lessons learned by employees in the course of working. Happily, knowledge leaders will have the advantage of standing on many great knowledge teachers and leaders who, as we will describe in this book, have already blazed the path for them.

The new knowledge leaders will need to organize their companies to be perpetual knowledge-creating systems. Why is this necessary? In the organizations of the Machine Age, the shelf life of knowledge was relatively long. Things were so simple that a few experts could design brilliant systems that sustained the organization for decades. Those days are gone. The demand for new, high-quality knowledge for companies to remain competitive is no longer the exception—it is the rule.

The knowledge leadership challenge, then, is to lead the design of balanced business systems that continually create and use pragmatic knowledge to gain sustainable competitive advantage. In this way, knowledge leaders will transform their companies into *FAST* (*functional, adaptive, sustainable, and timely*) KBOs.

We invite you to use this book to help you explore the challenge—and the great opportunity—of becoming a knowledge leader.

## REFERENCES

Senge, P. (1990). *The Fifth Discipline: The Art & Practice of The Learning Organization*, New York, NY: Doubleday.

Wiig, K. (1993). *Knowledge Management Foundations: Thinking about Thinking—How People and Organizations Create, Represent, and Use Knowledge.* Volume 1 of Knowledge Management Series. Arlington, TX: Schema Press.

# 2

# THE EMERGING ERA OF THE KNOWLEDGE LEADER

## Executive Summary

Knowledge is not synonymous with information, nor is the management of knowledge the same as knowledge leadership. The competitive advantage for businesses in the future will depend on the ability of knowledge leaders to become more balanced in their leadership approach by learning from experience and inspiring others to do the same. In this way, knowledge leaders will help their companies develop *pragmatic knowledge* (the product of a scientific approach to learning from experience). Pragmatic knowledge turns business decision making into an ongoing experiment of discovering cause-and-effect patterns about what works best in practice. Pragmatic knowledge provides a highly effective competitive edge for businesses, which is why *knowledge-based organizations* (KBOs) are already beginning to dominate their industries. Indeed, as we move from the last stage of the Machine Age into "daybreak" of the emerging Knowledge Era, it appears that the corporate winners of the future will be *FAST* (*functional, adaptable, sustainable, and timely*) KBOs. In this chapter, we also discuss the story of how this book came to be written and provide an outline of its chapters.

Although most people acknowledge that dynamic leadership is a critical factor for the success of any organization, leadership and knowledge are rarely mentioned in the same breath. When conversations in the hallways of major corporations turn to the subject of knowledge, the focus is typically on the need to invest in computer networks that ensure the right knowledge gets to the right people at the right time.

14

Unfortunately, knowledge has become synonymous with information, and technology has come to be seen as the critical source of competitive advantage among companies. There was a time in the not too distant past when knowledge was thought to be the province of kindly white-haired, bespectacled scholars who worked in ivy-covered ivory towers. But now, many businesses think of knowledge as a commodity that is distributed by powerful technology throughout the organization in much the same way as mail, office supplies, or announcements of retirement parties.

The excitement that accompanied the advent of KM in the 1990s has given way to the realization that, to be worthwhile, knowledge must provide a source of sustainable competitive advantage. A more chilling discovery for many corporate executives is that if competitors are engaged in similar KM initiatives that simply leverage existing knowledge, they are not gaining any real advantage.

Using knowledge as a source of sustainable competitive advantage is a qualitatively different ballgame, and it requires much more than KM or super information technology systems. Competitive advantage for organizations in the future, we contend, will increasingly depend on knowledge leadership. The challenge for prospective knowledge leaders is to become more balanced in their leadership approach by learning from experience and inspiring others to do the same. Unfortunately, most managers have been trained to rely on data in ways that undermine their development as leaders and stunts their organization's capacity to innovate. In an interview with WalterKiechel and Andrew Grove, Harvard Business School's Clayton Christensen, co-author of *The Innovator's Dilemma* (2003), commented on the need for reform in the current data-driven models of management education:

The problem with the way we teach is that if a student makes a comment in class that isn't grounded in the data in the case, the instructor is trained to crucify her right on the spot. And so we exalt the virtues of data-driven decision making. And then many of the students go to work for consulting firms where they carry data-driven analytical decision making to an nth degree. Thus, in many ways, the whole teaching model condemns managers to act after the game is over. (p. 1)

Knowledge leaders are *both* data driven and informed by their intuitive senses of things as they continually build pragmatic knowledge. Pragmatic knowledge is created by taking a scientific approach to learning from experience; it turns decision making into an experiment of discovering cause-and-effect patterns that govern what works best in practice.

However, in complex systems (including most businesses), cause and effect rarely unfold as a simple, direct, or predictable chain of events. More often, indirect forces also influence outcomes. For example, the transition to becoming a KBO is not a straightforward process of installing the necessary processes and technologies. Everything that a knowledge leader does to create a KBO will be filtered through the company's identity, culture, and existing management systems. These forces can accept, reject, or modify how a new knowledge approach is actually expressed in the company.

So when there is so much at stake, so much competitive advantage to be gained, what could possibly prevent leaders from becoming knowledge leaders? We believe that there are a great many obstacles to becoming a knowledge leader. The first obstacle is a leader's way of seeing the world. For example, why do some leaders focus on exercising control over employees' activities, while others focus on liberating their creativity? Why do some leaders emphasize the importance of efficiency, while others emphasize effectiveness? Why do some leaders view employees as a cost to be economically utilized, while others see these same employees as a source of innovation and profitability? These are the kinds of questions that launched this book many years ago.

On his daily 2-hour drive to and from MIT's Sloan School of Management during 1991 and 1992, Steve Cavaleri mused about leadership and organizational issues. As a visiting scholar at the Learning Center, Steve was brought into regular contact with some of the greatest minds in organizational learning, such as Amy Edmondson, Ed Nevis, George Roth, and Peter Senge. These people agreed that organizational leaders were being confronted by opposing forces that made their work exceedingly complex and difficult. As a result of this complexity, actions that appeared to improve things at first, sometimes paradoxically made them much worse. Steve decided that his quest was to name these forces and discover whether these self-defeating patterns could be broken.

During this same period, the authors of this book met when they attended an introductory systems dynamics seminar at MIT's Sloan School of Management, which featured a speech by the famous systems theorist, Jay Forrester. After being paired on a management decision-making exercise, the two started a conversation that developed over the years into this book. Sharon had been the CEO of a heath care plan, so she was intimately acquainted with the forces these organizational theorists described. Steve, in turn, was interested in Sharon's unique approach of using personality archetypes to describe different types of leadership styles and organizational cultures. *Archetypes* are patterns in human behavior, human instincts, ways of thinking or being that can be found across the world. Steve and Sharon wondered if some of the forces that were making life so difficult for business leaders might be patterns of this nature. However, they did not know where to begin to define or name these forces. Little did they know at the time, that the answers to their questions would be found in a Polish bookstore.

## A Date with Synchronicity in Warsaw

In May of 1992, Steve was visiting Poland on a teaching assignment at the University of Warsaw. There he first encountered two of the central characters in *Knowledge Leadership*: the Yogi and the Commissar. On a beautiful spring day, Steve decided to take a stroll through downtown Warsaw. There he came upon a bookstore and decided to enter it, despite the fact that he could speak only a few words of Polish. He remembered musing at the time, "What on earth is the point of my going into a Polish bookstore?" Undaunted, Steve proceeded to browse the shelves of books, focusing primarily on photography and art books that he could enjoy despite his linguistic limitations.

Then, seemingly out of nowhere, the only book in the store that was written in English caught Steve's attention. It was British philosopher Arthur Koestler's classic *The Yogi and the Commissar* (1945). Delighted, Steve purchased it to pass the time. Little then did he realize the influence this book would have on his thinking about the respective roles of action, learning from experience, knowledge, and leadership in modern corporations.

Koestler used the "thinking styles" of the Yogi and Commissar to represent two divergent worldviews that he observed in the political systems of his era. Commissars believe that changing "the system" will force people to comply with the ideology of that system, whereas Yogis believe that people need to change their own thinking for behavioral or systemic changes to last. Yogis prefer to learn by reflecting inwardly on the meaning of their experiences to form new ways of thinking about future problems, whereas Commissars prefer to learn by experimenting, testing their actions on the world, and objectively analyzing their environment.

In the extreme, Koestler asserted, both the Yogi and Commissar leaders do tremendous damage to their followers. Although Koestler targeted his incisive critique on the political hot spots of his day (post–World War II Russia and India), we believe that the Yogi and Commissar are alive and well in business corporations all around the world. In fact, Commissar leaders, such as General Electric's Jack Welch, are in the business news every day. Effective Yogi leaders, such as the late CEO of Hanover Insurance, Bill O'Brien, also can be found with modest effort. Interestingly, both Yogis and Commissars can be good leaders, but they have distinctly different ways in which they learn from experience and create new knowledge.

The new knowledge leaders, we contend, are *balanced leaders*— one part reflective Yogi, one part active Commissar. These balanced leaders know how to create knowledge from experience. They value both the inner world of self-knowledge and outer world of information, and they know when to discount so-called objective data in favor of subjective principles. Such balanced leaders already exist. They include Fujio Cho of Toyota, Andrew Grove of Intel, and Louis Willem Gunning, president of Unilever Bestfoods. Intel's CEO Andrew Grove (2003) dispels the myth that corporate leaders should be data-driven analysts. He believes that it is equally important for them to draw on their own inner resources, which enable them to inspire and lead others in the face of uncertainty:

None of us have a real understanding of where we are heading. I don't. I have senses about it. But decisions don't wait; investment decisions or personal decisions don't wait for that picture to be clarified. You have to make them when you have to make them. (p. 1)

The more balanced knowledge leaders of the future will be better able to make good, enduring—pragmatic—decisions when they need to make them. But how do people become knowledge leaders? As a first step, leaders need to understand how they themselves learn and create knowledge. Steve and Sharon decided that they could employ the extreme leadership styles of Yogi and the Commissar to help people understand their own leadership styles—including how they learn and manage knowledge. The authors were joined by Steve's colleague in the Department of Management and Organization of Central Connecticut State University, Professor Lee W. Lee. Together the three developed and tested the *Knowledge Bias Profile* (KBP) on more than 500 individuals. This instrument proved very effective in helping people determine their preferred learning, perceptual, and leadership styles.

Leaders who seek to build the KBOs of the future must encourage their employees to remain productive while simultaneously enabling them to create knowledge. What a dilemma! Perhaps, leaders can learn a lesson or two about how to do this from bees.

Bees, you ask?

Of course. Knowledge is the "honey" of organizations, and who knows more about honey than bees?

## ORGANIZATIONS AS KNOWLEDGE HIVES

Knowledge creation is a deliberate process that involves thought, reasoning, and personal reflection. Businesses typically are designed more for efficiency and productivity than for knowledge. Indeed, given the many competing values in organizations, knowledge is often managed in ways that provide disappointing results and few sources of sustainable competitive advantage. It will become increasingly critical for organizations to have knowledge leaders who advocate for the value of knowledge. Knowledge leaders not only envision how a company's resources can be marshaled to support the creation and sharing of knowledge, they will also lead individuals in the development of new knowledge.

In many respects, knowledge leaders are like beekeepers. Beekeepers are always seeking ways to improve the quality of their bees' honey. There are many factors for beekeepers to consider: food sources for the bees, type of housing for the hives, climate, and location for the hives. But the most important factor of all is for beekeepers to remember that their bees already know how to produce honey. Therefore, the beekeeper must not disrupt the bees' natural processes. Otherwise, there will be problems—as Sue Monk Kidd (2002) describes in this story from *The Secret Life of Bees*:

That night I looked at the jar of bees on my dresser. The poor creatures perched on the bottom barely moving, obviously pining away for flight. I remembered then the way they'd slipped from the cracks in my walls and flown for the sheer joy of it. I thought about the way my mother had built trails of graham-cracker crumbs and marshmallow to lure roaches from the house rather than step on them. I doubted she would've approved of keeping bees in a jar. I unscrewed the lid and set it aside.

"You can go," I said.

But the bees remained there like planes on a runway not knowing they'd been cleared for takeoff. They crawled on their stalk legs around the curved perimeters of the glass as if the world had shrunk to that jar. I tapped the glass, even laid the jar on its side, but those crazy bees stayed put. (pp. 26–27)

Over time, workplace structures become embedded in employees—much as the bees in this story, who no longer remembered how to fly. When organizations create structures that unwittingly stop workers from creating new knowledge from experience, there is a failure of knowledge leadership.

Is your company one where KM is practiced, and, figuratively speaking, the lid has been lifted off the jar, yet the bees have not discovered they are free to fly again? This is all too common of a problem. Many times, what is missing in such situations is knowledge leadership. Knowledge leaders draw followers toward a vision of a renewed organization where everyone benefits by pursuing knowledge via work experiences. W. Edwards Deming, commonly regarded as the father of the quality movement, observed that the most valuable currency in any business was its employees' initiative and creativity. He argued that it was the highest priority and "solemn moral responsibility" of leaders to develop these qualities in all their people.

While it would seem to be a monumental achievement if corporations could reliably learn from their mistakes, this alone is not sufficient to achieve sustainable competitive advantages in the marketplace. The stakes are higher than ever, and the challenges to leaders are greater perhaps than any prior time in history. Leaders must not only inspire followers to develop solutions to existing problems; they must also design ways to create knowledge that will help people solve problems more effectively. The principle behind Einstein's notion, "The problems that exist in the world cannot be solved by the level of thinking that created them," implies that future problem-solving efforts must be driven by knowledge that helps people transcend their current paradigm limitations. Purposeful actions taken to achieve organizational goals and solve problems all help to create new knowledge about how things really work in practice. While new knowledge enables more problems to be solved, it simultaneously opens doors to more questions about these new solutions. Ultimately, performance improvement efforts and continuous quality improvement initiatives are driven by never-ending cycles of problem solving, knowledge creation, and experimentation that help leaders learn how things work best in practice.

## Blazing and Marking New Trails

Ideally, knowledge would be created as part of the natural flow of work processes, and also from customer interaction feedback. However, traditional scientifically managed organizations often short-circuit these learning cycles in the name of productivity and efficiency. This is the equivalent of hikers who are too busy blazing a trail to leave behind markers that would make the return to their base camp easier. Sometimes this marking could just be a timesaver, but on difficult terrain, or in rapidly changing or dangerous climates, these markers could be lifesavers. When we reflect and allow the effects of our prior actions to wash back over us, we create useful knowledge about what works best in practice. The learning process tends to occur more naturally in everyday living, as people are somewhat freer to design and manage their own lives. However, in most workplaces, the advent of mass production has truncated the potential of employees to make sense of the effects of their work.

In the past two centuries of the Machine Age, problems were regarded as being occasional exceptions to the rule of normalcy. Today, problems punctuate our organizational lives with regularity, and problem solving has gone from being the interest of a few leaders to being everybody's business. When looked at from the perspective of pragmatism, everyday problems provide the raw material for creating practical new knowledge that can improve business performance. This creative process changes our understanding of *how* and *why* things work as they do in practice, and it does so in a way that enables us to see solutions that were previously unrecognizable to us.

It is well known that what we see depends on what we believe is possible. Moreover, what we know can change what we believe and how we act. Knowledge that develops as a result of our current actions can powerfully influence how we act in the future. It can also shift what we believe is true. As the Pareto "80/20" principle indicates, once we recognize a problem, we are 80% of the way to solving that problem. As the legendary American scholar and pragmatist, John Dewey (1933) once put it:

A question well put is half answered. In fact, we know what the problem exactly is simultaneous with finding a way out and getting it resolved. Problem and solution stand out *completely* at the same time. Up to that point, our grasp of the problem has been more or less vague and tentative. (p. 140)

Being effective at what we do is mainly a function of seeing things differently. And, we see things differently by allowing the results of our prior action to inform our thinking about what works best. This process of allowing ourselves to be informed by the feedback of knowing what really works is the first step in creating knowledge for effective action. What could be more practical for the interests of leaders than solving problems and acting in ways that are reliably effective at getting their desired results?

The most convincing argument for knowledge leadership is that KBOs are beginning to dominate their industries. For example, awareness of the importance of knowledge to the economic success of the European Community has created an impetus for corporate leaders to build on the rich intellectual capital in this continent. The shift toward European businesses becoming more knowledge-based can be seen from the north in Scandinavia through the Netherlands to the south in Italy and Spain. A prime example of a KBO that creates pragmatic knowledge through the process of continuous improvement is the automobile manufacturing company, Toyota. Even though Toyota is the fourth largest company in terms of industry sales, it is *the leader in profits*. At Toyota, leaders aspire to be builders of "learning organizations." According to researcher Jeffrey Liker (2004) of the University of Michigan, Toyota's leaders are not only technically competent. They also develop, mentor, and lead their people, not by giving orders but "through questioning" (p. 182). While some people might argue that such an approach to leadership would only be effective in Eastern cultures, the need for knowledge leadership has been recognized in the West as well. For example, in an interview with Steven Cavaleri, the then CEO of Hanover Insurance, William O'Brien (1996), reflected:

Leaders in this emerging future will act to create organizations that can provide a context of meaning for what people already know. They will then proceed from this shared understanding to act and learn together. (p. 534)

Clearly, there is an emerging cadre of elite organizations whose leaders not only have discovered the importance of creating knowledge for performance and innovation; they also have achieved some amazing results. These knowledge leaders have transformed traditional organizations into *FAST* organizations that are *functional, adaptable, sustainable, and timely. FAST* organizations use knowledge to achieve results that are almost impossible for their competitors to duplicate. These highly successful corporations are characterized by knowledge leadership, organizational openness, linking knowledge to continuous improvement efforts, knowledge development, and innovation. We argue that, in the emerging Knowledge Era, it will be up to organizational leaders to transform themselves into knowledge leaders who are capable of pragmatically creating these *FAST* KBOs. Clearly, knowledge-based strategies can work to drive performance, yet it would be a mistake to believe that organizations can move quickly from relying on strategies and systems that implicitly devalue knowledge to organizations that emphasize its importance.

Even now, some industries are increasingly populated by companies that have committed to knowledge-based strategies. In the U.S. pharmaceutical industry, for example, Biogen, Boehringer-Ingelheim, Bristol Meyers-Squibb, Burroughs-Wellcome, Merck, Pharma, and Pfizer have invested heavily in knowledge-based strategies to improve everything from drug development to marketing. Similarly, in the petroleum industry, companies such as BP Amoco, ChevronTexaco, and Shell view knowledge-based initiatives as critical to their success. It should come as no surprise that, in both the petroleum and pharmaceutical industries, products are processed through highly automated systems, and the human component is focused on developing new products and marketing them more effectively. On the other hand, in industries with low-margin, commodity-like products, knowledge-based strategies are understandably less attractive. Clearly, every industry has different knowledge needs that cannot effectively be addressed with a one-size-fits-all mentality. When it comes to knowledge, organizations have multiple and sometimes competing needs to address—such as survival, profitability, waste reduction, new product development, and improving the quality of products and services. Effective knowledge leaders define the types of knowledge needed at various levels in their companies. Not only will they have to determine the performance and knowledge requirements of their domain, they will also need to work with peers to influence employees and design systems that translate into more effective performance across the whole organization. The reasons for pursuing such a diverse knowledge strategy are greater than ever as companies around the world face unprecedented competition.

## THE BEST AND WORST OF TIMES

Describing the French Revolution, Charles Dickens keenly observed, "It was the best of times, it was the worst of times." Dickens's famous phrase seems just as applicable to describing the state of many organizations in this second millennium. A revolution of another sort has reached a fever pitch, fueled by the clash of managerial paradigms. In a sense, this clash is an inevitable result of the ending of the Machine Age and the emergence of the Knowledge Era, which has brought with it both confusion and opportunity.

Since the beginning of the Machine Age, the predominant view among managers has been that efficiency was paramount, that markets changed little, and that organizational survival was guaranteed. The borderless world that we are living in now is characterized instead by free trade, intense international competition, and volatile markets. Around the globe, the number of companies being formed is growing exponentially, with waves of firms that can implement their agile business strategies at breakneck speed. The days are over when a business can be managed effectively by mimicking the methodical operation of a stable machine that is designed to serve a well-established, well-defined, and enduring market. Just as the writings of the great scientist Sir Isaac Newton represented a profound breakthrough for his time, only to be replaced by models of quantum physics developed by Werner Heisenberg, Max Plank, and Niels Bohr, the principles of the machine organization are being eclipsed by those of the knowledge-based organization, and will become progressively less relevant over time.

The single greatest lesson of this transitional time is that while machines are stable, predictable, and efficient, they are not adaptive, sustainable, or capable of innovation. Now that organizational survival can no longer be taken for granted, knowledge leaders are needed to bring both art and science to bear on circumstances that a short time before could not have been imagined, much less prepared for. In the emerging Knowledge Era, the importance of effectiveness and innovation will surpass that of efficiency and stability.

The first generation of commerce we discuss in this book is the Age of Arts and Crafts, where product and service *quality* were of chief importance. During the Machine Age that followed, *productivity and efficiency* were requirements for success. In the Knowledge Era, organizations will need to reliably act in a highly *effective* manner, and knowledge and clear reasoning will be the basis for all effective action. By necessity, knowledge-based organizations will be more open, democratic, and experimental than ever before. Companies will increasingly be organized around ways to improve the quality of their knowledge. Most important, such organizations will depend on knowledge leaders *at every level* to facilitate the process of creating and leveraging knowledge system-wide.

Such a transformation represents nothing less than a sea change in what it means to a leader. The knowledge leaders in this new era will not only lead knowledge-based initiatives—they also will create and apply knowledge to enable their organizations to perform ever more effectively. Moreover, knowledge leaders will not only spur the development of knowledge in other people, they also will be active participants in the creation of their own personal knowledge. The noted management scholar Henry Mintzberg (2000) argued that the managers of the future will need to become more capable of reflection. In a *Fast Company* interview, he stated:

The last thing managers need from us is boot camp—intense, high-pressure classroom activity. . . . They live boot camp every day! What they need is to step back from the pressures and to reflect on their experiences. (p. 286)

Mintzberg's prescient observations signal that the days of the manager as analyst are nearly over. Moreover, the distinctions that previously have separated "managing" and "leading" are breaking down. For over a century, modern workplaces have been marked by barriers between the routine work processes and those efforts that were focused on inquiry, discovery, and experimentation. Efficiencies derived from the work simplification movements of the Machine Age effectively dismantled the way people ordinarily learn from their own experiences. The ordinary feedback mechanisms, opportunities for learning through reflection, experimentation, and interaction with peers were all summarily removed from the designs of most work systems.

It is no wonder, then, that solution-resistant problems plague many modern organizations. After all, work has unwittingly been designed in a way that has forced employees to be *chronically unknowledgeable*, despite the best intentions and capabilities of these employees. This tradeoff has been made willingly in traditional corporations, because efficiency and productivity were paramount—and there were large differences between the education levels of managers and other organization members. However, in most economically developed nations today, those conditions no longer hold true.

## THE REST OF THIS BOOK

*Knowledge Leadership: The Art and Science of the Knowledge-Based Organization* provides a practical approach to developing and leading a knowledge strategy for your organization. Our goal is to provide a new way of thinking about the role of knowledge in your business and an innovative framework that will help you design a tailored knowledge strategy to best fulfill your organization's performance needs. This book goes beyond the narrow focus of KM to consider how knowledge can be integrated into the entire *operating logic* of your company to make it more competitive.

*Knowledge Leadership* is not a handbook or a cookbook. However, it does provide a conceptual structure that will assist you in integrating strategies and knowledge-based initiatives with your existing management systems so that they all are more closely aligned with the performance needs of your organization. Special features of the book include the results of a major cross-cultural research study that examined the knowledge styles of leaders, self-assessment and organizational diagnostic tools, actual case examples, and practical guidelines for implementing a pragmatic knowledge strategy. We would like to point out that this book is organized sequentially, with each section building on the prior one, so that its key elements are not fully integrated until the final chapter.

In Part I of *Knowledge Leadership*, we answer the question: "Why Should You Care about Knowledge?" In Chapter 1, "The Knowledge Leadership Challenge," we made the case for the importance of knowledge leadership to the future viability of businesses. In this chapter, "The Emerging Era of the Knowledge Leader," we explain how knowledge leaders are becoming the most important people in knowledge-based organizations (KBOs) because they connect knowledge to everyday performance. Most current KM approaches are more general—they attempt to raise the overall level of knowledge in an organization by leveraging and sharing existing knowledge. By contrast, knowledge leadership targets specific strategic needs by developing knowledge and by creating a knowledge mix that suits the unique knowledge needs of that organization.

Part II of this book focuses on the process of "Becoming a Knowledge Leader." In Chapter 3, we help you with the process of "Discovering Your Knowledge Leadership Style." In most businesses, there are tensions between leaders who prefer to utilize existing resources (for example, knowledge managers) and who those want to innovate and create new products, processes, and programs (knowledge developers). This tension is embodied in the worldviews of two colorful archetypal leaders—and archenemies—whom political philosopher Arthur Koestler described in his classic book, *The Yogi and the Commissar*. Effective knowledge leaders must find a way to balance and integrate the capabilities of both Yogi and Commissar leaders. This chapter also provides a short form of the *Knowledge Bias Profile*; this instrument will help you to identify your *knowledge leadership style*—that is, how you look at the world, learn from experience, and lead others.

What can we learn from the battles that have occurred over the millennia between Yogi and Commissar leaders? Chapter 4, "Learning from Commissar and Yogi Leaders," provides key lessons about knowledge leadership by analyzing the strengths and weaknesses of both Yogis and Commissars. Both of these leaders create problems for themselves because they steadfastly adhere to extreme beliefs about human nature. Although their worldviews contain elements of the truth, they both are incomplete—and therefore destined to fail.

Another way to say this is that Yogi and Commissar leaders are often unable to see themselves or situations in a clear light. Chapter 5, "Stepping Back to Envision New Possibilities," points a way out. We all form habitual ways of looking at or thinking about things— perceptual patterns—of which we are unaware. While it is natural to develop such habits, over time we unnecessarily narrow our field of vision and cut ourselves off from potentially useful information. When we take a deliberate step back to look at things with fresh eyes, we are often able to find new ways to solve old problems.

Chapter 6 is titled "Studying Knowledge Leadership Behavior: Lessons from Cross-Cultural Research." It provides the exciting results of a research study of 517 participants. This chapter is designed to give you feedback about your own knowledge leadership style. It will help you understand how perception, knowledge development, and leading styles are all related. This comprehensive cross-cultural study considers tendencies to be either more of a Yogi leader or Commissar leader in ways of looking at the world, learning from experience, and leading. It will also show you how to compare your sample *Knowledge Bias Profile* results from Chapter 3 with the data from participants in our cross-cultural research.

Part III, "Putting Knowledge into Action," begins with Chapter 7, "Aligning Knowledge with Business Strategies," which focuses on how you can develop knowledge strategies that are more closely aligned with your company's goals so as to enable higher levels of organizational performance. A key element of this approach is to understand the different types of knowledge and which processes are able to generate these types of knowledge.

Chapter 8, "Understanding the Role of Knowledge in Organizations," provides a brief history lesson. It explains the three different ages of organizational strategies and how knowledge has played a central but very different role in each age. This chapter also explains how each type of knowledge can be targeted so that organizations develop *a knowledge mix*—that is, a careful selection of various types of knowledge-developing and knowledge-managing processes that can be used concurrently for different purposes.

In Part IV, "Developing Pragmatic Knowledge," we delve into greater detail to explain how knowledge leaders can help their organizations attain sustainable competitive advantage by creating pragmatic knowledge. Chapter 9, "Putting Action into Knowledge," explains how leaders can enliven knowledge with action—by employing the principles of pragmatism. Pragmatism provided the conceptual foundation for TQM, action learning theories, and organizational learning. It is a performance-oriented philosophy that was developed in the 20th century by Charles Sanders Peirce, William James, John Dewey, C. I. Lewis, Donald Schon, and noted systems thinkers Russell Ackoff and C. West Churchman.

In Chapter 10, we discuss the process of "Learning to Make Knowledge Pragmatic." While it is normal for individuals to learn from experience, it is *conscious learning* (an understanding of what has been learned or how something has been done) that is most important to organizations. The most valuable kinds of knowledge are those that are within our awareness and the products of our own reasoning efforts. For example, we learn to ride a bicycle through trial and error. However, if we understand *how* we maintain our balance on the bicycle, we have gained a richer and more useful kind of knowledge. The knowledge leaders of the future will be responsible for creating the organizational conditions that will foster this valuable learning-to-knowledge process.

"Leading Knowledge Processing" is the subject of Chapter 11. In most organizations, KM approaches lack ongoing processes that give purpose and meaning to the information they store. Only by linking knowledge directly to performance can knowledge leaders create the pragmatic knowledge that is needed for sustainable competitive advantage.

Part V addresses the topic of "Leading *FAST* Knowledge-Based Organizations (KBOs)." As stated earlier, *FAST* is an acronym that means *functional, adaptive, sustainable, and timely*. It is our contention that KBOs with pragmatic knowledge initiatives are most likely to achieve the four criteria necessary for sustainable competitive advantage. Unfortunately, most business managers are under great pressure to perform, and they often respond by trading off adaptability and sustainability for functionality and timeliness. If this trade-off is made on a large scale throughout the company, or on an ongoing basis, it is likely to result in a decline in organizational vitality. Over time, creative forces that drive innovation are systemically removed, and sources of cost reduction, process improvement, and new products are overlooked.

In Chapter 12, we describe the process of "Developing *FAST* KBOs." Special focus is placed on Toyota, where quality improvement, learning from experience, model redesign, and waste reduction are all continuous processes that operate simultaneously. Through its long-term commitment to the pragmatic practices of TQM and relentless organization learning, Toyota is becoming a *FAST* pragmatic KBO.

Chapter 13, "Learning from Experience: A Case of Mistaken Identity," features the critical role for knowledge leaders in interpreting and shaping an organization's identity. This chapter underscores our belief that corporate identity is the starting point and touchstone for all knowledge-based initiatives. This is why it must be reflected in all systems, processes, and knowledge-based initiatives. In this chapter we discuss a particular case where organizational identity was not taken into consideration—with devastating results. The dilemma of Yogis and Commissars resurfaces in this case study, as represented in the tensions between the organization's "pioneers" and "settlers."

Chapter 14 will help leaders with the challenge of "Balancing Knowledge and Management Systems." Outstanding organizational performance is reliably the result of using high-quality knowledge as the basis for decisions. This chapter explains the role of management systems as a context for both knowledge development (KD) and knowledge management (KM). It also looks at how knowledge leaders can enable their businesses to move toward being more effective by helping them develop knowledge that continues to be refined over time.

Chapter 15 points out the necessity of "Constructing Effective Knowledge Infrastructures" to assure that high-quality knowledge is available throughout the organization. Here we argue that the prime function of an organization is to develop actionable and pragmatic knowledge—because it is this knowledge that will make it most effective, provide it with a significant competitive edge, and thereby ensure its survival.

Finally, in Part VI, "Putting It All Together," we weave together all the threads we have developed in this book. Chapter 16, "Using 5-Point Dynamic Mapping to Lead *FAST* KBOs," integrates the principles we have discussed throughout *Knowledge Leadership* and presents a powerful tool you can use to make your business a *FAST* KBO. The 5-Point Dynamic Mapping process moves with your organization to keep it *FAST* despite changing circumstances. By using organizational identity as the starting point, this innovative dynamic mapping process will help you design highly integrated strategies and knowledge-based initiatives that will make your company more pragmatically performance-driven, thereby providing it with a significant competitive advantage.

## Our Invitation

We invite you to use the ideas contained within this book as a basis for exploring new ways of thinking about what it means to be pragmatic. We also suggest that you develop your own approach to using knowledge for high performance. We ask you to consider many questions as you read this book: What does it mean to you to be "pragmatic"? What is your habitual way of looking at things? Are you more of a Yogi leader or a Commissar leader? What is your organization's identity? Moreover, many more questions will occur to you as you try out this material in the laboratory of your workplace.

We recommend that you make notes in the margins of this book as thoughts arise in response to these questions. Then come back at some point and review your notes to see how they compare with what you now believe about how things work best in practice. We think you may be surprised with what you learn.

After all, being surprised by the unexpected is an invitation to become a pragmatic knowledge leader. The surprises you encounter every day allow you to learn, try out new behaviors, form new knowledge, and more successfully adapt to the changes that confront you.

We will begin this learning process in the next part of this book (Part II), where we will help you discover your knowledge leadership style, uncover your knowledge-creating biases and perceptual limitations, and learn how to become a well-balanced knowledge leader.

## References

Dewey, J. (1933). *How We Think*, Revised Edition. Boston: D.C. Heath.

Koestler, A. (1945). *The Yogi and the Commissar*. London: Jonathan Cape.

Grove, A. (2003). Interview with Kiechel, W. "Andy Grove on Confident Leaders," *Working Knowledge for Business Leaders*. April 14, Harvard Business School, Cambridge, MA.

Kidd, S. M. (2002). *The Secret Life of Bees*. Harmondsworth, England: Penguin Books.

Liker, J. (2004). *The Toyota Way*. New York: McGraw-Hill.

Mitzberg, H. (2000, November). "You Can't Create a Leader in a Classroom." *Fast Company*, 286.

O'Brien, B. (1996). Interview with Bill O'Brien by Steven Cavaleri. *Managing in Organizations That Learn*. Cambridge, MA: Blackwell Business Books.

# Part II

# Becoming a Knowledge Leader

# 3

# DISCOVERING YOUR KNOWLEDGE LEADERSHIP STYLE

Executive Summary

A key element of becoming a knowledge leader is to be able to effectively transform one's learning experience into knowledge. This requires that you become equally comfortable with the process of personal reflection as you are with more outward activities, such as experimentation—and also that you free yourself from self-limiting intellectual prisons by finding new ways to look at how things really work best in practice. This section of *Knowledge Leadership* is dedicated to helping you in this learning-to-knowledge process by discovering your knowledge leadership style. In this chapter, we will provide an abbreviated version of the assessment instrument we developed precisely for that purpose, the *Knowledge Bias Profile* (KBP). The KBP not only will help you identify potential knowledge biases, it also will introduce you to the "Yogi" and the "Commissar," two colorful, polar opposite leaders who have specific contributions and liabilities for knowledge leadership. In the KBP, you will discover your tendency to be more of a reflective leader (Yogi) or an action-oriented leader (Commissar). Understanding your knowledge leadership style will help you learn from your experience and become a more balanced knowledge leader who knows when to act and when to reflect, when to develop knowledge and when to manage it. At the end of this section, we will discuss the exciting results of 8 years of study on the KBP and show you how to compare your self-scores with those of 500 other individuals.

## The Natural Instinct for Learning from Experience

Becoming a knowledge leader depends on being able to consciously learn from your work and life experiences. Happily, the human instinct for learning is almost insatiable. Yet creating knowledge from learning is hardly automatic—it requires the ability to reflect and reason. Propagating knowledge among human communities is nearly as vital to the long-term survival of our species as human reproduction itself. Interestingly, if you observe how children learn, most of their learning is in service to action. As every parent knows, they fix their attention on something they want, then they do everything in their power to figure out how to get it. So if the process of learning from experience is naturally built into humans, why is the process of creating knowledge from learning so difficult? Why is it challenging to become a knowledge leader? And why is it difficult for knowledge leaders to develop a knowledge-based organization (KBO)?

The answers to these questions start with our educational institutions, which emphasize the importance of acquiring information so that students can learn how to function efficiently in society. We teach students how to master information and behave compliantly in the classroom; we do *not* teach them to think or act independently. (In fact, when children act outside given parameters, they are usually punished.) This pattern is further reinforced by companies that want employees to efficiently—and without complaint—carry out established work routines. This *enforced dependency* often reflects the prevailing views of science, education, and philosophy that have been adopted in our societies and that, over time, have remained largely unquestioned.

In businesses, where leaders are rewarded for their ability to make quick decisions and take bold action, the issues of science, philosophy, and even knowledge may seem irrelevant. Ironically, the famed economist John Maynard Keynes (1936) observed that "Practical men who believe themselves to be quite exempt from any intellectual influences, are usually the slaves of some defunct economist" (p. 383). A key element of becoming a knowledge leader is to be willing to free yourself from such self-limiting intellectual prisons by beginning to experiment with new ways of looking at how things actually work in practice.

Today, more than ever, success in business will come from learning what works best in practice and revising our knowledge to reflect these insights. Making the choice to become a knowledge leader and initiate an enterprise-wide knowledge-based strategy is not one to be taken lightly. Yet it is also potentially much more rewarding than any other path of action. The initial investment of time and energy is often high, but the likely payoffs are great. Fundamentally, adopting a pragmatic knowledge-based strategy will appeal to businesses that value continuous performance improvement and innovation. We believe that the handwriting is on the wall: taking a pragmatic knowledge-based approach to innovation is one of the most effective (and difficult-to-duplicate) means for gaining sustainable competitive advantage. This can be explained by the fact that organizations do not just *do* knowledge and innovation. The most successful companies actually *become* knowledge and innovation-centric in their strategies and design. This is because developing knowledge is not an event—it requires a commitment to an ongoing process. Although there are significant barriers to becoming a true knowledge leader or developing a KBO, there are few competitors who can follow on the trail that you blaze.

One of the first steps to becoming a knowledge leader requires that you become equally comfortable with the process of personal reflection as with action. In other words, it is important to become aware of your own thinking and reasoning process when you are making decisions about how to act. You can see the process of knowledge development beginning to work when you notice that you are becoming adept at both (1) experimenting with new ways of acting and (2) constructing new explanations that make sense of what happened as a result of your actions. Fundamentally, knowledge leaders are well balanced in their capacity to act, reflect, theorize, and experiment with new ways of acting. In other words, it is important for you to neutralize the amount of bias in the way you learn from experience. In this way, you will be able to create higher-quality knowledge and act more effectively.

Unfortunately, in many companies, learning and innovation are considered diversions from the "real work" of managers (that is, planning, organizing, and controlling to achieve optimal efficiency). We contend, however, that the days are over when organizations can be successful by encouraging managers to focus only on efficiency and cost reduction. Indeed, too many businesses are already quite efficiently doing all the wrong things! In part, this may be due to their prior history of focusing on efficiency and productivity at the expense of learning and innovation. The price for employing this unbalanced approach is now being paid by many companies where desperate efforts to squeeze out even more cost efficiencies are going dry and potential innovations continue to be unwittingly ignored. As a leader, you may have inherited such a situation. If so, you are probably seeking ways to find the balance that will ensure your company's viability and improve its future performance.

This section of *Knowledge Leadership* will help you start the rebalancing process for yourself, your department, or your business—by first learning how to capture the lessons of your own experiences. We are not suggesting there is a need for large system-wide knowledge-based initiatives at the outset. We understand that you need to walk before you run. Rather, we advocate starting a self-knowledge initiative—that is, learning your knowledge leadership style—so that you become continually more effective at whatever you do. After taking this first step yourself, you will be in a much better position to support your staff and colleagues in creating their own pragmatic knowledge from experience. Then, together, you will be better able to design and sustain successful knowledge-based efforts within your organization.

When we learn lessons from our own experiences, we are on the path toward custom-creating new knowledge. Such knowledge has the most potential to improve your work or personal performance. However, deliberately creating knowledge by learning from experience takes some time to master—and it is only one of several steps necessary for creating new knowledge. Even though it may appear to be an *inefficient* use of time at first, learning in this way develops your capacity to operate more *effectively* in the future. It is similar to learning how to most effectively swing a tennis racket or play a musical instrument in that, at first, it may feel very awkward to do it the right way after years of doing it the wrong way.

To prove our point about the value of knowledge, take a minute to think about those companies that have been able to sustain durable competitive advantages for the longest periods. Such competitive advantages rarely are based solely on efficiencies, because virtually every business has access to the same labor markets, technologies, and raw materials. In fact, the forces that confer sustainable competitive advantage to organizations are most often found in learning, knowledge, and innovation. Noted companies such as Apple Computer, 3M, John Deere, Siemens, Royal Dutch Shell Oil, and Virgin Atlantic have all marched to the beat of a different drum.

## A Tradition of Knowledge Leadership

Knowledge gained via millennia of experience has provided the necessary foundation for every form of human civilization. From building the Great Wall of China, to curing debilitating diseases, to composing beautiful music or poetry, to educating citizens of the world—all great accomplishments have resulted from humanity's ability to draw useful lessons from our experiences. The very survival of cultures around the world has depended on elder generations to support the natural human drive for learning and then to pass on vital information to succeeding generations. The innate drive for learning and the need for knowledge are not even unique to humanity. Indeed, all species of animals display an inborn curiosity and urge to learn. Moreover, our fellow creatures have found their own ways of sharing the information and knowledge they have gained from millennia of adaptive learning: through parenting practices, teaching peers new skills, and even passing the "rules of life" through DNA to their progeny. What is different today is that extraordinarily sophisticated technology increases our capacity to quickly share newly created knowledge. Advances in computing, declining prices for computers, and the emergence of the Internet and intranets as popular modes for communication and inquiry have all enabled leaders to move information literally at the speed of light throughout entire organizations. These sophisticated artificial systems call to mind futurist Arthur C. Clarke's words that any sufficiently advanced technology is "indistinguishable from magic."

It is the responsibility of knowledge leaders to manage these remarkable information systems so that they operate in the *service* of knowledge. Because technology cannot replace the fundamental ways by which humans learn from experience, those leaders who ignore the development of core knowledge processes and infuse their companies with "knowledge technologies" will only accelerate the underlying confusion. Making flawed knowledge processes work more rapidly is definitely not a good business strategy. It is a bit like trying to fix an old lawnmower by installing a jet engine on it. Yet this is precisely what many corporate leaders do every day. Unfortunately, these "solutions" only make the original problems much worse and mask the ineffectiveness of the underlying system. A primary task for knowledge leaders is to create environments where employees are creating new knowledge through experience. While it is critical for organizations to build cultures where knowledge is valued, that is not the goal of this book. Rather, our focus is on assisting knowledge leaders in mastering their own pragmatic knowledge capabilities first, so that they will, in this way, increase their capacity to design and maintain a KBO.

## KNOWLEDGE APPLICATION IN PRIOR ERAS

Unlike today's knowledge leaders who must demonstrate their performance in monthly reports, our ancestors had to meet an even more daunting task: assuring the survival of their society. Instead of the advanced technology available to us today, early knowledge leaders observed nature as a primary method of learning and gathering information. In many cases, they developed quite sophisticated systems for the oral transfer of knowledge—storytelling. The distinguished historian Will Durant (1935) once noted:

Simple tribes living for the most part in comparative isolation, and knowing the happiness of having no history, felt little need for writing. Their memories were all the stronger for having no written aids; they learned and retained, and passed onto their children whatever seemed necessary in the way of historical record and cultural transmission. It was probably by committing such oral traditions and folk-lore to writing that literature began. (p. 76)

It was by learning how nature works and which actions are most in concert with nature that our ancestors discovered many of the secrets to survival and prosperity that benefited their cultures. For millennia, the Chief Knowledge Officers (CKOs) of a society were known by much more colorful names, such as shaman, wizard, magician, or seer.

Unfortunately, human beings have not always managed knowledge particularly well. For example, an extraordinary amount of knowledge has been lost when civilizations conquered and destroyed others—including their literature, arts, architecture, and scientific and healing discoveries. Similarly, in our corporations today, we lose great amounts of knowledge when we reorganize departments, lay off employees, experience high turnover, lose top talent, and merge with other organizations. We also prevent the development of knowledge when we employ fear-based management techniques that are designed to keep workers in line and on time.

One of the things that knowledge leaders learn first is to value the knowledge of others in their organizations. They know that, because people are the creators of knowledge, employees have the potential to be the wealth generators of the future. When a knowledge leader treats employees with that understanding, the door of opportunity is opened—for the leader, the employee, and the company. The knowledge leader removes fear from the workplace and rewards curiosity and learning until they become innovation.

We look to Charles Sanders Peirce, the great American philosopher and scientist who is considered the founder of Pragmatism, for clues about how knowledge leaders can lead their employees into creating knowledge that is pragmatic. What will enable employees to heed their inquisitive instincts and become increasingly able to translate their experiences into knowledge? We believe that there is always some "natural selection" in this evolutionary process of moving from viewing employees solely as doers to seeing them as both doers *and* creators of knowledge. Some employees will be thrilled to make this transition, while others will dig in their heels or adopt a wait-and-see attitude. In the final chapter of *Knowledge Leadership*, we will detail precise action steps that we believe will help you encourage those in your charge to participate in the creation of a KBO. But for now, we will launch you on the journey to becoming a knowledge leader by helping you discover your own knowledge biases and knowledge leadership style.

## Introducing the Knowledge Bias Profile (KBP)

We now present abbreviated versions of the three parts of the Knowledge Bias Profile (KBP) to assist you in assessing your own knowledge leadership abilities. Please note that there are no right answers or wrong answers to the questions that follow. Our objective is to show you how your particular way of looking at the world might influence your experience of it. Having this feedback will make you more aware of your perceptual limits.

## The Knowledge Bias Profile, Part A— Worldview (Short Form)

Directions: Please answer how strongly you agree with each of the following statements by rating them from 1 (strongly disagree) to 5 (strongly agree). The more you agree with a statement, the higher your score will be on that item. Write your answers in the column to the right of each question.

| Response item | Score | Response item | Score |
|---|---|---|---|
| 1. What is important is to see and evaluate things accurately and objectively. | ____ | 1. The world can be viewed as anything (fishpond, clock, etc.): our worldview is only a metaphor. | ____ |
| 2. The ends justify the means. | ____ | 2. Means are most important because we cannot know ends accurately beforehand. | ____ |
| 3. It is most effective to change the system to change human behaviors in organizations. | ____ | 3. Cause-effect relationships are not always clear to human observers. | ____ |
| 4. In most systems, change has to come from outside, such as from external forces and surroundings. | ____ | 4. Before organizational change, we need to change ourselves and our own values. | ____ |
| 5. Organizational change efforts should focus on making people consistent with the needs of the organization. | ____ | 5. The focus of change must be how values of the team relate to those of individuals. | ____ |
| 6. Reasoning is the sole basis for actions. | ____ | 6. Logic is a useful tool, but it alone cannot reveal all that is true. | ____ |
| **Your Total Commissar Score→** | ____ | **Your Total Yogi Score→** | ____ |

## The Knowledge Bias Profile, Part B— Behavior (Short Form)

Directions: Please answer how strongly you agree with each of the following statements by rating them from 1 (strongly disagree) to 5 (strongly agree). The more you agree with a statement, the higher your score will be on that item. Write your answer in the column to the right of each question. If you are not in a designated leadership position, you may answer the questions by indicating how you believe you would act if you were a leader.

| Response item | Score | Response item | Score |
|---|---|---|---|
| 1. As a leader, I believe I am most effective when I have a clear vision for the future and direct all employees toward that vision. | ____ | 1. For me to make lasting change as a leader, I believe I must find the shared beliefs of my employees and build on them. | ____ |

| Response item | Score | Response item | Score |
|---|---|---|---|
| 2. I prefer to gather more information and learn best practices in order to gain competitive advantage. | ____ | 2. I prefer to learn through reflection and thinking; more information can be confusing rather than helpful. | ____ |
| 3. I am an empiricist: I believe only what I can see and experience. | ____ | 3. I look for hidden, implied meanings of what I see and challenge old ways of looking at things. | ____ |
| Your Total Commissar Score→ | ____ | Your Total Yogi Score→ | ____ |

## The Knowledge Bias Profile, Part C— Effective Leadership

After you have read the leadership profile of these two individuals, use the following scale to rate your preference for the one you believe would be the more effective leader.

| | |
|---|---|
| Mr./Ms. Patrick believes that problems can best be solved by redesigning the system to make it more efficient and productive. The lofty end justifies the use of all means. By reorganization of the system and strong top-down leadership, performance is improved. Logical reasoning is an unfailing compass. The world works like a very large machine, in which a large number of parts are interconnected in an integrated system. Any problem in the system can be corrected by analyzing it methodically, finding out precisely what caused the problem, and taking the action necessary to alleviate the symptoms. | Mr./Ms. Raphael believes that lasting change must come from within people. He/she believes that the end is unpredictable and that the means alone count, logical reasoning cannot find truth, and that only through reflection and inspiration can one come incrementally closer to any truth that matters. He/she believes that the world could be like anything—a machine or fishpond, where all elements in the pond contribute something unique to the whole. Little can be improved by changing an organization. Rather, it is critical to reach a mutual accord among the people who bind together all components in a system. |
| I believe Patrick is a more effective leader. | I believe Raphael is a more effective leader. |

| Very Strongly | Strongly | Neutral | Strongly | Very Strongly |
|---|---|---|---|---|
| 1 | 2 | 3 | 4 | 5 |

The KBP is designed to help you discover whether you favor the worldview and behaviors of the Yogi or the Commissar. These two colorful characters represent opposite worldviews, different styles of learning from experience, and different perceptual biases. Clearly, none of us is a "pure" type, exclusively Commissar or Yogi. However, the KBP can give you an indication of the *degree* of your preference for either one of these opposite leadership styles.

In both Parts A and B, the first (left) column represents your Commissar preference, and the second (right) column represents your Yogi preference. Part A measures your worldview or beliefs, and Part B measures behavioral patterns that you think are most effective. In Part C, the higher your score, the more you prefer the Yogi leader (Raphael). The lower the score, the more you prefer the Commissar leader (Patrick). You will be able to compare your results with those of more than 500 other individuals in Chapter 6.

In the rest of this section, we will describe how both the Yogi and the Commissar have knowledge biases that can influence your ability to become a knowledge leader and create the KBOs of the future.

## INTRODUCING THE YOGI AND THE COMMISSAR

*The Commissar's emotional energies are fixed*
*on the relation between individual and society,*
*the Yogi's on the relation between the individual and the universe.*
— *Arthur Koestler (p. 11)*

Arthur Koestler wrote his landmark book, *The Yogi and the Commissar* (1945), during the period that followed World War II. Koestler was highly critical of what he perceived as the dogmatic and ineffective worldviews adhered to by leaders at the two opposing polar extremes in human social systems. He believed that both types of leaders ultimately were destined to fail because of the innate flaws in their respective worldviews. The Commissars resorted to tight bureaucratic structures and used methods of thought control to govern the populace. On the other hand, Yogis, through analysis-paralysis, rarely took the timely action they needed to be effective at anything.

While Koestler was concerned with understanding the limits of political leadership, we find that his ideas are quite relevant for contemporary business leaders, especially for those who wish to become knowledge leaders. There are several reasons for our enthusiasm about the Yogi and the Commissar. The first is that they are *archetypes*, instinctive human patterns that are found the world over. That means that (1) they will already feel familiar to you, (2) you will be able to access both of them to become a more balanced leader, and (3) you will be able to easily observe them as they influence your own behavior and the behavior of others around you. This powerful imagery also provides a practical tool for you to more clearly identify the biases that are reflected in your own perceptions and actions.

We also discovered that these two types were particularly relevant to knowledge leaders because each has a strong preference for opposite knowledge approaches and ways of learning from experience. The Yogi prefers to develop new knowledge (KD), the Commissar to manage existing knowledge (KM). The Yogi tends to embrace the two stages of reflection and analysis in the standard action-learning cycle, whereas the Commissar favors the two stages of action and experimenting. (We will discuss these action-learning differences in greater detail in Chapter 5.) It is our hope that, by showing you the strengths and weaknesses inherent in these two leadership styles, you will be able to more systematically account for the sources of bias that would otherwise restrict the quality of your own knowledge. It will also help you decide when it is time to have the Commissar part of you take the lead by designing systems for creating and distributing knowledge (KM) and when instead you need the Yogi part of you to reflect on your own experience or address the subjective learning worlds of your employees (KD).

Through Arthur Koestler's colorful description of these two characters, we hope to illustrate a number of useful lessons about how you can learn from your own experience and achieve greater results from your efforts. We have chosen these images to emphasize the key lessons in this book because symbols convey much more meaning than can be gleaned from theories, examples, graphs, or techniques alone. We wanted the concepts in this book to come alive so you would find them truly memorable. It is as Charles Handy (1989) said in *The Age of Unreason*: "New imagery, signaled by new words, is as important as new theory; indeed new theory without new imagery can go unnoticed" (p. 25).

Commissars (including the Commissar tendency in each one of us) tend to believe that the world consists of a single transparent reality that can be objectively known by all people who employ rigorous methods of inquiry and precise measurement. There is nothing remotely mystical about Commissars' methods for knowing the world—they are precise and straightforward, everything is black and white to them. From the Commissar's perspective, efforts to change "the system" (including workplace systems) begin with the assumption that all systems behave in ways that can be easily measured, predicted, and controlled. Therefore, they are readily knowable. Commissars view systems as existing outside of (and independently from) the people within the system.

On the other hand, Yogis (again, including the Yogi part of each one of us) view human systems as having no intrinsically ideal structure and believe that we create our own meaning by subjectively interpreting "data" based on our own internal references. Whereas to the Commissar, an organization is surely a machine, to a Yogi it could just as well be a fishpond or a musical box. Therefore, Yogis believe that the world we perceive is mainly the result of our own subjective interpretations—and that making change in systems results from helping members of that system alter the perceptual lens through which they view the world so that they can transform themselves.

Needless to say, there is little mutual understanding, respect, or affection to be found between Yogis and Commissars. In fact, neither respects the other because they mutually regard each other as being delusional. (Similarly, these opposing parts of ourselves can cause considerable internal conflict as we weigh decisions, even causing us to become paralyzed.) This is because both Commissars and Yogis believe not just that they are right, but rather that they are *absolutely right*. Commissars believe that Yogis are emotional weaklings who lack the courage to act boldly and make the necessary system-wide structural changes that are demanded in crises and turbulent times. On the other hand, Yogis regard Commissars as being so detached from their own internal workings that they are not capable of dealing with the reality of a very complex world. Yogis view Commissars as providing simplistic solutions to complicated problems by assuring followers that the path to success is not only clear, but near. Commissars tend to view the world objectively, whereas Yogis see things much more subjectively.

Clearly, neither of these characters is right all the time—even though their perceptual limitations keep them from experiencing any irritation that would be caused by self-doubt. In their extreme form, neither type can be a good leader; they are *learning arrogant* and, in effect, learning disabled. By learning arrogant, we mean that they believe they know all of the answers and have no further curiosity to learn.

When taken together, however, the traits of the Yogi and Commissar can be beneficial to knowledge leaders. We will now examine the specific learning assets and liabilities, perception traps, and knowledge-creating capabilities of both the Yogi and the Commissar. We hope that this process will help you increase your understanding of your knowledge leadership style and make you more aware of the subtle ways you limit your own perception, learning, and leadership effectiveness.

## THE INFRARED COMMISSAR

Koestler states that the Commissar lies at one end of the spectrum of humanity—"obviously on the infra-red end." The Commissar thinks that all lasting change in any system must originate from *without*—in other words, from outside of people—then move inward. This is based on the Commissar's belief that people lack the requisite discipline, courage, and motivation to initiate and sustain lasting changes on their own. Commissars also believe that all the "pests of humanity" can and will be cured by revolution—that is, by a radical reorganization of the system. (You don't have to look far to see companies that have restructured in an attempt to solve their problems.) Commissars are convinced that the end justifies the use of any and all means necessary to accomplish it. In the extreme political example Koestler described, these means to an end included wide-scale violence and the imprisonment of the state's enemies. Commissars believe that logical reasoning serves as an "unfailing compass" in a universe that is similar to a "very large clockwork in which a very large number of electrons once set into motion will forever revolve in their predictable orbits." To make certain that no one can disturb this worldview, the Commissar part of us states that anyone who believes anything else is "an escapist."

Commissars are action-oriented people who believe that results are determined in predictable ways by prior causes. Consequently, Commissars are driven to initiate very tight controls because they view the system as operating with a mechanical precision that does not tolerate much variability. This causes them to seek discipline and hold on tightly to standard operating procedures, because people within the system cannot always be trusted to exercise good judgment in their own decision-making processes.

Commissars like to "keep score" because that way they know exactly where they are going and how quickly. This way there is no mistaking when they have "won" by arriving at their goal. Once Commissars believe they have finally discerned how a system operates, they do not hesitate to put their plans into action. In their view, available physical and human resources become instrumental as the means to accomplishing a goal, but have little intrinsic value of their own. Anybody who does not believe in the goal, or who resists this change, is regarded as a traitor—and is treated accordingly. This harsh treatment is particularly troubling to Yogis. They believe people should be liberated to reach their potential based on their own intrinsic merits and that leaders should not place the goals of the system above those of the system's constituents.

Commissars tend to be realists and *structuralists* who focus their attention on tweaking the mechanics of systems over time until they operate precisely as planned. Sometimes this results in apparent miracles and great acclaim, as when Mussolini got the notoriously late Italian trains to run on time. Ultimately, the Commissar desires, creates, and protects the highly valued sense of order. This can give the members of any organization a significant sense of pride and accomplishment. Commissars are notable for the bold actions they take. The strength of their actions comes from having a clear path laid ahead for reaching their goals. This clear path is, in turn, a result of conducting a thorough analysis of the situation. Furthermore, Commissars are spurred on by their belief that if they do not act boldly to offset the undisciplined habits of others, the system's performance will collapse. Finally, Commissars do not invest large amounts of time in trying to decipher what is "true" because they believe they already know what is true. After all, in the Commissar's view, the world operates in ways that are completely transparent. They feel they already know what needs to be done and that their time is best invested in preparing plans and organizing activities.

Commissars are convinced that their actions are right. Their followers consider them plainly spoken, courageous, and decisive. They live in a world where issues are sharply delineated between black and white. Situations are perceived as precipitating the need for obvious courses of action, and success is seen as limited only by one's courage to follow through on plans. Concern for the system always outweighs the objections or resistance of the few. Consequently, it is relatively easy for Commissars to commit to a strong course of action since the "right thing to do" is so clear to them.

Commissars also believe that a major obstacle to success is a lack of information needed to monitor and control the system. Consequently, they are unparalleled in digging for data about how things work. Because they view the world as being like a giant clockwork mechanism, they consider all systems as being subsystems of that great mechanism. They believe, therefore, that the information they need can be acquired just by finding its location in the world. It is like going to a library and finding the right book. Knowledge, then, needs to be *discovered*, not *created*. The Commissar part of you believes that gains in human knowledge occur when you access knowledge that other people have already found or when you experiment in ways that help surface the intrinsic rules for how the giant mechanism operates.

"There is *always* a right answer somewhere," says the Commissar in each of us, and "that right answer is knowable." If you can just identify the source of knowledge (and comprehend the information you find), then you can apply these answers to achieve your goals. Learning means acquiring information about how things work. As a result, Commissars are dedicated to mastering the tools and techniques that will help them more efficiently manage the system. These are the qualities, they believe, that make a good leader.

## THE ULTRAVIOLET YOGI

"On the other end of spectrum," Koestler continues, "where the waves become so short and of such high-frequency that the eye no longer sees them, colorless, warmthless but all-penetrating, crouches the Yogi, melting away in the ultra-violet" (p. 9). The Yogi would not object to the Commissar's description of the universe as a clockwork, says Koestler, but then adds that the Yogi also thinks that "it could be called, with about the same amount of truth, a musical-box or a fishpond" (p. 10). The Yogi believes that "the Means alone count" because the end is unpredictable. Who can tell what tomorrow will bring? Who knows what the effects will be of this particular action? The unpredictability of cause and effect is one of the reasons that violence is never justified in the Yogi worldview—what ends could possibly justify those means?

Yogis also believe that logical reasoning gradually "loses its compass value as the mind approaches the magnetic pole of Truth or the Absolute, which alone matters" (p. 10). This is why Yogis emphasize the maxim that personal transformation is the best way to achieve organizational revolution. Change must come from within, insists Koestler's Yogi; "nothing can be improved by exterior organization" (p. 10). It is as the great Yogi, Mahatma Gandhi, himself was once reported to have said: that is, that we each must become the change we wish to see in the world.

The rationale supporting the Yogi's worldview is that the external world we see is not the complete world, but merely a distorted reflection that is governed by our inner state of mind. Our mind filters what we can perceive, says the Yogi. Try it yourself. Stop reading, and for the next 30 seconds sit quietly and pay attention to what is happening within you (breath, heartbeat, thoughts) and around you (street noise, other people talking). Chances are you are now aware of more than you were 30 seconds ago. But you are still aware of much less than is really there. Our senses are simply not capable of taking in all the stimuli around us, so we tend to focus selectively and then interpret those selected perceptions in light of what we believe to be true (not always in terms of what *is* real or true).

Yogis believe that the inner beliefs, values, and ideologies that shape how people see the world are resistant to influence and manipulation by external forces. Indeed, they tend to change gradually, if at all, says the Yogi, and often only through significant life experiences that shake us to our core. From the Yogi's perspective, if you want to create organizational change, you and the members of your company must first examine which of your beliefs are trustworthy and effective in leading you to *personal* success. From this kind of individual examination, group success, and then organizational success can follow later.

Whereas Commissars believe that we operate within systems where the important goals are known, and that installing proper structures will *make* people behave in the way they should in order to reach these goals, Yogis believe that people will act with sincere intentions only when they have sufficient confidence in the truthfulness of their beliefs. Yogis focus their system-wide change efforts on helping groups of people who hold divergent opinions arrive at a *consensus*. To the Yogi, the meaning of an experience is not always to be found simply in data, results, or information. Rather, the Yogi would argue what something means is *whatever you interpret it* to mean. This attitude, of course, makes the reality-based Commissar ballistic.

Because Yogis believe that the process of finding the meaning in our experiences is a complex one, they ascribe particular value to the activities of reflection and sense making. Yogis' personal compasses start with their own identity and purpose. With the benefit of hindsight, Yogis often spend the major portion of their time analyzing their own thinking, logic, and rationale so as to capture the most valuable lessons from their experiences. It is easy to understand, then, why Yogis' actions tend to be cautious and guarded. There are so many variables and points of view to consider! Things are never clearly black or white, as they are for the Commissar. The world Yogis live in is colored with many subtle—and shifting—shades of gray. However, there is one thing of which the Yogi part of us is absolutely sure. Certainly with as much conviction as their Commissar nemesis, Yogis insist that anyone who thinks differently from them is "an escapist."

## THE COMMISSAR AND YOGI MEET WITH DISASTER

It is tempting for each of us, when confronted by such strongly divergent points of view, to pick a favorite, then paint the other character in this knowledge-creating drama as they do each other—the villain in an epic battle of good versus evil. As in every morality story, there is tragedy and heroism present in the tension between these two larger-than-life characters. What we contend, however, is that in anything but the short term, *the difficulty for both the Yogi and Commissar is that they usually fail—both as learners and as leaders.* Alone, neither one has the capacity to become a knowledge leader, largely because, to paraphrase the Upanishads, "They who think they know, know not."

Koestler's *The Yogi and the Commissar* is a compelling model for improving personal learning and leadership, as well as corporate knowledge development. It dramatically displays two common perceptual limitations inherent in divergent worldviews. Ultimately, these two polar worldviews control how people process their experiences and learn from them. Koestler's Commissar overemphasizes the importance of *action* and *experimentation,* while the Yogi overemphasizes *reflection* and *sense making* in their personal learning styles. These two extreme characters also illustrate the tendencies that leaders may need to correct if they are to do the kind of learning-through-experience that can pay the greatest dividends for themselves and their organizations. In the following chapters, we will use the images of the Yogi and the Commissar to demonstrate how you can avoid many common, self-imposed, perceptual limits by combining both inner-directed *and* outer-directed forms of learning from experience.

Because both the Yogi and Commissar are human patterns that are easily recognizable in everyday life, you may already be familiar with some of the ways they currently impact your learning and leadership behavior. That is, you may find yourself acting in Yogi-like ways some-times and in Commissar-like ways at other times. It is a good thing that we all have both the Yogi and the Commissar living within us as potential human patterns, because problems are more likely to arise when we lose touch with either type and embrace one of them to the exclusion of the other.

In the following chapters we will provide details about the contrasting worldviews and behavioral patterns of the Yogi and the Commissar so that you can create an ongoing dialogue between these two aspects of yourself. This will help you stay alert to the ways in which you limit your own potential to become a well-balanced knowledge leader.

## References

Durant, W. (1935). *The Story of Civilization: Our Oriental Heritage*, vol. 1. New York: Simon & Schuster.

Handy, C. (1989). *The Age of Unreason*. Boston, MA: Harvard Business School Press.

Keynes, J.M. (1936). *The General Theory of Employment, Interest, and Money*. New York: Harbinger Books.

Koestler, A. (1945). *The Yogi and the Commissar*. London: Jonathan Cape.

# 4

# Learning from Commissar and Yogi Leaders

## Executive Summary

There are seven core beliefs that distinguish the very different worldviews of Yogi and Commissar leaders. Commissar leaders prefer to focus on action and changing the behaviors of others (change from without). Yogi leaders prefer to build and revise theories of action and to change the beliefs of others as a path to effecting lasting change (change from within). Although Commissar leaders have been the gold standard of leadership in the West for centuries, Yogi leaders are becoming more valued for their complex problem-solving abilities and for their visionary leadership. The Yogi and Commissar also differ in their ways of looking at the world, learning, and leading others. Taken together, these two opposite leadership styles contribute to becoming a balanced knowledge leader. Commissars tend to rely on facts and measurements in making decisions, while Yogis focus more on impressions and social knowledge. For the Commissars, knowledge is created when information is effectively passed on through structures to others. Therefore, their strength is in designing and implementing knowledge management systems. For the Yogis, their focus is on creating and improving knowledge. Their strength is in the area of knowledge development. Unfortunately, under pressure, Commissars become more Commissar-like and Yogis become more Yogi-like. That is, these extreme leadership styles are only further polarized, often resulting in significant repercussions for their organizations.

The message for knowledge leaders from Arthur Koestler's book, *The Yogi and the Commissar*, is that any rigidly held worldview, although seductive on the surface, is inherently limited and likely to cause leaders their own demise. Both Yogis and Commissars steadfastly adhere to extreme assumptions about human nature. Commissars have a core belief that forcing change on people is the only way to alter their behavior because, sadly, most people lack the discipline or courage to make necessary changes on their own. Therefore, Commissars conclude, all lasting change must originate from outside of people. On the other hand, Yogis believe that people are quite capable of personal transformation. Consequently, sustainable change comes only from people's efforts to change themselves and how they think about the world. Yogis believe that people's personal development is only limited by their lack of self-confidence, or a dearth of knowledge about how to change. Koestler surmised that for millennia these divergent worldviews have plagued humankind's best efforts to create workable political and social systems.

The fundamental worldviews of the Yogi and the Commissar are so clearly polarized that it places their distinctions into bold relief. It would have been simpler for us if Koestler had developed a single measure that could be used to differentiate between the Yogi and the Commissar, for example, if we could judge that all Yogis are passive and all Commissars are aggressive. Instead, Koestler has developed rich and complex profiles of these two leadership styles, thereby providing us with multidimensional, full-spectrum profiles of people whose worldviews appear to be opposite in a great many respects. Indeed, our analysis shows that there are *seven core beliefs* that can help you distinguish between the worldview of the Yogi and that of the Commissar. They are listed in Table 4.1.

It is rare to find anyone who is a "pure" example of these rich archetypes (that would make that person a stereotype). Rather, each person has different combinations of these seven factors. This makes them look at the world, learn, and lead in sometimes dramatically different ways. All of the indicators discussed here would make us more effective at some types of learning and limited in other areas. (In the prior chapter you indicated your preference for the core beliefs of the Yogi or the Commissar via the Knowledge Bias Profile. In Chapter 6, you will be able to compare your scores with participants in our research study.)

It is our view that favoring either of these leadership styles to the exclusion of the other seriously hinders your ability to develop the self-awareness necessary to become a knowledge leader. As many of

Table 4.1

*Seven Core Beliefs of Yogis and Commissars*

| Primary beliefs | Commissar | Yogi |
|---|---|---|
| 1. Change comes from | Without. | Within. |
| 2. The way to make change is to | Change the system. Change people's relationships and roles within the system. ("Revolution is necessary.") | Change human experience. Help people connect to their own values and each other. ("Violence is not a viable alternative.") |
| 3. Values | The ends justify the means. | The ends are so unpredictable that the means are more important. |
| 4. Logic/reasoning | Is valued above other forms of knowing; reason is the basis for all action. | Has diminishing value as one approaches the truth. |
| 5. The world | Is an objective reality, orderly and knowable, with a predictable cause and effect (a mechanical-deterministic worldview). | Could as easily be described as a clockwork, a music box, or a fishpond (a subjective, social-constructionist worldview). |
| 6. Perception/learning | We see the world as it is. | Our beliefs shape what we see in the world around us. |
| 7. Other opinions | Anyone who believes otherwise is an escapist (and a wimp). | Anyone who believes otherwise is an escapist (and a Neanderthal). |

us have learned through painful personal and professional experience, our best-intended actions sometimes produce unintended consequences because we did not see the situation clearly at the outset. Both the Yogi and the Commissar want to do the right thing, but both can miss the mark because they do not really understand the situational intricacies. This point was eloquently observed by the French philosopher, mathematician, and scientist, Blaise Pascal, who noted that individuals are neither "angeles" nor "brutes," and their problems arise when those who would act the part of an angel, actually behave in ways that are more like the brute.

## THE WAY OF THE COMMISSAR LEADERS

The Commissar in each one of us is intrepid. Often acting with a great sense of purpose and clear direction, this part of us focuses on changing the behavior of other people—rather than our own—to suit our purposes. Granted, Commissars work diligently to expand their knowledge of the world and add to their own mental database, but they rarely question their own interpretations of how things really work in practice. Commissars act quickly, as they avoid dealing with potentially paralyzing questions about the rightness of goals or values that would only delay them further. Then, Commissars briskly advance to the next dauntless move—eschewing reflection on past failures as being a negative use of their energy and a "time waster." Commissars usually don't recognize a need for any type of inner change because they believe that their tasks, the system they work in, and its governing rules are self-evident and operate predictably—in the manner of clockwork. Since they understand "the game" of business as being played by a clear set of rules, Commissars see no need to question the accuracy of their perceptions. They become experts in their playing field, are often exhilarated by the competition—and typically, they win.

For Commissar leaders, the ends justify the means. They believe that what is needed to bring their system to a high performance level is simply to gain the full compliance of its people. The Commissar reasons, "If people will just cooperate with me, the brilliant system I have designed will operate flawlessly." Thus, by changing things around them, all else will follow. Many employees are loyal followers of the Commissar—they view this leader as a suitably dominant, take-charge person who is committed to turning things around by "making real change." Not surprisingly, powerful Commissars can attract "yes men" around them who ride in their wake and never challenge their opinions or actions.

Commissars rarely recognize a need to learn about their own inner workings. Indeed, they often devalue the importance of self-reflection or knowledge creation—that's for people who don't have the right stuff for leadership. Ultimately, Commissars fail because the energy required to keep their system in place grows exponentially to meet the increasing resistance of the masses who resent complying with often harsh directives. Although Commissars are typically high-powered people, the sheer amount of energy required to hold up their crumbling structure eventually overwhelms them, causing their downfall. When the resistance they've created is no longer containable, the organization often collapses on itself in order to go through another cycle of development. An example of a collapse of a Commissar-led system is the former Soviet Union, where the demise was sudden and dramatic. In Commissar-led businesses, some signs that the end is near include loss of executive and creative talent, widespread passive-aggressiveness or "low morale" in employees, increasing customer dissatisfaction, or rising costs due to production errors.

Many corporate leaders have strong tendencies toward the Commissar. Indeed, the Commissar's perceptual bias has long been the gold standard for management education and executive development programs. Commissars are disciplined, focused leaders who strive mightily to design and operate the brilliant design strategy to its ultimate conclusion—high performance. When the Commissar aspect of ourselves takes over our inner controls, we become aware of our own impatience with people's inability to comply with our directives or we bridle at their "lack of commitment." When faced with a crisis, the Commissar part of us responds by working harder to reorganize the system. The Commissar also attempts to minimize unpredictability by more tightly controlling other people's behavior and making them a "better fit" for the system. Commissars often succeed in achieving some immediate tangible improvements as a result of their brilliant strategies or by the sheer force of their iron will. This they can do with one hand tied behind their backs. However, their learning challenge lies in discovering ways to achieve longer-term, *sustainable* growth and to support cutting-edge innovation that will enable their systems to *adapt* to changing times.

The price Commissars pay for immediate success is often significant and temporarily hidden. That is, they solve the presenting problems by employing methods that do not engage the full commitment of other organizational members. Then, this lack of support and loyalty tends to create other crises that surface at a later date. For the moment, however, the problem is "solved," and the Commissar looks like a hero. Unfortunately, taking action without understanding how human social systems really work can unwittingly set in motion today the very wildfires that must be extinguished tomorrow. This vicious cycle keeps the Commissar constantly engaged in a series of heroic actions to fight the fires that seem to be threatening the organization. But it is difficult to escape from this addictive, adrenaline-pumping pattern for even a moment to breathe, reflect on experiences, or draw new meaning from what has transpired. The unenviable situation in which many Commissars find themselves is best captured by a quote from inventor Alexander Graham Bell:

When one door closes, another opens. But we often look so long and so regretfully upon the closed door that we fail to see the one that has opened for us.

## THE WAY OF THE YOGI LEADER

For Commissars, sitting quietly and reflecting in the middle of a crisis is inexcusably irresponsible and makes as much sense as Nero's taking time out to fiddle while Rome burned.

But while Commissars believe that "he who hesitates is lost," the Yogi counters that those who are hopelessly lost in a maze *should* hesitate and get their bearings before dashing blindly onward and smashing into the nearest wall.

Yogi leaders see the value of devoting their time and energy to making sense of their experience by reflecting in ways that enable them to find new explanations for why things work as they do. Yogis usually defer taking bold actions in favor of proceeding with caution, not because they lack self-confidence but because they believe that situations can be interpreted in multiple competing ways. Yogis believe that any action taken in this complex and mysterious world cannot have easily predictable results, so they consider it imperative to be careful, conservative, and patient before proceeding. To the Yogi, the ends are usually unpredictable—so it is *the means* that are of the greatest import. Yogis begin change within themselves, then develop a philosophy of action with which they try to create an ideal system. Unfortunately, Yogis often struggle to find the best philosophy for guiding their own actions and for determining the best actions for optimum systemic leverage. This process can take a lot of time.

While Yogis frequently discover deep insights, these are rarely grounded in the experience of having acted. This lack of action causes a corresponding lack of feedback from prior actions and experiments—feedback that is necessary to make Yogis' ideas pragmatic. Because Yogis usually lack practical data, they are often unable to determine what they seek so hard to understand (i.e., the future effects of their actions).

We don't see many Yogic business leaders in the West because Western corporations have traditionally placed higher value on the contributions of those people with Commissar tendencies. However, the Yogi leader is becoming more highly valued in today's increasingly complicated and more process-oriented organizations that require systemic, long-term solutions to complex problems. The late MIT professor Donald Schon (1987), eloquently stated the need for the Yogi to inform knowledge leaders of the future. He once observed:

In the swampy lowland, messy confusing problems defy technical solution. The irony is that the problems on the high ground tend to be relatively unimportant to individuals or society at large, however great their technical interest may be, while in the swamp lie the problems of the greatest human concern. (p. 3)

Whereas the Commissar is an expert in doing, the Yogi is an expert in *thinking about doing*. For this reason, Yogis may also feel more at home in leadership positions in universities, scientific research teams, or consulting firms that specialize in long-term visioning and the application of elaborate mental models.

Interestingly, leading critics of popular management practices, such as Dr. Henry Mintzberg, have pointed out that modern managers are taught how to conduct analysis and take bold action—but they do not know how to *lead* other people. Here is where leaders can learn from Yogis, who favor making methodical decisions by building consensus, creating an ongoing dialogue with followers, and envisioning a compelling ideal future that will inspire followers. Yogi leaders are not passive or incapable of acting. Rather, their actions are targeted, high-leverage, and driven by a clear personal vision that is strongly linked to the corporate vision.

We believe that the emergence of Yogi-style leadership in the East, in companies such as Canon, Honda, and Toyota, is an almost instinctive antidote to the Commissar-dominated traditional Western business model that has been exported worldwide. Moreover, we believe that this emergence of Yogi-style leadership is a good harbinger of the more balanced knowledge leaders of the future.

## KEY DIFFERENCES IN BEHAVIORS: LOOKING AT THE WORLD, LEARNING, AND LEADING

All leaders have within themselves access to both archetypal patterns of the Yogi and Commissar, with a natural preference for one or the other. However, a strong bias in either direction limits a leader's capacity for future learning from experience. Indeed, either bias can result in a learning disability and, subsequently, a leadership disability. As it turns out, neither the Yogi nor the Commissar is capable of engaging in what Chris Argyris (1993) called *leading-learning*. Even more tragically, the different leadership-learning disabilities of the Yogi and Commissar can produce businesses that have parallel learning disabilities and problems with developing new knowledge. This is because learning is necessary—but not sufficient—for creating new knowledge.

In our view, organizational success starts with a knowledge leader's ability to simultaneously access the strengths of *both* the reflective Yogi and the action-oriented Commissar. To help knowledge leaders avoid these two learning disabilities, we will illustrate in the rest of this chapter exactly how the Yogi and the Commissar differ in their ways of

1. *looking* at the world
2. *learning* new things
3. *leading* their followers

In Chapter 3 you indicated your preference for these three behavior patterns of the Yogi or Commissar. You can refer back to Part B of the Knowledge Bias Profile for your looking, learning, and leading scores.

In *Knowledge Leadership*, we define *looking* as "exercising the power of vision." In our view, people acquire the power of vision by actively surfacing, testing, and refining their cherished beliefs about how the world works. *Learning* refers to the process of "action learning," which combines and balances the Yogi's reflection and the Commissar's action. *Leading* is a process of personal influence in which a person's sense of clarity develops a sort of power that is recognized and valued by others and makes them willing to follow that person.

Table 4.2 presents a detailed summary of the contrasting looking-learning-leading styles of the Yogi and the Commissar. These three activities of looking, learning, and leading can best be understood as separate functions with considerable overlap, as shown in Figure 4.1.

As Table 4.2 underscores, the way leaders look at the world dramatically affects when and if they learn, how they learn, what they learn, and how they help others learn. The opposing worldviews of Yogi and Commissar leaders are rooted in their distinctly different

**Figure 4.1**
*Looking-Learning-Leading Style*

**Table 4.2**
*The Looking, Learning, and Leading Styles of Yogis and Commissars*

| Commissar looking | Yogi looking |
|---|---|
| ■ Look at the revealed truths of the world to understand reality. | ■ Look for the hidden or implied meaning in search for the real truth about the world. |
| ■ Empiricists (actively seek the truth of the outer world). | ■ Reflectionists (actively seek the truth of the inner world). |
| ■ Actively seek the truth of the outer world with passive eyes; tend to believe only what they can see-touch-feel. | ■ Actively seek the underlying, hidden meaning of the revealed world; tend *not* to believe only what they can see, touch, and feel. |
| ■ Believe that the world has already unfolded the transparent truth before their eyes. | ■ Believe that the tangible/visible world is only a small portion of the truth. |
| ■ Desire to witness or observe what unfolds before their sensors with greater attention to the details. | ■ Desire to understand the meaning of what they see by paying greater attention to the subtle nuances. |
| ■ The process of looking is "purposefully seeing" and ordering the visual systems. | ■ The process of looking is just the beginning of "sense making" (i.e., making meaningful connections to other constructs). |

| Commissar learning | Yogi learning |
|---|---|
| ■ Searching for new ideas; reviewing the latest and best practices for both leading and managing in order to gain a competitive advantage. | ■ New ideas come from inner self-development (i.e., discovering the truth about their aspirations and what part of themselves to share in the organization). |
| ■ Acquisition of information (as much as possible) and its careful dissemination is the primary means to learning. | ■ Exploring the hidden/implied meaning of any piece of information is the primary means to learning. |
| ■ More information, therefore, is better than less to understand/learn what action to take. | ■ Less is more. More information is not necessarily better as an action guide; often it only causes confusion. |
| ■ Is interested in and quickly adopts sophisticated analytical tools, whether mathematical, statistical, or graphical. | ■ Is not particularly interested in and tends to disregard sophisticated analytical tools because they often only distort the truth. |
| ■ Experience (real-life trial and error) is the best way to learn; experimentation is the second best alternative. | ■ The best way to learn is through reflection, connection, and then making sense of all known variables. |
| ■ Holds a strong belief in the value of tangible/measurable outcomes as evidence of truth in any piece of knowledge. | ■ Holds a strong belief in the value of exploring the as-yet-unrevealed truths of all tangible/visible things. |
| ■ Must see, touch, feel, and experience to believe and learn; enjoys most action-based experiential learning. | ■ Must reflect and think deeply to uncover the truth. Enjoys most sense-making learning exercises. |
| ■ In general, action-based experimentation and experience are the basic tools of learning. | ■ In general, reflection and hypothesizing are the basic tools of learning. |

Table 4.2
*Continued*

| Commissar leading | Yogi leading |
|---|---|
| ■ Focus on structural work, develops and implements new initiatives, policies, structures, and systems. | ■ Focus on organizational development; works with individuals in system to assure cohesion, shared vision, and core values so everyone collaborates on common goals. |
| ■ Empiricist: Experiments with new tasks/ behaviors to see the tangible, measurable improvement of organizational outcomes. | ■ Humanist: Employees need to find their own personal truths and act on them together, thereby building enduring organizational success from shared truths. |
| ■ Change comes from the top downward. | ■ Change comes from the inside out— and sometimes from the bottom up. |
| ■ Leading starts from assessment of current observable realities and ends in improvement of all measurable parameters. | ■ Leading starts from understanding and revealing current shared beliefs then shaping them into a new social reality. |
| ■ The primary tools for successful leadership are control, strong direction, and (when necessary) appropriate punishment. | ■ The primary tools for successful leadership are continuous interaction with—and feedback from—the workers. |

points of view, guiding philosophies, and underlying beliefs about what is true. We will now examine these underlying beliefs in more detail.

## THE OBJECTIVE-EMPIRICIST COMMISSAR AND THE SOCIAL-CONSTRUCTIONIST YOGI

At one extreme of the worldview continuum is the Commissar *objective-empiricist* who believes that truth can be discovered and verified through experience because an undeniable objective reality exists. This point of view, which seems dominant in Western businesses, is predicated on the notion that truth is verifiable through the rigorous use of logic, precise measurement, and scientific experimentation. From this perspective, learning usually means finding the correct answers to well-defined problems and then providing this information to others who can use it for solving the same kinds of problems. Accordingly, "knowledge" is gained when people discover the basic working principles that govern the operation of the Commissar's clockwork universe. To them, all that is needed for success is an owner's manual or its equivalent. The key to making this approach successful is to get the precise information communicated to the right people at the right time. Commissar leaders step forward with confidence to offer their point of view, saying things such as: "For the vast majority of problems I encounter in my company, my approach works. It is easy for people to follow me because they appreciate my straightforward method. I am a doer—and as far as I am concerned without people like me calling the shots, this company would go to hell in no time at all."

At the other end of the leadership spectrum lies the *social-constructionist* Yogi, whose point of view is that all knowledge comes as the result of a complex, personalized process of perception and interpretation of what is true. We call Yogis social-constructionists because they see knowledge in organizations as being built on the shared perceptions of people about what is true. In other words, to Yogis, whatever people as a group *believe is true*, for all intents and purposes *is true* for them. The Yogi proudly claims, "We are all biased in how we see the world, and we all act based on the illusions of how we think things work. We will not be effective in changing the world until we first change ourselves so we may see the world afresh." To their Commissar colleagues, the Yogi sardonically complains, "If life were so simple, then we could break complex problems down into a finite series of more manageable problems. But, as we've seen time and again, reducing problems to bite-sized pieces does *not* tell us how the whole works. People see only what their beliefs enable them to see. Commissars see only what they want to see. Life is just not that simple."

According to Yogis, your interpretation of a situation flows from whatever you expected and believed *in advance* of that encounter. We all inevitably approach our work or life situations committed to some prior assumptions about how things really work in practice. In the Yogi's worldview, truth is a relative concept because it is nearly impossible for anyone to know the absolute or complete truth about anything that is complicated. Most of the important questions of life and work are matters of great intricacy, so the Yogi's opinion is that "Commissars are Masters of the Obvious." Our perceptual and learning style biases exist for many reasons, including sensory limitations, rigid beliefs, and bounds on our rationality. Moreover, we are not capable of knowing how much our own biases color our perceptions. In other words, people are, by definition, unaware of their perceptual blind spots: simply put, we do not know what we do not know.

The Yogi humbly suggests to the Commissar, "Even your Western science guru, Albert Einstein, said that problems cannot be solved by the same level of thinking that created them. So, you see, this conflict we're having is because you stubbornly refuse to look at yourself." While Commissars forcefully argue that the truth is knowable, Yogis observe that we can only get closer to or further from the truth—we will never arrive at the pure truth. The Yogi advises, "Okay, I admit there are some absolute truths that we can all know quite readily, but they are of little consequence to the big issues that plague humankind and organizations. What matters most to the success of organizations is not easily attainable. This is why people need to prepare themselves for seeing the world clearly by cleansing themselves of illusory thinking."

To further detail the looking, leading, and learning styles of the Yogi and the Commissar, Table 4.3 presents the distinctions made between empiricists and social-constructionists that were listed by Dixon (1994) in her book, *The Organizational Learning Cycle*.

These two types of leaders each make a significant contribution to creating effective KBOs . . . for an empirical-knowing Commissar leader, it is essential to include some sort of archive where people can store bite-sized pieces of vital information so others can easily look up the "right" answers or potential solutions to common problems. This creates great efficiency in busy work environments and keeps people from continually having to reinvent the wheel. Clearly, in this approach it is vital to put technologies in place to accelerate knowledge sharing and the distribution of best practices.

In contrast, the social-constructionist Yogi leader is not so focused on information or efficiency. There is a much greater likelihood that Yogi leaders will emphasize increasing organizational effectiveness

Table 4.3

*The Objective-Empiricist versus the Social-Constructionist*

| | Objective-empiricist (Commissar) | Social-constructionist (Yogi) |
|---|---|---|
| Source of knowledge | Learn from experts who have the answers | Group creates meaning |
| Timing of action | Act, then learn | Learn through acting |
| Human nature | Theory X | Theory Y |
| Uniformity versus diversity | Uniformity: Wide acceptance for correct answer | Diversity: Development of new knowledge; overcome tacit assumptions |
| Causality | Linear; scientific method | Systemic; action research |

by employing socially interactive, team-oriented activities such as communities of practice, organizational development programs, story telling, and engaging in dialogue—all to generate knowledge for innovation. Through these interactions, people become aware of the incoherencies in their own thought patterns. Japanese management approaches, such as creating *Ba* (a quiet place for reflection), *genchi genbutsu* (deeply knowing a situation in detail), and *hansei* (reflection) are also useful for Yogi leaders in designing KBOs.

## THE UNDERLYING WORLDVIEW OF THE COMMISSAR LEADER

The Commissar leader believes the following:

1. Cause and effect follow clear patterns over time (determinism).
2. These relations are largely visible for the noting (positivism).
3. An objective reality exists and can be seen by anyone (objectivism).
4. The workings of the objective reality can be reliably known through experimentation and observation (empiricism).

Because Commissars adhere to a mechanical worldview (still the dominant paradigm in the Western business world), they see organizations as being like elaborate machines. This "machine model" worldview holds that the causal relations in the world are predictable because they follow well-established paths of cause and effect. Unfortunately, human behavior is less aptly described using machine metaphors, but this does not deter Commissars, who reason that people are the weak link in the machine system and, thus, need to be more tightly controlled.

According to Commissars, reality can be distilled to a few self-evident universal truths, and these truths are the a priori assumptions on which all subsequent inquiry should be based. Therefore, in this view, the success anyone experiences in uncovering additional truths depends first on the rigor of the scientific process by which one inquires and then on one's unswerving fidelity to these fundamental truths.

Therefore, from the Commissarial perspective, learning is the process of transferring information about that which has become known to those who are (as yet) unknowing. This is a reciprocal process where some individuals pass on information, while others take in this "information." Paradoxically, because this knowledge is actually externally derived, it would be better named *ex-formation*! Therefore, in the Commissar view, knowledge is created when ex-formation is effectively passed on from one individual or group to another. In many ways, Commissars are like miners—they believe that the best ore is found by digging deeply in the external world. This makes them active investigators in the objective outside world (yet passive perceivers of it).

One of the most notable aspects of the Commissar's worldview is the role that structure plays. Structure, preferably hierarchy, is believed to be tangible, stable, and enduring. To the physician, for example, the human skeletal system is regarded as a superstructure, a solid, supportive framework within which the body's internal organs and systems (nervous, respiratory, digestive) can most effectively operate. Consequently, the preferred way for physicians to fix problems of the skeletal system is similar to how engineers would repair a machine—in this case, surgery. On the other hand, osteopaths believe that the natural state of the skeletal system is not solid, but rather flexible, dynamic, and constantly changing. This is why they prefer to use techniques that promote the natural resilience of this living skeletal system. This approach, they believe, will better support the health of all the other interconnected body systems.

Because Commissars assume the primacy of structure in a system, they often select structural changes as a starting point for other secondary changes. In organizations, this worldview results in hierarchical, top-down management styles and its organizational equivalent—surgery. Often the Commissarial leadership style is misunderstood as a power play or an unfeeling attempt to dominate and control subordinates. However, the underlying motivation of most Commissars is utilitarian: they want to work with the most tangible, "real," and fundamental variables at their disposal so they can change the way their corporations function. Commissar leaders are attracted to management approaches such as business process reengineering (BPR), operational research, and systems analysis. In general, these leaders are hard-edged, analytical thinkers who value the role of measurement in organizations. The Commissar lives by the credo, "If it can't be measured, it doesn't exist" (or, perhaps, "If it can't be measured, I don't want to be bothered with it").

Commissars borrow from well-known laws of nature (such as the physical laws of gravity and motion) manage the daily operations of their companies. They believe that the truth can only be found through *scientific* reasoning. However, what is scientific reasoning to the Commissar is considered bad science by the Yogi. The best way to make sense of an all-too-complex world, says the Commissar, is first to simplify it, then to learn about its essential building blocks. If everything has a place, then the leader's job is to put everything that is broken back into its proper place. This way all sorts of otherwise-fuzzy things can be measured and monitored, trends determined, and results quantified.

In the Commissar's philosophy of *objectivism*, the individual is the ultimate authority on what is true because reality is transparent, the world is knowable, and its "objects" are quite visible. The great system theorist C. West Churchman (1971) proposed that the credo of the objectivist would be: "I and I alone can know the inner states of my own mind and can only *infer* the states of other minds." In other words, I trust my own experience because that is real for me, whereas what others say only allows me to guess about their experience. Commissars trust and value the lessons gained from their own experiences. Such conviction enables them to act with confidence because they believe absolutely that they are correct in how they have seen the world. The only thing that could possibly be doubted is whether they used logic correctly to draw reasonable conclusions from their experience.

## THE UNDERLYING WORLDVIEW OF THE YOGI LEADER

While Commissars might regard themselves as impartial, objective, and scientific, Yogis counter that the Commissar's brand of science is a very specific exception to an otherwise much broader definition of science. Yogis favor the subjective, socially constructed view that "the truth" is a relative concept and, in many cases, the truth is just not knowable. The Yogi leader believes the following:

1. The effects of our actions (causes) in complex systems cannot always be known in advance. (Whereas the Commissar believes that effects will follow from causes in a consistent manner because there is order to the universe.)
2. Solutions to difficult problems and assertions of truth are best determined by a community of practitioners who share their interpretations of how they think things happen. When the outcomes of actions are governed by probabilistic systems,

past experience becomes progressively less useful. (In contrast, Commissars believe that difficult problems are simply conglomerations of simple problems, and once understood, have simple solutions.)

3. The best way to understand these relations is through reflection on how things actually work in practice, sharing theories, and listening to possible explanations of organization members who challenge conventional wisdom by piecing together ideas into a more cohesive and understandable whole theory. (To the Commissar, perceptions are irrelevant because rigorous inquiry and experimentation, following tight procedures, will tell us all that needs to be known.)

4. An objective reality exists, but it is of little significance to our greatest concerns. (Whereas, the Commissar believes that all systems are goal-seeking and the goals as they understand them are the ones that should be achieved.)

The social-constructionist Yogi believes in the philosophy of *subjectivism*, a perspective that was developed by the Scottish philosopher David Hume and popularized in the writings of Thomas Hobbes (*Leviathan*). Whereas the objective-empiricist is inclined to adhere to absolutes, the subjectivist proposes that everything is relative—that is, how you receive something depends on your values. The subjectivist argues that although you may know your own mind, this does not enable you to infer from the outward behavior of others whether your experience is the same as theirs. Thus, we arrive at a main precept of the doctrine of subjectivism: It is impossible to compare the values of two or more members of a society, other than in the form of preference ordering.

To social-constructionists, finding the truth is like putting together a jigsaw puzzle with each piece representing one person's idea of some aspect of the whole. Once the puzzle has been assembled, there must be some basic consensus among the people who contributed to the puzzle that they have arrived at an accurate representation of the world. Social-constructionists do not trust rigid structure, but rather the process of achieving a consensus among a group of people who are committed to searching for the truth. They believe in the power of having members of a community share their interpretations of what is true and how they think things happen. This is the Yogi's version of cause and effect.

The socially constructed view originates with our willingness to test the validity of alternative beliefs and to look at the world from the different perspectives of others. This creative process enables us to experience our world in new ways that may yield new realizations. This is a deliberate process of "enlightening" whatever was previously hidden from our awareness. In the socially constructed worldview, therefore, leaders need to (1) encourage others to experiment with new assumptions and (2) challenge unproven or untested beliefs. This approach allows social-constructionists to try on many different interpretations of the meaning of their experience. Social-constructionists are active internal investigators who then choose other people with whom they can dialogue to further discover the "incompletenesses and incoherencies" of their views.

Some might say the social-constructionists' mission is to *clarify* how they see the world, whereas empiricists seek to *simplify* the world they see. The spirit of the social-constructionists might be expressed by the question posed by Lao-Tzu:

Do you have the patience to wait till your mud settles and the water is clear? Can you remain unmoving till the right action arises by itself?

## THE STRUCTURALIST COMMISSAR VERSUS THE HUMANIST YOGI

Another significant dichotomy between the Yogi and the Commissar is the preference for either structuralism or humanism. In businesses, this is often evidenced in how people approach changing their systems—through structural work or through organizational development. These two activities reflect very different philosophies about the most effective ways to make human activity more consistent with the goals of an organization.

Commissars are typically structuralists who believe that it is most effective to start with concrete mechanics (organization charts, rules, procedures, and systems) and align those with corporate goals. After this is accomplished, people's behavior can then be molded to fit what is "known" to have the highest value, namely achieving the organization's goals. Commissars believe that the structure of a system governs the behavior of those working within it. For example, if you work in a company and break the rules, then you must be controlled: you could be removed from further consideration for promotion, assigned to unfavorable work, or dismissed. In the eyes of Commissar leaders, these are powerful incentives for making sure that workers comply with directives. Most structuralists are also empiricists because the tangible, mechanical, and measurable nature of structure makes it the management tool of choice. For example, during the 1980s, the Russian leader Mikhail Gorbachev often spoke of the needs for *glasnost* and *perestroika* in order to reform the Soviet Union. The system that had become so inefficient and bound up by bureaucracy now would be *restructured* (perestroika) to achieve greater openness (glasnost).

Yogi leaders prefer an organizational development (OD) approach to change because they believe that there are no quick fixes to problems nor any easy ways to win people over to their side. Unlike the structuralists who envision employees as thinking as they do (and therefore complying with the overwhelmingly unpleasant consequences of violating structure), Yogi leaders tend to be humanists who believe that lasting change occurs only when people have internal incentives to make changes themselves. The humanist argues that structuralism leads to *compliance*, but not *commitment*—and that compliance lasts only until the boss's back is turned. The Yogi humanist leader gives workers opportunities to express their feelings and engage in dialogue with management so as to arrive at common ground around a shared vision. To the humanist, peak performance results when enthusiastic members of an organization work together as a team to realize a shared vision of what is possible.

## RECONCILING THE DIVERGENT APPROACHES OF YOGI AND COMMISSAR LEADERS

Clearly, the Commissar takes one approach to learning and knowledge creation, whereas the Yogi takes another. Neither even bothers to sing, "You take the high-road and I'll take the low road, and I'll be in Scotland before you," because each thinks the other is on a completely wrong path and will never manage to get there. The Commissar thinks that once the unknown becomes known (learning occurs), then knowledge application is a simple matter of understanding the newly discovered facts so that the organization can accomplish its desired goals. In the case of the Yogi, the successful path to learning and knowledge application is to progressively reveal more of the truth by uncovering the tacit beliefs that obscure it.

In summary then, neither the Yogi's nor the Commissar's perspective alone affords the insights that knowledge leaders can achieve when both of these perceptual lenses are used in combination. In our view, both lenses are very useful—and both lenses are dangerous if they are used exclusively. Indeed, either of these divergent perspectives can calcify into immovable dogma, and dogma is deadly in a rapidly changing environment. As the great British scientist and philosopher Francis Bacon (1944) observed,

Surely every medicine is an innovation; and he that will not apply new remedies, must expect new evils; for time is the greatest innovator; and if time of course alters things to the worse, and wisdom and counsel shall not alter them to the better, what shall be the end?

As Koestler noted, the unfortunate tendency when under pressure (and we're all under pressure) is that Commissars become more Commissar-like and Yogis become more Yogi-like. In other words, most of us will just continue doing more of what we already prefer doing. These two worldviews then become increasingly exclusive, primal polar forces that can never meet to be balanced and integrated. This, then, is the challenge presented by the divergent worldviews of the Yogi and Commissar. Prospective knowledge leaders who can learn from both of these colorful archetypal characters will have the advantage in generating and applying knowledge and leading KBOs. It is as Thomas Crum (1998) once stated, "Being willing to change allows you to move from a point of view to a viewing point—a higher, more expansive place, from which you can see both sides."

Although it is no small task, becoming a knowledge leader requires you to become more aware of—then reduce the dysfunctional effects of—your own worldview and perceptual blocks. In the next chapter, we will provide you with specific ways you can take a few steps back so that you will be able to more clearly see, then deal with, your own learning limitations.

## REFERENCES

Argyris, Chris. "Education for Leading-Learning." *Organizational Dynamics*, Winter, pp 5-17.

Bacon, Francis. *ESSAYS*; New York Heritage Press (1944). Intro. by Christopher Morley.

Churchman, C.W. (1971). *The Design of Inquiring Systems*. New York: Basic Books.

Crum, T.F. (1998). *The Magic of Conflict*. New York: Simon and Schuster.

Dixon, N. (1994). *The Organizational Learning Cycle*. New York: McGraw-Hill.

Schon, D. (1987). *Educating the Reflective Practitioner: Toward a New Design for Teaching and Learning in the Professions*. San Francisco: Jossey-Bass.

# 5

# STEPPING BACK TO ENVISION NEW POSSIBILITIES

## Executive Summary

To envision new possibilities for their organizations, knowledge leaders must step back so that they can first see, then address, their own perceptual limits to learning. Perceptual limits occur when our beliefs determine both what we choose to perceive and also how we will interpret the meaning of what we have perceived. Individuals and organizations must move out of their comfort zones if they are to create new pragmatic knowledge. *Inquiry* (seeking alternative solutions) results when the *irritation of doubt* occurs about our beliefs because our actions do not produce the results we expect. Both the Yogi and Commissar have learning arrogance—a *learning disability* where they mistake their beliefs for "truth" and become masters of defensive thinking and "skilled unawareness." The Yogi and Commissar have completely different processes of perception and learning—yet each has precisely what the other lacks. Similarly, each favors one-half of the standard *action-learning cycle* where we can learn through our experience. (Commissars prefer action and experimenting; Yogis prefer reflection and constructing new meaning.) *Robust learning* is an optimal learning style that can develop new pragmatic knowledge (by learning how to align our beliefs with our experience of how things really work in practice). Robust learning results in continually combining the externally focused (grounding) activities preferred by Commissars with the internally focused (enlightening) activities preferred by Yogis.

To envision new possibilities for their organizations, knowledge leaders must step back so they can more clearly see, then address their own perceptual limits to learning. These learning limitations are often subtle—taking form as stylistic preferences for how people think and learn. We refer to them as limits because they restrict our freedom and the degree of flexibility in how we act. *Perception traps* are created when we hold on to beliefs that prevent us from taking full advantage of the opportunities available to us. Unfortunately, this tendency to stay inside a comfort zone of habitual thinking and perceiving is largely at fault for the difficulties we experience.

It is natural to develop habitual patterns and routine ways of learning that originate in our perceptual biases and stylistic learning preferences. We all can get into difficulty when we fail to see how our existing patterns of perception limit our field of view. A great irony is that not only do these beliefs determine what we will choose to perceive, they also will determine how we interpret the meaning of what we have chosen to perceive. Often, an unfavorable reinforcing cycle results where self-limiting beliefs color our interpretations. This, in turn, only has the effect of further reinforcing the self-limiting nature of those beliefs by excluding any feedback from our actions that is contrary to them.

Arthur Koestler observed this tendency when he noted that, under pressure, the Yogi becomes more Yogi-like and the Commissar becomes more Commissar-like. This *single-loop learning* sets off a self-limiting spiral that can neither generate new knowledge nor be successfully challenged without some kind of compelling outside stimuli. It's a bit like living in a hypnotic trance, but it is a spell that we cast on ourselves! If we view our experience via an ungrounded or rigidly defined process, then we are unwittingly setting ourselves up to unconsciously limit the amount of information we can access about the world. This sort of perceptual trap was described by Thomas S. Kuhn in his famous book, *The Structure of Scientific Revolutions.* Kuhn observed that even the most sincere scientific investigators were prone to distort the evidence from their research by overlooking any findings that ran contrary to their beliefs or by discounting them as trivial side effects. The old saw that "what one sees depends on what one believes" seems to hold true. American pragmatist Charles Sanders Peirce also noted that scientists often behaved in quite *unscientific* ways due to the perceptual biases caused by their distorted or incomplete beliefs.

For many of us, the way we have chosen to design our lives and work has already accommodated our existing perceptual limitations.

We are in our comfort zones—and most of us prefer staying there. However, Mary Lou Retton, former U.S. Olympic champion, advises that we move out of them:

We all live our lives in comfort zones, avoiding risky situations, avoiding the potential to fail. But in order to get ahead of your competition, you've got to go out of your comfort zone. Now your comfort zone is something that you live your whole day, your whole life in. You go to work and do what has to be done to get by. You've got to try to do more. Try that little new thing, that different approach. Get out of your comfort zone and see if it works. It may, it may not, but you'll never know if you don't try.

Perceptual limits do not always pose a problem. They can, in fact, be quite functional, allowing us to get on with our daily tasks without being distracted or overwhelmed by new information. But for those leaders or businesses whose survival depends on their capacity to generate and apply new knowledge, it is imperative that these perceptual limits be constantly addressed.

All ways of knowing the world can contribute to developing the fullest possible understanding and experience of reality. The more we are aware of our perceptual biases, the greater our chance to approach the ideal that historian Matthew Arnold recognized in the ancient philosopher Sophocles—that is, "He saw life clearly and whole." To break through many of our self-imposed perceptual limits, each of us needs to expand the range and depth of our learning experience. Different avenues may be needed by different people to open up new windows onto the world. For example, scientists may find that music helps them break through learning blocks. Artists may need a course in business to help expand their view of the world. Other helpful ways to create perceptual breakthroughs include (but are not limited to) logical inference, reasoning, scientific inquiry, playing, systems thinking, listening to intuition, reading scripture, performing or listening to music, reading or writing poetry, studying a brand new topic, using subjective-interpretative methods, and learning chess, a new language, or how to dance. Any of these modalities might provide a fresh perspective from which we could learn how to see the world anew.

Interestingly, as we become willing to examine the perceptual filters inherent in our worldviews, we are likely to discover that some of our most rigidly held beliefs are actually hand-me-downs from family members, early teachers, former bosses, or other authority figures. There is nothing intrinsically wrong with such beliefs. However, they may have become outdated or obsolete as the world has changed—that is, they may now be incomplete or distorted in some important way. An example is how research into quantum theory has dramatically altered the field of modern physics, resulting in theories that have eclipsed, encompassed, and replaced the old theories.

Our beliefs are tools that are (more or less) effective in truly explaining how and why things work as they do. If they are less effective, we need to revise them so that they more accurately reflect how things really do work in practice. Fortunately, most beliefs that we use in everyday life do not need to be scientifically validated. However, when we are about to make important decisions that involve grave risks or outstanding opportunities, it is sensible for us to question our beliefs, subject them to scrutiny, and reflect on their value. This is not to say that many of the beliefs handed down to us by our predecessors are without value. On the contrary, many of these beliefs have stood the test of time and scrutiny, and have proven themselves robust and reliable.

However, when we automatically default to looking at life through a very narrow lens, it eventually becomes impossible for us to appreciate the wholeness of life. The world is composed of many complex systems, where sets of interconnected parts dynamically interact to produce the behavior of the whole. When we use only a microscope to focus solely on a single part of the whole, we are likely to develop overly simplistic, erroneous notions about the interrelationships that govern how things actually work. The beginning of any real effort to see things as they are (clearly and whole, rather than as we wish them to be) begins with our willingness to experience what Charles Sanders Peirce calls the *irritation of doubt*.

Feelings of authentic doubt usually arise from nonperformance. That is, when things do not work the way we expect them to, we begin to doubt whether our actions are correctly matched to the problems we are hoping to solve. True doubt is not simply the experience of being skeptical. People experience true doubt as being emotionally disconcerting. The desire to assuage this discomfort often prompts individuals to take action (such as seeking alternative explanations, theories, or solutions to the situation that is causing the irritable doubt). This process is known as *inquiry*. Inquiry and performance are opposing forces that tend to balance each other's effect (Figure 5.1).

Engaging in inquiry is like shining a flashlight on a dark space in search of a particular object. If you allow this healthy doubt and inquiry to shine a bright light on the problems you are solving, then

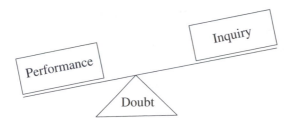

**Figure 5.1**
*The Mediating Effect of Doubt*

you will discover the unexamined assumptions and beliefs that limit your performance. However, this effort requires courage and a will to learn. *Choosing*, after examination, to favor your prior beliefs over potential new ones is fine. However, doing so unconsciously, out of routine or inertia, is a self-limiting pattern that will prevent you from creating the results you desire.

While people are quite capable of seeing things in a number of different ways, it does seem to be a deeply imbedded human tendency to lock into one way of seeing things at the exclusion of others. The difficulty in perceiving the world in new ways can be illustrated by the pictures that show two images. What you see depends upon how you look at it. A famous example is the drawing that contains facial profiles of both a young woman and an old woman shown in Figure 5.2. Once you see the first profile, it is very difficult to shift perceptual gears and see the second profile. This process is comparable to the way rain

**Figure 5.2**
*Facial Profiles of an Old Woman and Young Woman*

runs down the side of a mountain, eventually creating a gully that funnels future downpours into the same path. Similarly, if left un-examined, the self-organizing structures of perception will lead to illusory (and incomplete) understandings of the world you live in.

This is why physicist David Bohm asserted that all worldviews are inherently self-limiting. When they function alone, they can not possibly provide the scope of views we need to fully understand the whole. This is especially true of the complex, vexing issues knowl-edge leaders face today. Unfortunately, many leaders have been conditioned by educational systems and workplace routines to think in ways that do not increase their capacity for problem solving or learning from experience.

Obviously, the challenge of looking at things in unaccustomed ways can be so uncomfortable initially that it is easier to stick with the tried-and-true methods that got you to the level of success you enjoy now. Indeed, why should you bother to do something new when simply getting the task done might be sufficient for your goals? Such is the way of habit. Human beings are creatures of routine in our thinking, perhaps more than in any other respect. Actually, these behavioral patterns are a good thing: They enable us to be efficient by assuming that we can act the same way each time we encounter the same situation. The problem with routines comes when our effec-tiveness at getting what we expect, want, or need starts to diminish. Changing habitual ways of thinking is like learning to walk all over again. Who wants to be a novice when they have already mastered a particular approach to living and working? However, the heroic journey to becoming a knowledge leader requires a commitment to continually improving the quality of your knowledge for action. This is not always easy or comfortable. It means a willingness to be a learning-novice when you enter unknown territory, and also a will-ingness to change beliefs and behavior when you discover they are no longer effective. Consultant Denis Waitley noted that:

We make our habits and our habits make us. Practicing bad habits over a long period of time can ingrain attitudes, beliefs and feelings so firmly that escape seems impossible. In such cases, you must exhibit change—do it, perform its outward manifestations—before you can learn to believe in it. You will find that by learning and repeating new behavior patterns you can change your habits and your life.

The absence of doubt can have the effect of *fixating* our beliefs in ways that are neither adaptive nor sustainable. People who rigidly subscribe to dogmatic beliefs are usually right some of the time because, as the old adage goes, even a broken clock shows the correct time two times a day. Once we are convinced by our success that we know what works best, we have no further incentive to engage in inquiry. This can result in a decline in the capacity for learning, as M. Scott Peck (1978) so eloquently noted:

The more effort we make to appreciate and perceive reality, the larger and more accurate our maps will be. But many do not want to make this effort. . . . Their maps are small and sketchy, their views narrow and misleading. By end of middle age most people . . . feel certain that their maps are complete and their Weltanschauung is correct (indeed, even sacrosanct), and they are no longer interested in new information. It is as if they are tired. Only a relative and fortunate few continue . . . enlarging and refining and redefining their understanding of the world and what is true. (pp. 44–45)

Some people believe that if they are not actively learning, they are at least in a holding pattern. We do not think this is true. Leaders who are not growing suffer a sort of internal dry rot. In turn their companies suffer because they are not nourished by a constant flow of invigorating new ideas that can come only from leaders who are courageous enough to move out of their comfort zones into new knowledge territory.

## LEARNING ARROGANCE

On the surface, it would appear that there is very little Yogis and Commissars have in common. But they do share one fatal flaw—a subtle form of learning disability, a perceptual trap that we refer to as *learning arrogance*. That is, both the Yogi and the Commissar confidently mistake all their beliefs for truth, and in so doing prevent themselves from either learning or leading effectively. Consequently, both characters are masters of defensive thinking and self-deception. They go to great ends to avoid seeing any feedback that indicates their ineffectiveness at accomplishing what is most important to them.

Over time, both the Yogi and the Commissar adapt to this lethal learning limitation by cultivating what Chris Argyris (1990) referred to as *skilled unawareness*. By deftly applying their distorted theories about how things work, they are able to secure at least some of the results they desire. However, it is this deliberate unawareness, and the distorted perception of success it creates, that blocks them from ever seeing the broader consequences of their actions. The ability of the Yogi and Commissar to remain blissfully unaware of the effects of counterproductive actions only serves to sustain their learning arrogance. Clearly, this way of thinking is not helpful over time for any business that needs to create and apply knowledge.

The perceptual traps inherent in the learning styles of Yogis and Commissars can be described with the following analogy. The Yogi part of us is like a golfer who obsessively analyzes his swing but rarely practices or plays. Yogis may develop useful insights into how they could improve their game, but they rarely develop enough skill to enact their plans. Conversely, the Commissar part of us is more like a frequent golfer who improves his or her game through sheer will but never learns to play differently and has very few "breakthrough" moments. Both characters need outside intervention to see themselves clearly.

Sports psychologist Tim Gallwey tells how he helped a golfer become aware of his swing by placing a full-length mirror in front of him as he practiced. Because his perceptual block was so suddenly shattered by the image reflected back to him, this man could no longer ignore, discount, or deny his problem. Through (in this case, literal) reflection, this golfer was finally able to integrate his perceptions with his actions—and actually learn. We have had similar breakthrough moments while coaching executives who allowed us to videotape their presentations. Truly, this sort of "candid camera" feedback is worth more than a thousand words when it comes to eliminating perceptual blocks and changing behavior.

The art of connecting action and reflection through the process of receiving feedback is not always as easy as seeing yourself in the mirror. Perceptual feedback is only as useful as your openness to receive it and your willingness to accept it. Unfortunately, both the Yogi's and the Commissar's learning arrogance can result in a kind of blindness that prevents them from processing the vital sensory input that would help them learn and lead more effectively.

Yogi leaders build elaborate conceptual models and self-understandings based mainly on impressions of their relationship to a world they prefer to see from afar. They are somewhat like people sitting around the fire in Plato's mythical cave, where reality was no more than the flicker of shadows dancing on the rock walls of the cave. Yogis delude themselves that their intricate mental models provide an accurate map of the world—a map that they often mistake for reality. In contrast, Commissars believe that there are no mysteries in life. They are guilty of thinking that their watered-down, simplified theories of how things work are robust enough to capture the complexity of the real world. This is a bit like people who know what a sunset looks like and therefore decide that they never need to actually *look* at a sunset again. For Commissars there are few mysteries in the universe that need further exploration. What is important to them is learning the rules about how the world's mechanisms work.

## THE PROCESS OF PERCEPTION

Our perceptual processes are vital in shaping both our actions and our beliefs. The Commissar would regard perception as the (passive) act of receiving information from the environment. This is highly ironic since the empiricist Commissar is actively seeking the truths of the outer world—but with passive eyes. Commissars regard all the details of how the world works to be completely transparent. In their view, all you need to do is to look in the right place and what you're looking for will reveal itself to you. The way to understand the world, therefore, is simply by observing it with the courage to face things as they really are.

The Yogi believes that, even in the simple act of perceiving, we have interacted with the world. By focusing on a given aspect of reality, we enliven it and then later ascribe meaning to it. The Yogi thinks that the process of looking at the world is "purposefully seeing" it. What you perceive is also governed by your belief system, contends the Yogi, in that it orders your visual system to value certain aspects of the world over others. The Yogi believes that your *perceptual filters* are the mechanical extension of your own existing worldview.

We argue that perception is a much more complex process than is understood by either Yogis or Commissars. Research by behavioral optometrists Shapiro, Gottlied, and Mancini suggests that the physical process of *seeing* involves an entire visual system that is interconnected with a person's identity, beliefs, and values. Your visual system, they contend, is not a physiological apparatus that acts in a value-neutral manner. It is a much broader system of mind–body interactions that enable complex dynamics between yourself and your environment.

## IRRECONCILABLE DIFFERENCES?

Though they are usually unaware of it, the perceptual styles of the Yogi and the Commissar are enduring, defining characteristics of their identity. Yet despite their seemingly irreconcilable differences, the Yogi and the Commissar have much to learn from each other. Indeed, in their different ways of seeing the world, each one has precisely what the other lacks!

We propose that by deliberately integrating these two distinctly different learning tendencies, knowledge leaders can significantly improve their learning capacity. Senge (1990) referred to this as *generative learning*. However, much as with oil and water, the action-oriented Commissar and reflective Yogi are more likely to go their separate ways. Therefore, the integration of other ways of thinking into our personal system is an ongoing process rather than a permanent accomplishment. It is not unlike making a fine quality vinaigrette by combining olive oil, vinegar, and spices. The whole combination must be shaken vigorously to achieve the transitory state that we find so appealing. The lesson of the vinaigrette is that the temporary blending of oil and vinegar is beneficial, even if it doesn't last. It just has to be shaken again later on, when we next need it.

But then, your work environment is probably shaking you up quite a bit these days. While it is natural to resist this shaking, we encourage you instead to reframe such ongoing turmoil as an opportunity for learning in the midst of action. This action-based learning approach can help you find ways to adapt and grow. We propose that the path toward increased capacity for knowledge leadership is to experiment with new actions and behavior that will, at first, seem less natural to you. This is not merely to promote balance in the way you learn. It is also a way of honoring the principle that leaders have much more to offer their organizations when their own inner and outer work is integrated. Chris Argyris (1993) argued that "learning should be in the service of action." We concur. However, we add that the converse is true: action should be in the service of learning. *Indeed, combining action and reflection is in service to optimum individual and organizational learning—and the development of knowledge.*

Charles Sanders Peirce suggests that learning through experience helps us escape our perceptual traps because it has the potential to enable us to create pragmatic knowledge. Pragmatic knowledge is ad hoc knowledge that results from our experience of taking a certain action to achieve a goal, then receiving the feedback about whether that action was effective in reaching that goal. *Ad hoc* (Latin, "for this") *knowledge* is important to our success in the workplace because it is useful for a specific purpose. In contrast, most knowledge that people employ each day is *generic knowledge*. For example, once you learn how to drive an automobile, it does not matter which brand of automobile you drive because the generic knowledge you gain in a standard driving course will work effectively with almost any kind of vehicle. This is because most automobiles are roughly the same.

The problem comes when you are doing something new and complex or when there is not a single best practice for getting things done. Here is where things can get conceptually difficult. Commissars will argue that because all systems are variations on some theme and composed from the same building blocks, all you have to do is to identify the theme, break the problem down into its components, and "voila!"—the solution becomes apparent. On the other hand, Yogis believe that there are an infinite number of unique and fundamentally different problems we can encounter in life. One way to effectively cope with new or complex problems is to treat each situation as an experiment where you continuously try new approaches and, over time, learn from your ongoing experience. This approach will allow you to incrementally develop ever-improving ways of treating the problem.

Because management theories focus on simplifying the complex and reducing the "fuzzy" to its elements, they often create an illusion of certainty. The problem is that managers are often misled to believing that they *already* know what works best in practice. Consequently, as long as they view their performance as acceptable, there is no reason for them to feel the irritating sensation of doubt that would drive them to seek new solutions. This learning arrogance is a primary block to improving the usefulness of our beliefs and the quality of our knowledge. It gives people the illusion of being in control. During a classroom discussion of this topic, one student replied angrily when we asked him to consider the validity of his beliefs. "You can't think about whether everything you believe is true," he said, "or you'll go crazy." While we agree that it is not a terrible thing to believe in what you believe, people and organizations who do not regularly test their closely-held beliefs against their real-life experience wind up unable to learn, adapt, or innovate.

The pragmatic view is that learning is the process of aligning your beliefs with your experience of how things really work in the world. Unfortunately, both the Yogi and the Commissar are convinced of the correctness of their particular view based solely on its intellectual resonance with their core beliefs—without ever knowing if these beliefs will work in any given situation. This reflects their commitment to a specific ideology. Throughout the world in various professions, such as medicine, education, and management consulting, practitioners typically adopt an ideology that they identify with as their own, and then use it in all situations. The old adage that seems to apply here is that "If all you know how to use is a hammer, then all the world will look like nails to you." If people believe they already know what works best in all circumstances, then they have no incentive to learn, much less to engage in action-learning. Instead, they just have to apply what they already "know" to various new realms. Unfortunately, they then become incapable of either improving the quality of their existing knowledge or creating new knowledge.

A more pragmatic perspective is that learning by deliberately mining your experiences, capturing lessons learned, reflecting, and creating new theories of action can transform your work performance into a continuous experiment with an upward directed arc of improvement. Just as scientists continually change the conditions of an experiment to see what will happen, knowledge leaders can make their workplace a laboratory to discover what works best *for them.* Unfortunately, many leaders have been socialized to act in ways that are expedient but not pragmatic (as relates to organizational performance). The purpose of any pragmatic approach is not only to discover via experience what works best, but also to allow the new learning about how things work to inform your existing beliefs and rewire your brain to enable you to imagine new possibilities.

Obviously, many problems may crop up to short-circuit the fragile process of knowledge creation and improvement. These include the following:

1. Not having time to reflect, brainstorm, or imagine new possibilities.
2. Fear of taking the risks necessary to try new things.
3. Having strong preferences that favor one step in the learning cycle over others.
4. Believing that what is now true about something will be true forever.

This last problem is a particularly sinister perceptual trap because a person may know part of the truth, or a temporary truth, and mistake this partial truth as being complete and enduring.

## THE ACTION-LEARNING CYCLE

Knowledge leaders need to stay alert for the perceptual traps that can occur at any stage in the action-learning cycle to limit their learn-

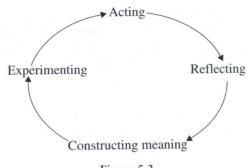

**Figure 5.3**
*Action-Learning Cycle*

ing capacity. The action-learning cycle (Figure 5.3) reflects the natural learning process for human beings. It depicts the ways we actively seek to create new meaning by putting our beliefs and expectations to the test of experience. The cycle typically consists of four stages: Acting → Reflecting → Constructing meaning → Experimenting.

The term *action* can mean two different things: to act purposefully or the active part of life's experience (i.e., doing things). Because it is impossible to not do things while you are alive (even when you are completely still, you are still breathing), we will use action to refer to purposeful action, to doing something with a goal in mind.

*Reflection* means not only looking back at the significance of the action you took. It also means looking ahead to imagine how things would work differently, in the future, if you took different actions under similar conditions. It is a review of some set of events or relationships. It is a recounting of your past in a way that allows you to organize that event in your mind so that you understand exactly what transpired—and can learn from it.

*Construction* refers to the construction of meaning. Construction may be defined as building a structure, creating an interpretation, or "sense-making." In the construction process, we take what we have reflected on and ask questions such as: "What does the way things worked in this case say about how things work in general, or about how they are likely to work again in the future? How and why did these results occur? What was my theory or hypothesis about how things should work? Did that hypothesis accurately predict the actual results this time around?"

In *Man's Search for Meaning*, psychologist Viktor Frankl (1959) proposes that human beings are in a constant search to create meaning from their experience. By creating meaning, you build reliable structures and gain new insights into reality. Constructing new meaning from your experience results in new lessons learned and reframed situations. You can then see familiar circumstances in a new light. This phase of the learning cycle results in a new road map through a complex world—a map you can rely on until your next learning replaces it.

*Experimentation* is the process of focusing your will and attention on changing some of your actions by testing the effects of new actions, perhaps on a pilot basis—*just to discover what happens*. As opposed to the action phase of the cycle, experimentation is mainly for the purpose of discovering whether your theories turn out to be true. For example, a company that is set to launch a new product may first test-market it on a limited basis in several locations to determine early consumer response to the product.

## COMPARISON OF THE LEARNING STYLES OF YOGI AND COMMISSAR LEADERS

We found something quite interesting about the relationship of the four elements of the action-learning cycle to each other. If we slice the cycle in half (Figure 5.4), we can see that one-half of the cycle is inwardly focused and favored by the Yogi, and the other half is outwardly focused and favored by the Commissar.

People with the Commissar's outwardly directed perceptual biases actively engage in search behaviors (to reveal the facts of the matter and to determine whether a prior solution exists). March and Simon (1958) have written extensively about this type of behavior. If the search fails to turn up a prior solution, then a process of experi-

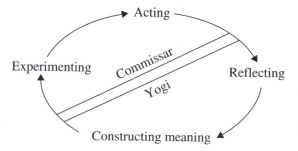

**Figure 5.4**
*Action-Learning Biases of Yogi and Commissar*

mentation is commenced to deduce an answer. If we look at the verbs that characterize this perspective, we see "active" language, emphasizing only action and experimentation. The other two parts of the action-learning cycle, reflection and construction of meaning, are virtually ignored in the linguistic array of the Commissar.

On the other hand, Yogis suffer from a different sort of limitation. They devalue the experimenting and acting phases of the action-learning cycle. They miss these grounding activities that would keep them in touch with the reality around them. They can become paralyzed by the complexities and possibilities they see. As a result, they avoid choosing an action because it just might be a misstep that will create unintended consequences. Yogis favor reflecting and constructing (enlightening activities) because these help them see more clearly—or in a different light—the problems they are encountering.

Obviously, no person learns by exclusively using one of these two archetypes. However, the more you combine, blend, and balance grounding and enlightening learning activities, the greater your ability will be to avoid perceptual traps—and the more "robust" your learning will be.

## ROBUST LEARNING

*Robust learning* is a profound knowing that derives from an ongoing movement between an exploration of the external world and your internal world. Robust learning thrives on curiosity, open mindedness, and the paradoxical quality of detached enthusiasm. People who learn in this way are drawn to figure out what really works, thereby coming ever closer to discovering what is true. As the great educator and pragmatic philosopher John Dewey (1916) observed:

The nature of experience can be understood only by noting that it includes an active and a passive element peculiarly combined. On the active hand, experience is *trying*—a meaning which is made explicit in the connected term experiment. On the passive, it is *undergoing*. When we experience something we act upon it, we do something with it; then we suffer or undergo the consequences. We do something to the thing and then it does something to us in return: such is the peculiar combination. The connection of these two phases measures the fruitfulness or value of the experience. Mere activity does not constitute experience. (p. 139)

The problem then is that the preferred learning styles of the Yogi and Commissar are both severely limited. The downfall of both Yogi and Commissar leaders is that they fail as action learners. Yogis take limited amounts of data from the outside world and process it internally over and over—questioning its meaning and validity. Commissars take in a large amount of data from the outside world and manipulate it in programmed and predictable ways—regardless of the circumstances. Left to their own devices, both of them ignore one-half of the learning cycle, which prevents them from ever learning fully from their experiences. Indeed, only by completing the full action-learning cycle can any of us learn in robust ways that will enable us to achieve the results we desire. It is interesting that between the Yogi's and the Commissar's preferred learning styles lies both the *best* (robust learning) and the *worst* (learning disability) of possible worlds (Table 5.1).

**Table 5.1**
*Types of Learning Styles*

|  |  |  |  |  |
|---|---|---|---|---|
| High | | Type 1 | | Type 4 |
| Grounding | | | | |
| Low | | Type 2 | | Type 3 |
| | | Low | Enlightenment | High |

## Type 1: High Grounding/Low Enlightenment (Commissar)

Leaders who prefer this style of learning can easily attain a sense of mastery because they live in an objective world where all that matters is obvious to them. Grounding is the result of a steady diet of dealing with practical concerns, such as finding out what works and then making it happen. Usually this mode is very effective for discovering "facts," such as numbers and rules that are related to what makes tangible things tick. In this world, leaders with the most data and best technology are the winners. The goal is to steep one's self in learning the intricacies of method, rule, and procedure. Along with being grounded comes a feeling of certainty and correctness—sometimes even complacency. Leaders who focus on learning in this manner will likely be very competent within a narrow scope of information, but not very adaptable or flexible as contrary ideas appear. This mode of learning has the following core precepts:

- A preference for exploring the "outer world"
- A fascination with finding out what works
- A focus on concrete, tangible aspects of the world

- A feeling of clarity derived from dealing with discrete, easily definable items
- An adventuresome desire to "change the system"
- An emphasis on mastery of technique

## Type 2: Low Grounding/Low Enlightenment (Learning Disabled)

This mode represents a true learning disability. Some people, through physical, mental, or emotional damage, have lost the natural desire to learn. This leads to stagnation, staying stuck in preconceived notions about what is correct and how things ought to be. In the extreme, people using this style become detached from all but the most basic characteristics of reality and never develop deeper insight about themselves or the world they live in. They do not question. They get by, but that's about it. This mode has the following core precepts:

- Apathy, lack of interest, a loss of the natural drive to learn
- Defensiveness about what they have been taught
- Head in the sand; naive ("What—me worry?")
- Feeling disempowered, having low morale; a lack of joy in learning or a devil-may-care attitude ("Live, drink, and be merry, for tomorrow you may die.")
- Belief that the world does not really change ("There's nothing new under the sun.")
- Attitude that all new knowledge and innovations are "the same old wine in new bottles"

## Type 3: High Enlightenment/Low Grounding (Yogi)

This learning style leads to the construction of elaborate models and theories about how things work. Unfortunately, these are built largely on untested assumptions. Here, there is a very loose connection between theory and practice. Yogis are prone to dwell on their own subjective feelings about what they have observed in the world and what it means to them. Since such inner dialogues are often incapable of being fully resolved without taking further action, Yogis often become caught in a circular, closed-loop pattern that leads them ever further away from the actual world they are contemplating.

With some extremely intellectual Yogis, the "ivory tower" effect takes over, and they may become specialists who analyze what *other* people do. Yogis who practice this mode of learning can be quite articulate when explaining their views, but they rarely extend themselves to putting their theories into action. What Yogis say may look great on the drawing board, but unanticipated practical flaws typically show up in the real world because their formulae often have not accounted for some important variable (for example, human nature). This then throws the real-world application of the theory into total disarray.

By remaining separate from the outer world, Yogis have to rely on finding answers within themselves. Unfortunately, they may only be able to offer stock answers (perhaps from favorite books). Yogis' lack of experience results in a stunted or atrophied development of their ability to judge what is true. This makes it possible for them to go on happily "chasing rainbows" and endlessly contemplating esoteric questions. They may never realize that their intellectual pursuits are drifting further and further from the mark of what is useful, of service, or true. This learning mode includes the following core precepts:

- Desire to fully think through every problem and solution (analysis-paralysis)
- Belief that the world can be known by standing apart from it and thinking about it, rather than by engaging with it
- Attachment to/fascination with elaborate theories and models
- Need to pursue rigorous methods in constructing complex theories
- Oversimplified view that implementation of solutions is quite easy, whereas developing solutions is the more difficult, and certainly the more noble, task
- Preference for detached methodical analysis

## Type 4: High Grounding/High Enlightenment (Robust Learning)

Robust learning requires constantly balancing, and staying in touch with, both the inner and outer worlds. Here, practice informs theory and theory informs practice in a virtuous, upward spiral of learning. This is a rich world of ever-deepening experience in which new explanations for why things happen are being constantly developed, tested, and refined. Robust learning occurs where feedback from the world informs your ideas about cause and effect and also triggers reconsideration of your beliefs. Clearly, robust learning is required for the development of pragmatic knowledge.

In this final learning style, *your capacity for learning expands concurrently with your knowledge base.* This is the key distinction of the robust mode of learning. In the other three learning modes, either capacity (grounding or enlightenment) improves at the expense of the other. In this fourth type of learning, both grounding and enlightenment are optimized, yielding a full-spectrum style of learning and resulting in the generation of new (pragmatic) knowledge. This learning mode includes the following core precepts:

- Willingness to live with the "irritation of doubt" until inquiry produces new (pragmatic) knowledge
- Eagerness to learn; excitement at learning
- Confidence in one's ability to learn
- Reasonable ease with stepping out of comfort zone
- A willingness to change—to shed old beliefs and incorporate new ones
- A balance of outer and inner learning; concrete and abstract; application and theory

In summary then, a dynamic, balanced combination of "grounding" and "enlightenment" is necessary to gain the optimum (pragmatic) knowledge of the world. Robust learning is full-spectrum learning—the kind that will reveal the limits of your existing beliefs so that you can generate new knowledge or improve your existing knowledge.

In this section of *Knowledge Leadership,* we have described how the worldviews of the Yogi and Commissar can significantly influence how leaders look at the world, learn from experience, and lead others. Do you know people at work who appear to strongly prefer the leadership style of the Yogi or the Commissar? Do these people fit the looking-learning-leading profile we have described here? Can you see aspects of the Yogi and Commissar in yourself? The more you recognize the Yogi or Commissar in yourself and others, the more you will be able to take advantage of the gifts they have to offer, expand the ways you learn, improve the quality of your knowledge, and become a well-balanced knowledge leader.

In the next chapter, you will be able to compare your Yogi and Commissar scores on the abbreviated form of the Knowledge Bias Profile with those of other participants in our research of this instrument. We believe you will enjoy this process and that it will provide you with helpful feedback on your perceptual, learning, and leadership style.

# REFERENCES

Argyris, C. (1990) *Overcoming Organizational Defenses*. Boston, MA, Allyn and Bacon.

Argyris, C. (1993). "Education for Leading-Learning." *Organization Dynamics*, Fall, 5–17.

Dewey, J. (1916). *Democracy and Education*. New York: McMillan.

Frankl, V. (1959). *Man's Search for Meaning*. Revised and Updated Edition, New York: Bcacon Press, Boston, MA Pocket Books.

March, J. and Simon, H. (1958). *Organizations*. New York: Wiley.

Peck, M. S. (1978). *The Road Less Traveled*. New York: Simon & Schuster.

Retton, M. L. Retrieved from www.managersforum.com/Quotes/. http://www.managersforum.com/Quotes/QuoteAll.asp.

Senge, P. (1990). *The Fifth Discipline*. New York: Doubleday.

# 6

# STUDYING KNOWLEDGE LEADERSHIP BEHAVIOR: LESSONS FROM CROSS-CULTURAL RESEARCH

## Executive Summary

Our study of the worldviews of the Yogi and the Commissar led us to speculate that these two colorful characters would have distinctly different *knowledge leadership styles*. To scientifically test our hypothesis that what Yogis and Commissars *believe* influences their leadership *behavior*, we spent eight years developing the *Knowledge Bias Profile (*KBP) and testing it on 517 managers and business students in both the United States and China. In this chapter, you will be able to compare your scores on the abbreviated version of the KBP in Chapter 3 with participants in our research study. The results of our study provided us with strong evidence of a clear relationship between the worldviews of these two kinds of leaders and their behaviors—that is, how they perceive (*look* at) situations, *learn* from experience, and *lead* others. The data revealed not only that there are significant behavioral differences that result from the worldviews of Yogis and Commissars, but also that these differences can be discriminated by using the KBP (which proved to have strong internal validity). Interestingly, most respondents in our study scored in the midrange, indicating a preference for a more balanced business leadership style both for themselves and for their leaders. We believe these results signal good news for the future of knowledge leadership, which requires a strong integration of the Yogi's knowledge development (KD) preferences and the Commissar's knowledge management (KM) abilities.

## THE STUDY

Our early investigations of the worldviews of the Yogi and the Commissar led us to speculate that the fundamental beliefs held by these two leaders would influence how they perceive organizations, learn from experience, and, ultimately, lead others. We hypothesized that Yogis would focus on *change-from-within* strategies of leadership and that their learning style would be biased toward reflecting and creating new meaning from their experiences. On the other hand, we hypothesized that Commissars would lean toward *change-from-without* leadership strategies and that their learning style would be biased more toward experimentation and action. To test our hypothesis that what leaders *believe* influences their *behavior* (specifically how they *look*, *learn*, and *lead*), we decided to study both managers and aspiring managers (business students). Over several years, the authors (and our colleague Lee W. Lee) first developed, then tested a standard structure questionnaire, that we named the *Knowledge Bias Profile (KBP)*. To minimize the effects of cultural bias, we made the study a cross-cultural one, with a sample equally divided between people in the United States and China.

## DATA COLLECTION

We collected data by surveying a large sample of business managers and business students. The questions contained in the KBP asked people to indicate, on a 5-point Likert scale, the extent to which they agree or disagree with statements about two leadership profiles that were modeled on Koestler's Yogi and Commissar. A total of 517 questionnaires were completed for inclusion in the study. (A detailed description of the development of the KBP—and information about how you can obtain the full instrument—is presented in Appendix A.) The data we gathered were analyzed by Dr. Lee W. Lee, using standard statistical methods, to test the strength of the relationships we had hypothesized at the outset of the study.

## THE RESULTS

The results of the study provided us with strong empirical support for the Yogi and Commissar models, two styles that represent very distinct leadership philosophies—and behaviors that are guided by these philosophies. The study provided strong evidence of a clear relationship between the beliefs, or worldviews, of these two kinds of leaders and their behaviors—that is, how they perceive (*look* at) situations, *learn* from experience, and *lead* others.

The data revealed significant differences in the worldviews of Yogis and Commissars, and also that these differences can be discriminated by using the KBP. The responses of participants varied widely—from those who had an extreme preference for the Yogi profile to those who had an extreme preference for the Commissar profile. However, most respondents fell somewhere between these two extremes.

The data also suggested a high degree of internal validity in the KBP. Indeed, over 94% of the correlations were significant at the level of .01. From the results we obtained, we feel confident about this instrument's reliability and validity in measuring these two leadership styles that have such major implications for knowledge leadership. As you recall, Yogis tend to be more adept at KD processes, whereas Commissars are more likely to favor KM approaches. Both approaches, of course, are necessary for well-balanced knowledge leadership.

Interestingly, most of our respondents were neither extreme Yogis nor extreme Commissars. They scored somewhere in the midrange—that is, moderately high on both scales. This preponderance of individual midrange scores hints that there may indeed be an evolution occurring now toward a preference for a more balanced business leadership style—one that moves away from the dominant Commissar worldview to an inclusion of the Yogi worldview. Another set of data that suggests a preference for a more balanced leadership approach is the strong midrange response of people to their "preferred leader" profile. Taken together, these two sets of data suggest the potential of an emerging business climate that is ready for more balanced leaders.

Although most people scored in the midrange between Yogis and Commissars for their preferred (more balanced) leader, we did find some interesting demographic differences in the study. For example, there was a strong gender difference in leadership preference. Although both men and women in the United States had a slight preference for a Yogi leader, this preference was much truer of women than their male colleagues. And this gender gap was even more accentuated in China, where men preferred the Commissar leader, and women preferred the Yogi. We also discovered that Americans who were older and had more education leaned slightly toward being more Commissar-like in their leading style.

The study revealed a significant correlation between most items that measured people's worldview identity and their behavioral orientation (looking, learning, leading). Interestingly, worldview was even more strongly correlated with behavioral orientation in people who preferred the Yogi than in those who preferred the Commissar (see Figures 6.1 through 6.3). These data suggest that Yogis may have a greater need to align their personal beliefs closely with their behavior—that is, their beliefs serve as an internal compass for choosing their actions. We speculate that perhaps Commissars' external and structural focus makes them more sensitive to taking cues about how to behave from their organization's existing structures, systems, and policies.

The worldviews of Yogis and Commissars were measured by six variables. These included (1) general worldview/beliefs, (2) core values, (3) the nature of the change (internal development versus structure), (4) the source of change (self versus external), (5) the focus of organizational change (from within versus from without), and (6) the type of reasoning used (open-ended versus a structured, mechanical approach). The three tables that follow indicate the degree to which the Yogi's or Commissar's worldview is correlated (percentage on the y-axis) with behaviors of looking (Figure 6.1), learning (Figure 6.2), and leading (Figure 6.3).

The KBP results we have gathered thus far provide us with some tantalizing data—information that has to be further tested before it

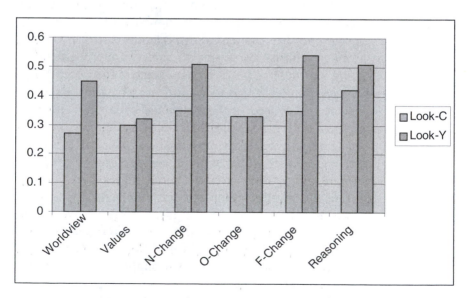

**Figure 6.1**
*Relationship between Perception (Looking) and Six Components of Worldview*

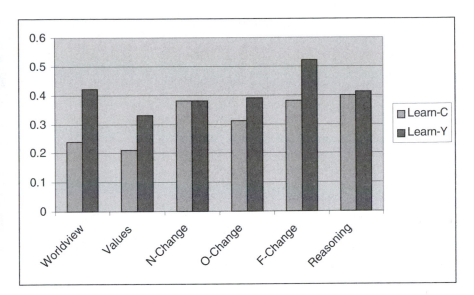

Figure 6.2
*Relationship between Learning and Six Components of Worldview*

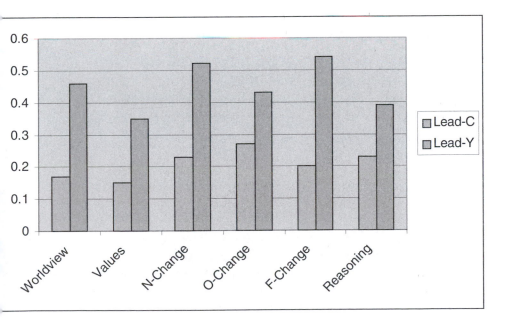

Figure 6.3
*Relationship between Leading and Six Components of Worldview*

**Table 6.1**

*Descriptive Statistics of the Knowledge Bias Profile, Part A: Worldview*
*(Short Form)*

| | Mean | Standard deviation | Your scores |
|---|---|---|---|
| *Total Score—Commissar* | *17.84* | *3.79* | Total:_____ |
| Q 1. Worldview—Commissar | 3.29 | 1.14 | 1. _____ |
| Q 2. Values—Commissar | 2.75 | 1.02 | 2. _____ |
| Q 3. Nature of change—Commissar | 2.81 | 1.07 | 3. _____ |
| Q 4. Origin of change—Commissar | 2.80 | 1.10 | 4. _____ |
| Q 5. Focus of change—Commissar | 3.46 | 1.04 | 5. _____ |
| Q 6. Reasoning—Commissar | 2.74 | 1.12 | 6. _____ |
| *Total Score—Yogi* | *21.11* | *3.79* | Total:_____ |
| Q 1. Worldview—Yogi | 3.21 | 1.18 | 1. _____ |
| Q 2. Values—Yogi | 3.47 | 0.93 | 2. _____ |
| Q 3. Nature of change—Yogi | 3.43 | 1.14 | 3. _____ |
| Q 4. Origin of change—Yogi | 3.73 | 1.10 | 4. _____ |
| Q 5. Focus of change—Yogi | 3.41 | 1.00 | 5. _____ |
| Q 6. Reasoning—Yogi | 3.86 | 1.01 | 6. _____ |

can be turned into knowledge. However, as you compare your own scores from the sample KBP in Chapter 3 with the scores of our research participants, you can start to do some of this knowledge development yourself. We invite you to first see how your scores rank with those of other participants in our research, then test this feedback about your worldview biases within the experiential laboratory of your own work. Our hope is that this process will provide you with feedback that will help you become a better knowledge leader. The remainder of this chapter explores the details and specific discoveries of this major research study.

## COMPARING YOUR SCORES WITH PART A OF THE KNOWLEDGE BIAS PROFILE (WORLDVIEWS)

Table 6.1 presents data from the full Part A study translated into a format that will allow you to compare your scores from the short form in Chapter 3. You can insert your total score for both Yogi and Commissar, or, if you choose, you can also compare each item within that category. The short form of the KBP has one representative question per worldview category (whereas the full KBP instrument has two to seven questions per category).

Out of 162 people surveyed on Part A of the KBP, 17.84 is the mean for Commissar. If you score higher than 17.84, you have a stronger preference for the Commissar than most of the 162 people we surveyed. If you score lower than 17.84, you have a below average preference for the Commissar. The degree to which your scores are higher or lower than the mean is measured by the standard deviation of 3.79. The standard deviation helps you see the strength of your preference. According to this bell-shaped distribution (Figure 6.4), if your score is above 21.63 (17.84 plus one standard deviation of 3.79), you are a stronger Commissar than 95% of our test sample. If your score is above 25.42 (the mean plus two standard deviations), your Commissar preference is stronger than 99% of our sampled population.

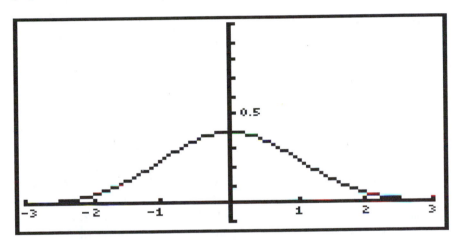

**Figure 6.4**
*Standard Distribution of Scores in a Bell-Shaped Curve*

If you have a less strong preference for the Commissar leadership style, simply do this math in reverse. That is, if your Commissar score is below 14.05 (17.84–3.79), you are less likely to prefer Commissar traits than 95% of our sample population. If your score is below 10.26, you are two standard deviations below the mean, which means that you have less preference for the Commissar than 99% of our population.

By the same token, 21.11 is the Yogi mean. The standard deviation is 3.79. (The standard deviations of the Commissar and Yogi are slightly different, but exactly the same when rounded to the two decimal points. The closeness of the Yogi and Commissar standard deviations is an indication of the stability of the Knowledge Bias

Profile.) Therefore the standard deviation benchmarks in the direction of a stronger Yogi preference are 24.90 (95th percentile) and 28.69 (99th percentile). For a less strong Yogi preference, the benchmarks are 17.32 (95th percentile) and 13.53 (99th percentile).

Although it is possible for a person to have both a high Commissar score and a high Yogi score, we discovered that it was unlikely. It is far more likely for people to be moderately high in both scales, reflecting the normal distribution for both Yogis and Commissars. Table 6.2 reflects the distribution that occurred in our testing of Part A (n = 162). The scores are adjusted to reflect the short form so that you can see where your scores fall in comparison to our sampled population.

Table 6.2
*Distribution of Scores in KBP, Part A: Worldview (Short Form)*

| Worldview | Very weak | Weak | Somewhat weak | Somewhat strong | Strong | Very strong |
|---|---|---|---|---|---|---|
| | 16% | 17% | 17% | 17% | 17% | 16% |
| Commissar | <14.1 | 14.1–16.2 | 16.2–17.8 | 17.8–19.5 | 19.5–21.6 | >21.6 |
| Yogi | <17.3 | 17.3–19.4 | 19.4–21.1 | 21.1–22.8 | 22.8–24.9 | >24.9 |

Finally, we present Table 6.3, which demonstrates the internal validity of Part A of the Knowledge Bias Profile—that is, its strength in measuring what we set out to measure: the worldviews of the Yogi and Commissar. The correlations exhibited in Table 6.3 show that the vast majority of statements in all six components of the Yogi or Commissar were significantly correlated with each other (94% at the level of .01). Another way to say this is that if you preferred one component of the Yogi worldview (for example, values), you also were strongly likely to prefer another component of the Yogi worldview (for example, focus of change).

Correlations at p < .05 are represented by a single asterisk. This indicates a 95% or greater confidence, for example, that this particular Commissar worldview category is compatible with the other Commissar worldview category. Correlations at p < .01 are represented by a double asterisk, which indicates a 99% or greater confidence level that these categories are compatible.

The complete Knowledge Bias Profile, Part A, includes several items for each subscale of the worldview construct (from two to seven items per category). Table 6.4 shows the basic descriptive statistics with means, standard deviations, and ranges of each subscale on the full Part A of the KBP. Just like any other psychological construct, the

Table 6.3

Complete Correlations for KBP, Part A (Internal Validity of Instrument)

| | WV-C | VA-C | NC-C | OC-C | FC-C | RE-C | WV-Y | VA-Y | NC-Y | OC-Y | FC-Y | RE-Y |
|---|---|---|---|---|---|---|---|---|---|---|---|---|
| WV-C | 1.00 | | | | | | | | | | | |
| VA-C | 0.54** | 1.00 | | | | | | | | | | |
| NC-C | 0.35** | 0.41** | 1.00 | | | | | | | | | |
| OC-C | 0.43** | 0.42** | 0.47** | 1.00 | | | | | | | | |
| FC-C | 0.43** | 0.44** | 0.50** | 0.58** | 1.00 | | | | | | | |
| RE-C | 0.39** | 0.50** | 0.40** | 0.46** | 0.52** | 1.00 | | | | | | |
| WV-Y | -0.30** | -0.18 | -0.20 | -0.18* | -0.03 | -0.01 | 1.00 | | | | | |
| VA-Y | -0.17 | -0.35 | -0.12 | -0.12 | -0.05 | -0.11 | 0.40** | 1.00 | | | | |
| NC-Y | -0.05 | -0.02 | -0.13 | -0.05** | 0.18* | 0.15* | 0.48** | 0.36** | 1.00 | | | |
| OC-Y | -0.03 | -0.06 | -0.04 | -0.22** | 0.07 | -0.02 | 0.28** | 0.38** | 0.50** | 1.00 | | |
| FC-Y | -0.01 | -0.11 | 0.02 | -0.09 | 0.08 | 0.13 | 0.33** | 0.47** | 0.60** | 0.62** | 1.00 | |
| RE-Y | -0.01 | -0.14 | -0.05 | -0.07 | 0.14 | 0.02 | 0.27** | 0.47** | 0.47** | 0.41** | 0.54** | 1.00 |

Note: *p < .05; **p < .01
Key: For Commissar: WV-C: Worldview, VA-C: Value, NC-C: Nature of change, OC-C: Origin of change, FC-C: Focus of change, RE-C: Reasoning.
For Yogi: WV-Y: Worldview, VA-Y: Value, NC-Y: Nature of change, OC-Y: Origin of change, FC- Y: Focus of change, RE-Y: Reasoning.

Commissar and Yogi worldview scales show a wide range of distribution and indicate a bell-shaped normal distribution in the population.

Table 6.4
*Complete Descriptive Statistics for Part A of KBP, Full Instrument (n = 162)*

|  | Mean | Standard deviation | Minimum | Maximum |
|---|---|---|---|---|
| Worldview—Commissar | 2.79 | 0.61 | 1.00 | 5.00 |
| Value—Commissar | 2.79 | 0.74 | 1.00 | 5.00 |
| Nature of change—Commissar | 2.88 | 0.82 | 1.00 | 5.00 |
| Origin of change—Commissar | 2.85 | 0.87 | 1.00 | 5.00 |
| Focus of change—Commissar | 2.96 | 0.78 | 1.00 | 5.00 |
| Reasoning—Commissar | 2.98 | 0.77 | 1.00 | 5.00 |
| Worldview—Yogi | 3.45 | 0.61 | 1.00 | 5.00 |
| Value—Yogi | 3.40 | 0.72 | 1.00 | 5.00 |
| Nature of change—Yogi | 3.43 | 0.95 | 1.00 | 5.00 |
| Origin of change—Yogi | 3.49 | 0.96 | 1.00 | 5.00 |
| Focus of change—Yogi | 3.42 | 0.76 | 1.00 | 5.00 |
| Reasoning—Yogi | 3.41 | 0.76 | 1.00 | 5.00 |

## THE YOGI AND COMMISSAR AT WORK

From our years of study, we have observed how much the Yogi and Commissar affect the way people see the world and how that worldview affects not only their lives but also the lives of their colleagues and customers. Let us examine a few examples of how these tendencies influence people in everyday life.

## School Principal 1

Mr. Kane is a retired grade school principal. He received his education in the colonial Japanese system and even worked for the Japanese colonial government in Korea when he was a young man. He later became an educator. When Mr. Kane was a grade school principal, he was a stern disciplinarian because he believed that young children needed to learn how the world works in their early years. People describe Mr. Kane as a "man of principle." He does not tolerate any deviation from what he thinks is right. He believes everything has its own place in this world. In both his home and school environments, everything must be in the right place and the right order. He repeatedly says, "a match and a candle must be exactly at the place they are supposed to be, so that they can be reached even in the darkest night. An emergency can happen any time or any day."

When Mr. Kane completed Part A of the KBP (short form), he scored 28 in the Commissar worldview and 10 in the Yogi worldview. Mr. Kane's Commissar score is higher than two standard deviations from the mean (17.84). He reports himself as an extreme Commissar, less than 1% of the population. He also scores very low in the Yogi scale (7), which is also two standard deviations from the mean (21.11) and less than 1% of the population.

## School Principal 2

Mrs. Rizzo was born to Italian-American parents and grew up in the New England region of the United States. She has been a principal the past 10 years and is currently a middle school principal. Many people consider her quite successful in her career. Mrs. Rizzo believes that every student has his or her own merit, which has to be realized to its fullest extent in the education system. She is strict when it comes to handling students' disciplinary matters, yet she focuses more on identifying and recognizing each child's unique talents. She enjoys music and sometimes plays with the students in school concerts.

Mrs. Rizzo scored a high 26 in the Yogi scale (95th percentile) and a very low 13 in Commissar (99th percentile).

In the examples provided by these two distinctly different principals, the KBP seems to accurately reflect their worldviews and behavior. This example of two different school leadership profiles also is reflective of an important demographic difference we discovered in our testing of the KBP.

### DEMOGRAPHICS OF THE KNOWLEDGE BIAS PROFILE, PART A

For all the parts of this study, we surveyed many different groups of people. Table 6.5 shows the demographic distribution of the KBP, Part A, research sample. It reflects a wide distribution among gender, age, and education levels. Seventy men and 91 women completed the survey. The largest age representation in our study was from people 21 to 30 years old, yet the sample covered ages beyond 40. Education levels range from high school graduates to those with graduate school degrees. (Specifically, participants ranged in age from 16 to

Table 6.5
*Demographics KBP, Part A: Full Instrument (n = 162)*

| Gender | Male | Female | Missing data | Total |
|---|---|---|---|---|
|  | 70 | 91 | 1 | 162 |

| Age | 16–20 years | 21–30 | 31–40 | 41+ |  |
|---|---|---|---|---|---|
|  | 45 | 65 | 25 | 26 | 162 |

| Education | 0–12 years | 13–14 | 15–16 | 17+ years |  |
|---|---|---|---|---|---|
|  | 49 | 43 | 52 | 17 | 162 |

59, with 75% of the participants being between 20 and 40. forty-nine participants nad completed their high school education; 95 completed college or junior college; and 17 had aquired post-graduate degrees.)

Our research indicated a strong gender difference in both Commissar and Yogi scales. Men tended to be more Commissar, whereas women tended to be more Yogi. For the five scale items (Commissar worldview), men showed higher scores than women, and the differences are statistically significant. On the other hand, for the next five scale items (Yogi worldview), men scored lower than women, and the differences are all statistically significant. You can use Table 6.6

Table 6.6
*Demographics, Gender Differences on the Two Worldview Scales
(Sample from Full Instrument)*

| Scale item | Men | Women | Difference |
|---|---|---|---|
| Worldview Commissar 1 | 2.60 | 2.25 | 0.35 |
| Worldview Commissar 2 | 2.56 | 2.17 | 0.39 |
| Worldview Commissar 3 | 2.72 | 2.35 | 0.37 |
| Worldview Commissar 4 | 3.65 | 3.61 | 0.04 |
| Worldview Commissar 5 | 3.35 | 3.26 | 0.09 |
| Worldview Yogi 1 | 3.45 | 3.74 | −0.29 |
| Worldview Yogi 2 | 3.38 | 3.73 | −0.35 |
| Worldview Yogi 3 | 3.77 | 4.02 | −0.25 |
| Worldview Yogi 4 | 3.71 | 4.03 | −0.32 |
| Worldview Yogi 5 | 3.03 | 3.35 | −0.33 |

to compare your own scores and determine if they reflect this same gender bias.

We also found differences in worldview preference by age and educational level (Table 6.7). It is interesting to note that the correlations of these first five items of the Commissar worldview all show slightly in the positive direction for both age and education, whereas correlations with the Yogi worldview scale all show slightly in the negative direction for both age and education. These differences are not as strong as the gender differences we discovered in worldview preference, but it clearly suggests a direction—that is, as age increases, so does the preference for Commissar. Education has less effect, although the direction is the same (the more schooling, the stronger the preference for Commissar). Without further analysis, we are uncertain what these data could mean. We do find ourselves wondering, however, if people become increasingly Commissar the longer they stay in the traditional (Commissar-biased) business and educational systems.

Table 6.7

*Correlations of Worldviews with Respondent's Age and Education Level*

|  | Age | Education |
|---|---|---|
| Worldview Commissar 1 | 0.19* | 0.07 |
| Worldview Commissar 2 | 0.07 | 0.04 |
| Worldview Commissar 3 | 0.08 | 0.07 |
| Worldview Commissar 4 | 0.08 | 0.10 |
| Worldview Commissar 5 | 0.13 | 0.08 |
| Worldview Yogi 1 | −0.18* | −0.03 |
| Worldview Yogi 2 | −0.17* | −0.03 |
| Worldview Yogi 3 | −0.14 | −0.03 |
| Worldview Yogi 4 | −0.13 | −0.11 |
| Worldview Yogi 5 | −0.06 | −0.01 |

* Indicates statistical significance at the level of $p < 0.05$.

## DIFFERENCES BY OCCUPATION OR INDUSTRY

Next we asked the question: Does one's worldview have anything to do with one's occupation? Is it a stereotype to say that military soldiers are more like the Commissar and that church pastors hold beliefs that are more Yogi-like? Or, if you already have a Commissar worldview, are you more likely to decide to become a soldier than a pastor? Or, as a result of 20 years in the military service, do you become a stronger Commissar? This presents us with a classic chicken-and-egg riddle, but it surely is an interesting question we would like to explore further.

Table 6.8 and Figure 6.5 show some interesting occupational differences in the Commissar and Yogi worldview scales. On six selected worldview items, healthcare workers rate themselves consistently lower on the Commissar worldview; while restaurant managers score consistently high as Commissars. Retail store managers stand in the middle.

Due to the limited sample size and representation in each industry, we cannot make any conclusions about industry or occupational

Table 6.8
*Difference by Industry in Strength of Commissar Worldview (n = 162)*

|  | WV-C | VA-C | NC-C | OC-C | FC-C | RE-C |
|---|---|---|---|---|---|---|
| **Restaurant** | 3.08 | 3.17 | 3.05 | 3.10 | 3.36 | 3.23 |
| **Retail store** | 2.75 | 2.97 | 2.98 | 3.13 | 3.20 | 3.13 |
| **Healthcare** | 2.46 | 2.46 | 3.00 | 2.38 | 2.75 | 2.76 |

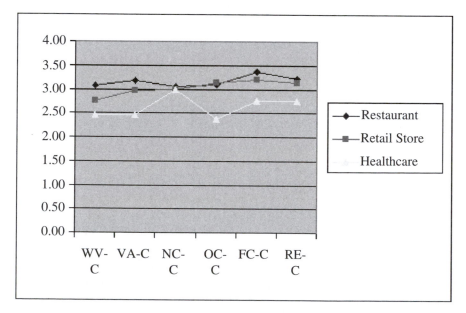

Figure 6.5
*Difference by Industry in Strength of Commissar Worldview (n = 162)*

differences. However, these early results do hint that occupational orientations may be related to the Commissar and Yogi worldviews. What we cannot know, without further study, is if some occupations require people who have certain worldviews to do the job that is expected of them, or whether these occupations inherently have a worldview bias and therefore attract people who already have certain worldviews.

## COMPARING YOUR SCORES ON THE KNOWLEDGE BIAS PROFILE, PART B (BEHAVIORS)

We had hypothesized that people with strong Commissar worldviews would tend to show strong Commissar behavioral pattern and that, conversely, people with strong Yogi worldviews would tend to show a high Yogi behavioral pattern. To test our theory, we designed Part B of the KBP to measure three behavioral patterns—that is, the way Yogis and Commissars (1) look at the world, (2) learn from experience, and (3) lead people in their organizations. Part B of the Knowledge Bias Profile relates the worldviews of the Yogi and Commissar to these three behaviors. To find out how your scores compare to the 222 respondents in this second part of our study, please transfer your KBP, Part B, scores from Chapter 3 to Table 6.9. You can compare just total scores, or, if you choose, you can also examine the three questions that represent the three behavioral categories in Part B. Then you can look to Table 6.10 to see where your scores fall in comparison to the distribution of scores in our research sample.

Table 6.9

*Descriptive Statistics of the Knowledge Bias Profile, Part B: Behaviors (Short Form)*

|  | Mean | Standard deviation | Your score |
|---|---|---|---|
| *Commissar behavior* | 10.40 | 2.31 | Total:_____ |
| Q1. Leading—Commissar | 3.42 | 1.09 | 1. _____ |
| Q2. Learning—Commissar | 3.89 | 0.92 | 2. _____ |
| Q3. Looking—Commissar | 3.19 | 0.92 | 3. _____ |
| *Yogi behavior* | 9.72 | 2.66 | Total:_____ |
| Q1. Leading—Yogi | 3.45 | 1.07 | 1. _____ |
| Q2. Learning—Yogi | 3.21 | 1.06 | 2. _____ |
| Q3. Looking—Yogi | 3.14 | 1.04 | 3. _____ |

**Table 6.10**
*Distribution of Scores of Commissar and Yogi Behavior Pattern (n = 222)*

| Worldview | Very weak | Weak | Somewhat weak | Somewhat strong | Strong | Very strong |
|---|---|---|---|---|---|---|
| | 16% | 17% | 17% | 17% | 17% | 16% |
| Commissar | <8.5 | 8.5–9.6 | 9.6–10.4 | 10.4–11.4 | 11.4–12.5 | >12.5 |
| Yogi | <7.3 | 7.3–8.7 | 8.7–9.7 | 9.7–10.9 | 10.9–12.3 | >12.3 |

Here are some illustrations of how these scores might be reflected in leadership behavior.

## Leader 1

Stacey Howard is CEO of a medium-sized electronics company, with annual revenues exceeding $120 million. Because she was always *looking* for opportunities for new products and markets, she has become a *leader* known for never ignoring any of her employees' opinions, no matter how silly they may appear at first. This is how she *learns* about new opportunities—by being receptive to her employees' ideas, then taking the time to reflect on them. On Part B of the KBP (behavioral scale), Ms. Howard scored 7 on the Commissar behavioral scale and 14 on the Yogi scale.

## Leader 2

In contrast, Mr. Matt Mackiewicz, the CFO of a large national not-for-profit organization, scored 13 on the Commissar behavioral scale and 6 on the Yogi scale. He practices his profession with precision, accuracy, and unequivocality. Mr. Mackiewicz *looks* to the empirical data contained in his accounting ledger to *learn* the truths these numbers reveal. Indeed, he believes that every number in the organization's books must have a justifiable story. This information provides him with the data he needs to determine his next *leadership* direction.

Table 6.11 shows our sample distributes on the behavior orientation scales and also contrasts scores between men and women respondents. The gender difference between Yogi and Commissar leaders that surfaced in Part A of the KBP is reflected also in Part B. Men are slightly higher than the mean in Commissar behaviors, and women are slightly higher than the mean in Yogi behaviors. (Most of these differences are statistically significant at the p < .05 level.) Use this table to see how the gender biases in behavior that we discovered do, or do not, reflect your own scores.

**Table 6.11**

*Gender Differences in the Behavioral Orientation Scales*
*(KBP, Part B, Short Form)*

|  | Mean | Standard deviation | Men | Women |
|---|---|---|---|---|
| *Commissar behavior* | 10.40 | 2.31 | 10.46 | 10.34 |
| Leading—Commissar | 3.42 | 1.09 | 3.46 | 3.39 |
| Learning—Commissar | 3.89 | 0.92 | 3.86 | 3.91 |
| Looking—Commissar | 3.19 | 0.92 | 3.23 | 3.16 |
| *Yogi behavior* | 9.72 | 2.66 | 9.52 | 9.60 |
| Leading—Yogi | 3.45 | 1.07 | 3.51 | 3.31 |
| Learning—Yogi | 3.21 | 1.06 | 3.09 | 3.31 |
| Looking—Yogi | 3.14 | 1.04 | 3.04 | 3.13 |

## Now Things Get Really Interesting for the Yogi and Commissar

When we gathered the data from the research on Parts A and B of the Knowledge Bias Profile, we were able to see the correlations between Yogi and Commissar worldviews and behaviors. As we had hypothesized, there were strong correlations between worldview and behaviors—but the strength of the answers surprised us. As Table 6.12 illustrates, the Yogi and Commissar worldviews and behavioral orientations are highly correlated and statistically significant. The top-left quadrant of Table 6.12 shows how the six worldview subscales of Commissar are positively and significantly correlated with the behavior orientation of Commissar. And the bottom-right quadrant of the table shows that the six worldview subscales of Yogi are positively, and significantly, correlated with the behavior orientation of Yogi. Indeed, 34 of 36 of these correlation coefficients are statistically significant at p < .01, and the remaining two are statistically significant at p < .05.

## Comparing Your Scores on the Knowledge Bias Profile, Part C

We developed two narrative profiles (one paragraph each), which described the leadership style of a composite Commissar leader (Mr./Ms. Patrick) and composite Yogi leader (Mr./Ms. Raphael). We

Table 6.12

*Correlations between Worldviews (KBP, Part A) and Behavioral Orientation (KBP, Part B)*

|  | Lead-C | Learn-C | Look-C | Lead-Y | Learn-Y | Look-Y |
|---|---|---|---|---|---|---|
| Worldview—Commissar | 0.17* | 0.24** | 0.27** | 0.01 | −0.04 | −0.07 |
| Values—Commissar | 0.15* | 0.21** | 0.30** | −0.07 | −0.13 | −0.11 |
| Nature of change—Commissar | 0.23** | 0.38** | 0.35** | −0.11 | −0.06 | −0.09 |
| Origin of change—Commissar | 0.27** | 0.31** | 0.33** | 0.03 | −0.02 | −0.04 |
| Focus of change—Commissar | 0.20** | 0.38** | 0.35** | 0.16 | 0.08 | 0.05 |
| Reasoning—Commissar | 0.23** | 0.40** | 0.42** | 0.21 | 0.09 | 0.08 |
| Worldview–Yogi | −0.15* | −0.04 | −0.18 | 0.46** | 0.42** | 0.45** |
| Values–Yogi | −0.07 | −0.03 | −0.09 | 0.35** | 0.33** | 0.32** |
| Nature of change—Yogi | 0.07 | 0.27** | 0.01 | 0.52** | 0.38** | 0.51** |
| Origin of change—Yogi | −0.30 | 0.09 | −0.03 | 0.43** | 0.39** | 0.33** |
| Focus of change—Yogi | 0.07 | 0.23** | 0.05 | 0.54** | 0.52** | 0.54** |
| Reasoning—Yogi | 0.19* | 0.19* | −0.04 | 0.39** | 0.41** | 0.51** |

* $p < .05$; ** $p < .01$.

conducted rigorous statistical analyses and concluded that these two narrative leadership profiles well represented the itemized scales of the two corresponding worldviews in Part A of the KBP.

Respondents in Part C of the study were asked to choose the profile that was closer to their image of a successful leader. The response pattern was a scale from 1 (strong preference for Patrick the Commissar) to 5 (strong preference for Raphael the Yogi). In Part C, a higher score indicates a stronger preference for the Yogi leader.

In Table 6.13, you can note your KBP, Part C, score from Chapter 3. In our sample of 222 respondents, the preferred leadership styles were quite evenly split between the two leaders (106 for Commissar/Patrick and 116 for Yogi/Raphael). This strong midrange response to people's preferred leader profile hints that people do indeed prefer a more balanced leadership style. Interestingly, respondents preferred a Yogi leader. While cynics might argue that, of course, people would want the "easy" Yogi boss who would let them get away with lesser productivity, we suggest that workers themselves know that

Table 6.13

*Preferred Leadership Profile, KBP, Part C (n = 222)*

|  | Preferred leader | Percentage preference | Score | Your score |
|---|---|---|---|---|
| **Commissar** | 106 | 48% | Below 3.0 | _____ |
| **Yogi** | 116 | 52% | Above 3.0 | _____ |

if left more to their own devices, they (like the bees) know how to "make honey." In any case, the data may indicate some good news for emerging knowledge leaders who strive to combine and balance the Yogi's strength in KD with the Commissar's strength in KM.

In this part of the study, there was a wide spread in the ages in our respondents, from people in their 20s to people in their 60s. Out of 222 respondents, 134 men and 86 women completed the survey (2 participants did not complete the gender question). Interestingly, *both* men and women preferred a Yogi boss (Table 6.14). However, Part C of the KBP study also revealed a gender bias. Women showed slightly higher preferences for Raphael, the Yogi (mean score of 3.54—where the exact midrange preference would be 3.0). Men also preferred the Yogi as a boss, but less so than their female colleagues (mean of 3.44). This gender preference difference of −0.10 is statistically significant at the $p < .05$ level.

**Table 6.14**
*Gender Difference in Leader Preference, KBP, Part C*

|  | Men (134) | Women (86) | Difference |
|---|---|---|---|
| Patrick-Raphael Leadership Profiles | 3.44 | 3.54 | −0.10 |

The third part of our study raises some interesting questions that we would like to explore further. For example: Does the data indicate an emerging preference for a more "balanced" leadership style? Is the slight preference for Yogi leadership the result of an instinctive counterbalance to prior centuries of Machine Age leadership by Commissars? How might the number of women in leadership positions effect an appreciation of what the Yogi leader has to offer? What other factors might be at work, such as sample anomalies?

# A Cross-Cultural Comparison Between American and Chinese Managers

In an early discussion among the authors, we discussed a question that intrigued us: "How do Chinese managers compare with American managers on the Yogi/Commissar scale? We think of China as traditionally being a Yogi-like culture, but for the past half-century, the country has been a Commissar communist state. Now china is changing again as its new economy emerges."

This question triggered our cross-cultural study of the Knowledge Bias Profile. For the sake of simplicity, and because we had found that Part C was highly valid, we decided to use only the profile paragraphs rather than all three parts of the KBP. First we translated these paragraphs into Chinese, then back-translated them from Chinese into English, and tested both translations with bilingual students to assure the validity of the translated version of our instrument. Finally we had a chance to survey Chinese managers in business enterprises in Beijing and Shanghai.

We also expanded the KBP, Part C, narrative of two leadership profiles to ask the three following questions: Which of the two profiles (Patrick/Commissar and Raphael/Yogi):

1. Best represents your image of successful leadership?
2. Is more effective as your boss (or a manager of your company)?
3. Is more effective in running your country as president of China?

It is interesting to see that Chinese respondents (n = 134) indicated slightly more preference overall for the Yogi as a self-image, as a manager, and as president of the country. Again, we would need further research to determine what these data might mean (Table 6.15). (Note: The midrange is 3.0. Scores above 3.0 show a preference for the Yogi; scores below 3.0 indicate a preference for the Commissar.)

Table 6.15
*Preferred Images of Leadership: Comparison between Chinese and American Managers*

|  | Chinese mean | (*n* = 134) Standard deviation | American mean | (*n* = 280) Standard deviation |
|---|---|---|---|---|
| My self-image | 3.15 | 1.01 | — | — |
| My boss (manager of company) | 3.09 | 0.97 | 3.49 | 0.83 |
| Desired president of the country | 3.03 | 1.10 | — | — |

Because we had only asked American managers (n = 280) only the one question regarding who they preferred as a leader, we can only compare that one item cross-culturally. From that comparison, we can see that Chinese managers show a higher preference for a Commissar boss than do their American counterparts. (The Chinese mean was 3.09, and the American mean was 3.49—where a lower score indicates a preference for a Commissar boss.)

There are some tantalizing hints in the Chinese data that might speak to one of the questions that originally launched this cross-cultural study. We had wondered out loud if there might be significant Yogi versus Commissar differences between Communist China and the emerging "new China." We received 77 responses from Beijing and 57 from Shanghai-based organizations. The respondents from Beijing were managers in a privately owned enterprise, whereas those from Shanghai were managers in a state-connected enterprise. There were some consistent differences between the two samples in terms of their preferences for leadership profiles—that is, respondents in Beijing (private sector) consistently showed higher preferences for the Yogi than those in Shanghai (state-connected sector) (Table 6.16).

**Table 6.16**
*Preferred Leadership Styles between Managers in Beijing and Shanghai*

|  | Beijing (Private) | Shanghai (State run) |
|---|---|---|
| My self-image as leader | 3.39 | 2.82 |
| My boss (manager of company) | 3.31 | 2.79 |
| Desired president of the country | 3.16 | 2.86 |

These data hint at a potential shift from a preference for the Commissar to more preference for the Yogi—and a better balanced leadership profile—as the "new China" emerges via its new economy.

Among the Chinese managers were 81 men and 53 women (ages ranging from 17 to mid-50s) (Table 6.17).

**Table 6.17**
*Sample Demographics of Chinese Managers*

| Gender | Male | Female | Missing |  |  | Total |
|---|---|---|---|---|---|---|
|  | 91 | 53 | 0 |  |  | 134 |
| Age | 17–19 years | 20–29 | 31–40 | 40–49 | 50+ |  |
|  | 14 | 45 | 62 | 11 | 2 | 134 |
| Area | Beijing | Shanghai |  |  |  |  |
|  | 77 | 57 |  |  |  | 134 |

Table 6.18 shows an intriguing gender difference in preferred leadership image among Chinese and American managers. Chinese men preferred a Commissar leader much more than their American counterparts. Indeed, Chinese men show a slight preference for the Commissar in their self-image, their boss manager's image, and desired president of the country. Their scores were counterbalanced, however, by their female colleagues, who significantly preferred the Yogi in all three of the same categories (self, boss, president). The gender difference in preference between male and female American respondents, although significant, was not as dramatic as the difference between male and female Chinese managers.

Table 6.18
*Gender Difference in Preferred Leadership among Chinese and American Managers*

|  | Chinese Men | Women | Chinese Difference | American Men | Women | American Difference |
|---|---|---|---|---|---|---|
| My self-image | 2.93 | 3.49 | 0.56 | — | — | — |
| My boss/company manager | 2.89 | 3.40 | 0.51 | 3.44 | 3.54 | 0.10 |
| President of the country | 2.85 | 3.30 | 0.45 | — | — | |

## SUMMARY OF KEY LESSONS

The Knowledge Bias Profile has demonstrated its effectiveness in helping managers understand two opposing worldviews that contain key understandings for knowledge leaders. (For more information about the KBP, please look to Appendix A.) Our research on the Knowledge Bias Profile presents the following key lessons:

- There are significant differences in the worldviews of Yogis and Commissars.
- These differences can be discriminated by using the Knowledge Bias Profile.
- Both of these leadership styles have important implications for knowledge leaders.
- The study provided strong evidence of a clear relationship between the beliefs, or worldview, of leaders and their behaviors, specifically, how they *look* (perceive), *learn*, and *lead* others.

- The data indicate that there are gender and cultural differences in preferences for these two leadership profiles.
- The research supports our contention that people prefer a balance between these two extreme profiles for themselves and for their leaders.

In the remaining sections of *Knowledge Leadership*, we will build on the lessons of these two colorful leadership types, the "ultraviolet" Yogi and "infrared" Commissar, to support you in learning how to become a well-balanced knowledge leader who can develop and manage the pragmatic knowledge necessary to create a highly competitive, *FAST* knowledge-based organization.

# Part III

# Putting Knowledge into Action

# 7

# ALIGNING KNOWLEDGE WITH BUSINESS STRATEGIES

## Executive Summary

Knowledge leadership will become increasingly recognized as knowledge-based initiatives become more strategic and less operational in their focus. To align knowledge with business strategies, knowledge leaders need to integrate their understanding of how the many components of an organization—its people, processes, and systems—can work together most effectively. In this way they will be able to develop a comprehensive *knowledge strategy* that pulls workers forward toward an ideal vision of what they may achieve collectively. Knowledge leaders are responsible for designing a *knowledge mix* of activities that target their organization's needs and are cost-effective. To be effective, knowledge-based initiatives must be aligned with the company's identity, strategy, and existing management systems. Knowledge is an excellent investment, indeed one of the few investments that offers companies strong payoffs on *both* the revenue and cost side of the profit equation. There are five major challenges to successful knowledge-based initiatives, but when these initiatives are well designed, they can result in sustainable competitive advantage. This chapter concludes with a case study and a list of criteria for developing pragmatic knowledge that meets the *FAST* criteria of being functional, adaptable, sustainable, and timely.

This third section of *Knowledge Leadership* provides current and prospective knowledge leaders with a framework for envisioning how they can align pragmatic knowledge with business strategies to increase innovation and improve performance in their organizations. Pragmatic organizational knowledge (that is, knowledge that is capable of driving innovations in operations, reducing waste, or cutting product development times) does not result from KM nor is it the sole responsibility of CKOs. Rather, pragmatic knowledge results from effective and system-wide knowledge leadership.

Being a knowledge leader requires a willingness to personally transcend the simplicity of most KM approaches and instead embrace the complexity—and excitement—of leading people toward a vision of a KBO. Making the leap from knowledge manager to knowledge leader requires a willingness to support employees in their development of knowledge. This requires that you dialogue with people about what they do, how they reason, and what they believe about how things actually work best in practice.

Knowledge leaders develop a drive to understand the complexities of life and work; this desire blazes a learning trail for them that cuts through outdated practices and leads to more effective systems. In his book, *Leadership Is an Art*, author Max De Pree (1989) reports that the noted pragmatist and former U.S. Supreme Court Justice Oliver Wendell Holmes commented on this desire when he said,

I would not give a fig for the simplicity this side of complexity, but I would give my life for the simplicity on the other side of complexity. (p. 22)

Knowledge leadership will become increasingly recognized as knowledge-based initiatives become more strategic and less operational. For some readers of this book, its title *Knowledge Leadership* may appear to be an oxymoron. Indeed, knowledge and leadership are often considered only distantly related cousins. For most people, *knowledge* brings to mind the world of teachers, schools, and educational systems. For those with a more technical bent, *knowledge* may engender thoughts of information technologies, systems for managing a company's intellectual capital, or organizational processes for capturing or sharing knowledge.

To align knowledge with business strategies, knowledge leaders need to integrate their understanding of how the many components of an organization—its people, processes, and systems—can work together most effectively. In this way they will be able to develop a comprehensive *knowledge strategy* that pulls people forward toward an ideal vision of what they may achieve collectively. Steven Jobs, CEO and cofounder of Apple Computer, achieved such a seamless integration when he moved his company forward—on several occasions, against all odds. In a *Business Week Online* (2004) article, Jobs discussed Apple's phenomenal success with iPod:

First of all, Apple is the most creative technology company out there . . . almost all recording artists use Macs and they have iPods, and now most of the music-industry people have iPods as well. There's a trust in the music community that Apple will do something right—that it won't cut corners—and that it cares about the creative process and about the music. Also, our solution encompasses operating system software, server software, application software, and hardware. Apple is the only company in the world that has all of that under one roof. We can invent a complete solution that works—and take responsibility for it."

Knowledge leaders cannot mandate that employees share or develop knowledge. Instead, they need to create workplace environments and knowledge-based initiatives that foster optimal KD and KM. To achieve this, leaders need to select knowledge-based activities that are closely aligned with their company's identity, culture, strategy, management systems, operating systems, and leadership. These factors all interact to determine the types and mix of knowledge-based initiatives that are most likely to be successful in a given organization.

## DETERMINING THE KNOWLEDGE MIX

By designing knowledge-based initiatives that are compatible with the company's identity, mission, management systems, and performance needs, knowledge leaders play a critical strategic role. When a *knowledge mix* is designed so that it specifically targets the needs of an organization, it is likely to significantly increase the cost-effectiveness of the chosen knowledge-based initiatives. By carefully choosing among your organization's array of possible knowledge-based activities, you can better balance corporate resources between building KM systems and enabling employees to develop new knowledge.

A wide variety of potential knowledge activities are available for your company's knowledge mix. Each activity relies on a specific kind of learning, system design, and leadership—and each activity produces a particular kind of knowledge. The various knowledge-based activities that can be included in a knowledge mix are presented in Table 7.1.

Table 7.1

*Potential Knowledge-Based Activities in a Knowledge Mix*

| Individual | Organizational |
| --- | --- |
| 1. Training | Knowledge management |
| 2. Education and management development | Organization development |
| 3. Action learning | Organizational learning |
| 4. Pragmatic learning | Pragmatic knowledge creation |

There is a huge difference between measuring the specific quality of your own work and thinking about the quality of your company's work. Becoming a "quality thinker," a "systems thinker," a "service thinker," or a "strategic thinker" involves a personal process of thinking through your views about how things actually work best in practice. Leaders who define a vision for becoming such a thinker are critically influential in the knowledge-creation process. In this way, you can engage employees so that they can create their own knowledge from experience. Such knowledge is critical for business innovation.

If done well, innovation is not always about the distant future and long payback periods. There is a growing list of high-performance companies demonstrating that there need not be a major tradeoff between investments in innovation and improved corporate performance. The conventional management wisdom is that investing in knowledge creation does not pay. The logic of this prevailing view is that knowledge-based activities (1) are unreliable in improving performance, (2) take too long to produce desired results, and (3) drain scarce resources from productive activity. While this describes the experience of many corporations, there is growing evidence that—when a critical threshold in capacity is reached—investments in knowledge pay off handsomely. Leading our list of high-performing KBOs is Toyota, but it is closely followed by such well-known organizations as BP Amoco, Canon, Nokia, 3M, and Xerox.

Indeed, it is not innovation itself but rather *poorly done innovation* that has a minimal *return on investment* (ROI) because it does not generate significant organizational improvements (Figure 7.1). When knowledge-based operational innovations are well done, they can become the foundation of the Holy Grail of business—that is,

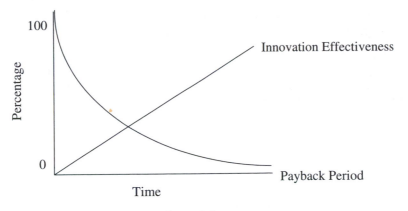

**Figure 7.1**
*Relationship between Innovation Effectiveness and Payback*

*sustainable competitive advantage.* Michael Hammer, one of the pioneers of Business Process Reengineering, has documented the effects of innovation at Progressive Insurance. In an article for the *Harvard Business Review* (April 2004), he stated:

The secret of Progressive's success is maddeningly simple: It out operated its competitors. By offering lower prices and better service than its rivals, it simply took their customers away. And what enabled Progressive to have better prices and service was *operational innovation,* the invention and deployment of new ways of doing work. (p. 86)

Clearly, if done well, both knowledge-based initiatives and innovation strategies can pay handsome dividends. For example, a 1999 *Fortune* article reported that BP Amoco's first year of using knowledge management yielded *more than $700 million in cost savings* as a direct result of using five of the simplest KM methods:

1. *After-action* post-project reviews, where actual results were compared to projected results, and results for gaps were analyzed.
2. *Peer-assist* programs, where experienced teams assist new teams in getting started.
3. *Retrospect* programs, in which lessons learned are captured.
4. *Connect,* a corporate Yellow Pages directory.
5. *Virtual teamwork,* real time distance collaborative group work that is facilitated by various technologies.

Since then, BP Amoco has moved to integrate KM into its business processes. As consultants Chris Collison and Geoff Parcell (2001) report:

BP is focusing on some key company-wide processes, Health Safety and Environmental (HSE), capital productivity, and operational excellence. KM principles are being embedded in each of these so that they become the normal way of doing business. (p. 173)

In addition, because it is people who create new knowledge, studies about the ROI in human capital hint at the potential economic return of knowledge-based initiatives (which are one subcategory of human resource investment). Researchers Jeffrey Pfeffer and John Veiga (1999) cite numerous studies that show dramatic ROI in human capital. For example, a study of 702 firms reported that a one standard deviation improvement in the human resources system led to a $41,000 rise in shareholder wealth per employee. Similar ROI results were shown in a study of 100+ German companies in 10 different industries. Finally, a study of U.S. companies that launched their public stock offerings in 1998 found that the value the firm placed on human resources was directly related to its likelihood of survival over the following 5 years. As these studies indicate, effective knowledge-based initiatives can offer rapid and substantial ROI.

In fact, we would like to underscore that *knowledge is one of the few investments a company can make that offers payoffs on both the revenue and cost sides of the profit equation.* This is because (1) increased revenues result from developing new products and enhancing old ones, and (2) costs typically decline as a result of process improvements. So now that we have demonstrated that well-designed knowledge initiatives can have excellent ROI and that poorly designed initiatives may leave companies even further behind than when they started, the question arises: What does it take to design effective knowledge-based initiatives?

We propose that the key to success is to embrace the value of all the components of a knowledge initiative. This includes KM architecture as well as knowledge processes and softer elements of business, such as organizational culture. As impressive as well-designed KM architectures can be, they reflect only a small portion of what KBOs need if they are to achieve sustainable high performance. In popular parlance, the *explicit knowledge* found in companies is often dwarfed by the magnitude of the *tacit knowledge* that has yet to be codified. This is why a well-balanced knowledge leadership approach is so critical to organizational success.

## KNOWLEDGE STRATEGIES: ONE SIZE DOES NOT FIT ALL

Just as people have different shoe sizes, personalities, and various hair colors, organizations are at least as distinct when it comes to their knowledge needs. Unfortunately, theorists have argued for years that organizations are essentially similar in most important dimensions. While this argument may be true with regard to many aspects of management, it does not hold up when it comes to knowledge-based strategies. In short, one size does not fit all. The odds of success for a knowledge-based initiative increases dramatically when it fits your company's identity, culture, strategy, and systems. Our hope is that this book will provide you with a conceptual framework to design a knowledge strategy that is tailored for your company.

Not only are all organizations not created equal when it comes to knowledge—not all knowledge is created equal either. In fact, there are many types of knowledge that arise from different kinds of sources. It is not surprising that, when it comes to the often-fuzzy domain of knowledge, many managers inadvertently do "A" while hoping for "B" and get the unintended result "C" that is off course from the organization's strategy. An essential element of knowledge leadership is the *targeting* of knowledge-based activities. Most companies rely on a shotgun approach to knowledge that is neither strategic nor cost-effective. The targeting of knowledge-based approaches avoids the costs of investing in unaligned knowledge efforts that do not produce the expected results (Figure 7.2).

Increasingly managers are discovering that knowledge is one of the most valuable assets a company can possess. Knowledge not only enables employees and managers to improve how they do things, it also is the fuel that drives innovation. Innovations can run the gamut from discovering ways of reducing costs, increasing operational efficiency, improving existing products and services, and creating new ones. Yet despite the importance of knowledge to business success, there is still a great deal of mystery that surrounds how knowledge is created and used in companies. In some cases, executives respond to their knowledge needs by adopting KM practices that are merely variants of information processing. While significant investments in state-of-the-art information technology software and hardware may give the aura that a business has implemented a cutting-edge knowl-

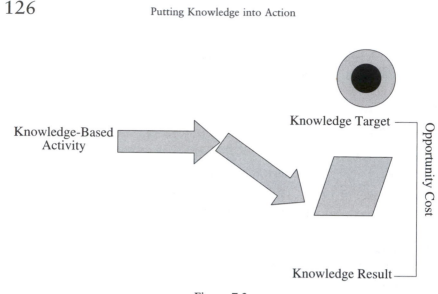

**Figure 7.2**
*Knowledge Alignment Failure*

edge initiative, these approaches usually provide no more than temporary incremental improvements. However, despite widespread frustrations with early KM approaches, there is still an undeniable thirst evident among business managers for the next knowledge-based "killer application."

Here we have listed several knowledge leadership challenges you may encounter as you launch knowledge-based initiatives in your organization.

*Challenge 1*: There are no guarantees that knowledge acquired from any external source will be understood or be effectively used in meaningful applications by your employees.

*Challenge 2*: For knowledge to be created there must first be individual learning. What is learned is ultimately determined by the intent of individual learners—not organizations. Moreover, there are no guarantees about what individuals will learn or whether they will apply it effectively to their work.

*Challenge 3*: The most powerful knowledge is knowledge that is created through experience and validated through use by peers. What is learned from experience is governed by the perceptions and biases of the learner(s), so there are no guarantees that what employees learn will be considered by leaders to be useful to the organization.[1]

*Challenge 4*: Knowledge is not the same as truth. Actions based on truth, if properly executed, are always effective at producing the expected result. Knowledge has a success rate somewhere between 1% and 99% in producing expected results. Therefore, there are no guarantees that actions based on knowledge will be effective 100% of the time.

*Challenge 5*: Some aspects of organizations and their environments are obvious and operate with such force that they exert their influence in concrete ways when employees take actions that are in accord with—or against—these forces. However, there are other, more subtle, aspects of the organizational milieu that can only be seen clearly with the aid of knowledge. Unfortunately, there are no guarantees that you will be able to tell the difference between these two sets of circumstances.[2]

## A FRAMEWORK FOR EFFECTIVE KNOWLEDGE STRATEGIES

Although *Knowledge Leadership* does not provide any killer applications, quick fixes, or hot new techniques, it does provide a framework for formulating an effective knowledge strategy—one that is comprehensive, systematic, and aligned with the future direction your company is pursuing. We propose that the ineffectiveness of prior knowledge-based initiatives in your company may be due in large part to two factors: (1) the knowledge activity may not have been appropriate or targeted for the desired results and (2) the knowledge approach (KM, training, action-learning, and organizational learning) may not have been aligned with other organizational forces and systems. The reasons for limited effectiveness of knowledge-based initiatives can most often be traced to (1) holding unrealistic expectations about what the different knowledge approaches can accomplish and (2) failure to effectively integrate these approaches with each other and with the capabilities of the organization as a whole.

Disappointing knowledge initiative results are often due to the absence of knowledge leadership. By this, we do not mean that CKOs are not doing their jobs well. Instead, we propose that knowledge leadership is a critical element of organizational success, one that has been inadvertently overlooked for the following reasons. First, the promise of KM technologies appears compelling at first blush. It is completely natural for managers to pursue what looks like a surefire winning information technology strategy. Second, up until now knowledge leadership has been narrowly defined as learning from your own experience to gain personal understanding. While some leaders may find this approach engaging, it is only a part of what is necessary to become a successful knowledge leader.

## Aligning Knowledge-Based Initiatives with Organizational Identity and Strategy

One of the greatest challenges for knowledge leaders is to design self-organizing and organic initiatives that energize knowledge creation and innovation. They also need to make certain these efforts are aligned with the organization's strategy, systems, and, most important, its identity. To return to our comparison of knowledge leaders and commercial beekeepers, everyone knows that bees already know how to create honey. It is the beekeeper's challenge to discover how to augment these natural capabilities. Within their community, bees also have leaders, especially the queen. The beekeeper must realize the queen's role as the central organizing force of the community. As L. Hugh Newman noted in *Man and Insects* (1965):

As L. Hugh Newman noted in *Man and Insects* (1965), the queen bee is the unifying force of the hive community—and the worker bees quickly sense her absence if she dies or is removed from the hive. In fact, after only a few hours, they will start showing unmistakable signs of being queenless.

So is there a similar "unifying force" in your business? We contend that an organization's identity can provide a strong center to hold together and make sense of all its activities. The identity of an organization contains the reason for its existence. It provides the answers to "why" it is in business and "what" function it has in society. (For example, "We are a management consulting firm" or "We are a health care center" or "We are a mutual funds company" are statements that reflect distinctly different organizational identities. ) Identity also helps with branding to determine what makes a company unique, different, one-of-a kind. (For example, "We are a management consulting firm that focuses on high-level executive coaching in the financial services industry. Our specialty is in helping executives improve interpersonal leadership skills.")

Identity is reflected in what the organization most values or considers important—and also how these values evidence themselves in the organization's culture and decision making. The identity of a business is the core of what it really *is*—not what anyone *says* it is or should be. Identity is the organization's "essence"—what is most *essential* to this system, that is, what must be sustained during any adaptation to change. In healthy organizations, identity functions as the unifying force—the self-referencing center that aligns and coordinates all of a company's activities, including its strategic planning and knowledge initiatives. Without a strong identity, organizations lack congruence in their behavior, and can act in inefficient, ineffective, and sometimes questionable or unethical ways. Due to abrupt changes in leadership or ill-conceived mergers, a firm's identity can become diffuse and cause the organization to act as if it were schizophrenic.

When this force is weak, leaders often feel they are trying to solve complex riddles that have no solutions—or that the "solutions" they've found raise new questions or create new problems. Often-times, lasting solutions to resistant problems can only be discovered by reframing how we view the problem. Such reframing can occur when we examine how well the company's knowledge-based initiatives fit the organization's identity.

Organizational identity is an issue that knowledge leaders need to keep in mind as they design and target their knowledge initiatives. (In the chapters that follow, we will provide more information to help you align knowledge initiatives with your organization's identity.) In a 1996 article, Fred Reed and Sharon Seivert described how vital identity is to organizational learning. Borrowing from the biological concept of *autopoesis*, they argued that organizations are autonomous (self-organizing, self-referencing) systems. Organizational identity is a powerful, but invisible, force that works below the surface to support or sabotage the efforts of knowledge leaders. Here are some of the key characteristics of organizational identity that Reed and Seivert identified:

1. The identity of an autonomous system is a closed (internal) network of relationships that define the organization of the system.
2. Autonomous systems adapt to maintain this internal network of relationships (its identity) in the context of its enclosing environment.
3. Interactions with the environment are not external inputs of information, but rather are potential disturbances of the network of internal organizational processes.
4. Learning, then, can be viewed as internal changes to the structure of the organization that allow it to respond to environmental perturbations in such a way as to successfully maintain its identity.

## INTEGRATING KNOWLEDGE WITH EXISTING MANAGEMENT SYSTEMS

Up to this point, we have focused on the importance of targeting knowledge-based activities so that they are aligned with the company's performance needs. While designing knowledge-based initiatives and targeting knowledge are both necessary processes for improving organizational performance, they alone are not sufficient for success. Knowledge leaders must also integrate their initiatives with existing management systems. A *management system* is a set of interconnected elements that link the ongoing process of managing to various aspects of the company through a mix of tools, methods, and routines. A management system operates as a set of functions that tend to either support or restrain each other. When an organization's management system is out of balance, it produces unintended consequences or outcomes that are counterproductive and cost-ineffective.

Figure 7.3 illustrates the interconnected elements that knowledge leaders need to consider when making changes anywhere in their

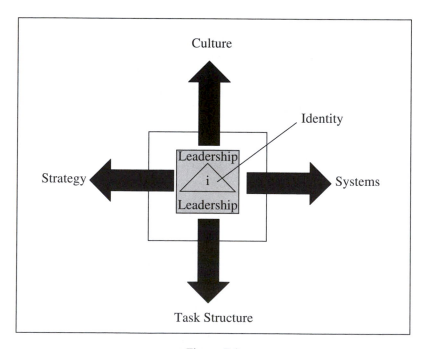

**Figure 7.3**
*Management System Model*

organization's management system. For example, when knowledge leaders propose a new KM system, it must be congruent with the organization's identity, culture, and overall strategy. It also must support the tasks that are to be accomplished as part of the knowledge strategy. By making certain all these interconnected parts of the management system are thoroughly integrated during change processes, leaders greatly increase the odds of success for their knowledge-based initiatives.

A high degree of *strategic knowledge alignment* is needed to integrate all aspects of an organization's management system and knowledge-creating processes. But when these are synchronized, businesses can achieve the synergy they need for success in today's hypercompetitive environments. Strategic knowledge alignment begins with examining the current identity of the organization, then clarifying the vision for what it seeks to become. This starting point is vital for success because it ensures that knowledge activities will build a bridge between the present corporate reality and the future it hopes to create. It also ensures a good organizational fit for the mix of knowledge activities that are chosen as vehicles to help the organization arrive at its goals.

## ORGANIZATIONAL STRATEGY CYCLES

Due to their systemic nature, organizational decisions often involve tradeoffs, and knowledge leaders need to develop strategies that take into account the likely effects of these tradeoffs. Over time, companies tend to cycle through most of the points on the organizational strategies grid shown below. For example, a corporation may choose at this time to focus on "performing-harvesting-utilizing" and later in its development to focus on "innovating-planting." Businesses can be distinguished by the amount of resources that they invest and the amount of time they spend in each strategic mode listed. As you may have already guessed, it is not a viable strategy for an organization to lock into just one combination of these strategies. In organizations, as in all of life, there is a time to plant and a time to sow. Figure 7.4 illustrates the basic strategies through which companies can cycle.

Each strategic cycle has particular benefits and disadvantages. The responsibility for knowledge leaders is to determine the appropriate knowledge activities for this stage of their company's growth. Knowledge leaders also must make certain that the strategy they choose

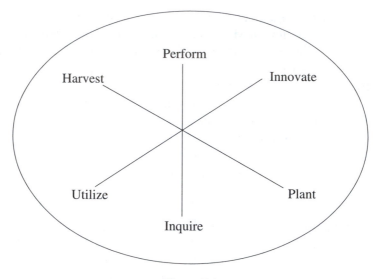

**Figure 7.4**
*Organizational Strategy Cycles Framework*

reflects the organization's identity. An organization's identity and strategy serve as the basis for answering many of the most fundamental questions about knowledge. For example, it can be argued that all questions pertaining to knowledge should be a board-level function and that all business strategies should flow from the organization's knowledge strategy.

The question of determining who within a company should be included in the process of defining an organization's identity is a critical one raised by various KM experts, such as Joe Firestone and Mark McElroy (2003). If an organization's members do not already have a strong sense of the company's identity, knowledge leaders need to develop a process that surfaces this subtle-but-powerful organizing force.

An organization's identity is often mirrored in (but is not the same as) its culture. For example, a startup business may have an *identity* as a "financial software development firm that specializes in supporting online checking services." Reflecting the values of its two entrepreneurial 30-something partners, this business could have a *culture* that is characterized by informality (casual dress), flexibility in hours worked, rewards for creativity, fun on the job, and autonomy for its self-directed work teams.

Clearly, an organization's identity also needs to be mirrored in the KM systems that are designed for it. Indeed, one of the worst things an organization can do is to undertake knowledge initiatives that run counter to its identity and values. The impact of this kind of misstep is clearly evident in the case of Bluestone Financial Services.

## BLUESTONE FINANCIAL SERVICES

"Bluestone Financial Services" was a premium quality life insurance company with a long and enviable track record of being highly profitable. It was an employer of choice for people in the area job market. Bluestone had a very conservative but relaxed corporate culture. This was in part attributable to the fact that Bluestone's superior reputation of products and services made most sales calls an "easy sell" for its low-key but respected sales force.

Most of Bluestone's sales representatives were men with many years of service. Eventually, Bluestone began to slowly lose sales as new competitors encroached on its market. In response, Bluestone created a special division that was designed to compete in this changing marketplace. The head of Bluestone's new division formulated an aggressive sales and marketing plan to help the company reclaim its market share. This new division brought over many people from its main sales division because they had such extensive knowledge of the company and its many products.

However, the emerging market conditions were highly competitive, and salespeople in Bluestone's new division were beaten at every turn. As it turned out, the identity, culture, and strategy of Bluestone's old sales force were not well aligned to the new sales strategy and the needs of the new market. This lack of alignment turned out to be a more important factor for success than the salespeople's considerable experience and product knowledge.

This issue raises a number of intriguing questions related to the firm's knowledge-based initiatives. Could Bluestone be managed in a way that integrated a new sales force that had different values and work style than the company as a whole? Was there any kind of knowledge that could have turned around the situation once Bluestone entered the new market with its low-key, but highly knowledgeable sales force? In a management systems problem, such as this one, alignment issues must be addressed *prior to* the change initiative so that knowledge-related questions can be more effectively dealt with.

## Generating *FAST* Knowledge

*FAST* is our acronym for knowledge that is functional, adaptable, sustainable, and timely. The terms that compose the acronym *FAST* can be defined as follows.

When something is *functional,* it is capable of operating properly or as designed to achieve a purpose. If a knowledge-based initiative is functional, it means that it is effective in reaching its goal. For example, if all of the students who took a course that prepared them for a professional certification exam passed the exam, then this knowledge-based activity (taking the class) can be said to be highly functional.

*Adaptation* is a process of change that derives from learning and that enables an entity (usually a person, team, or organization) to achieve a great accord with its environment. Knowledge-based initiatives that are adaptable help individuals and organizations adjust to different circumstances via the feedback that comes from learning through experience. For example, a corporate training program that provides employees with obsolete skills is not adaptive. However, a course that is constantly updated (based on what is most important for the employees to know now) would be considered adaptive.

*Sustainable* knowledge-based initiatives operate continuously at optimal levels of effectiveness. Most processes in life are subject to the forces of entropy, such as decay, aging, or fatigue. In contrast, sustainable processes are renewed with new sources of energy or critical resources. For example, a company may establish a community of practice for employees and schedule their meetings for Friday afternoons from 5 to 7 p.m. Such an initiative is not sustainable: it has preempted any natural self-organizing processes by employees, and they are likely to have little enthusiasm for meeting on their own time—and at the end of the workweek.

Finally, when activities are *timely,* it means that they occur when expected or needed—and also that they are appropriate for that particular time. For example, two passengers travel on a train that arrives in London at 6:10 a.m. The person with a 6 a.m. meeting is late, while the passenger who has a 7 a.m. meeting is likely to arrive on time. Taking the train was a timely activity for one passenger, but not the other.

Obviously, not all knowledge is *FAST* knowledge. Knowledge leaders can use the *FAST* criteria to assess the viability of different knowledge strategies. For example, let us consider a business that employs the strategy of sharing knowledge, but not creating new knowledge, and simultaneously focuses on harvesting performance without investing in innovation. To evaluate the potential efficacy of this strategy, we would simply follow two rules. First, we would employ the four *FAST* criteria, and then for each one of these criteria we would ask the question "Why?" five times. An example of this process follows.

Q1. Is the strategy *functional?* Will it achieve its short-term goal?
A1. We believe it is functional because it enables us to fill our orders and to be efficient.
Q2: Why does being able to fill orders and being efficient help us to be functional?
A2: Because filling orders increases revenues, and increasing efficiency reduces costs—both of which improve profits.
Q3: Why is achieving increasing profits functional?
A3: Because it enables us to pay more dividends to investors.
Q4: Why is paying greater dividends to our investors functional?
A4: Because more investors will want to buy our stock.
Q5. Why is it functional for more investors to buy our stock?
A5. Because an issuance of new stock can raise more money for our company.

The next step in determining whether a particular knowledge strategy is *FAST* is to go through the same process of questioning by asking five times, in turn, whether it is adaptable, sustainable, and timely. This process may seem at first to be laborious and time consuming, but it is actually a highly efficient and effective tool for making solid strategic decisions and avoiding costly rework.

In this example, it is likely that the organization's strategy of harvesting performance and sharing knowledge fulfills the *FAST* criteria of being functional and timely. However, the strategy does not increase the organization's capacity to adapt to change. Moreover, the strategy is not sustainable because little knowledge is created and there is a net drain on the knowledge resources of the organization.

By their very nature, all strategies have various limits and advantages that should be considered by knowledge leaders. In the next chapter, we examine the historical role of knowledge in the dominant business strategies that have prevailed over the past millennium. In particular, we explain the three most recent "ages" of organizational strategies, and how knowledge has played a central but very different role in each age.

# REFERENCES

*Business Week Online.* (2004, February 2). "Steve Jobs: It Feels Good." Retrieved from www.businessweek.com/magazine/content/04_05/b3868008_mz001.htm.

Collison, C., and Parcell, G. (2001). *Learning the Fly.* Oxford, UK: Capstone.

De Pree, M. (1989). *Leadership is an Art.* New York: Dell.

Firestone, J., and McElroy, M. (2003). *Key Issues in the New Knowledge Management.* Burlington, MA: Butterworth-Heinemann.

Hammer, M. (2004, April). "Deep Change: How Operational Innovation Can Transform Your Company." *Harvard Business Review,* 85–93.

Newman, L. H. (1965). *Man and Insects.* Garden City, NY: Natural History Press.

Pfeffer, J., and Veiga, J. F. (1999). "Putting People First for Organizational Success." *Academy of Management Executive,* vol. 13, 37–48.

Reed, F., and Seivert, S. (1996). "The Implications of Autonomy for Learning in Organizations." *Managing in Organizations that Learn* 383–387. Cambridge, MA: Blackwell Business Books.

Stewart, T. (1999, June 7). "Telling Tales at BP Amoco." *Fortune,* 220–224.

# NOTES

1. When we take actions that are reliably effective in producing the expected result, we can infer that it is a result of holding true beliefs about how things work. However, while true beliefs are necessary for reliably taking effective action, they are not always sufficient. For example, a manager may hold beliefs about conducting performance appraisals that are likely to prove reliably effective, but he or she may lack the sufficient skills in interpersonal communications to perform these appraisals well.

2. Oftentimes the brute force that accompanies the sudden feelings of doubt from experiencing unmet expectations can cause us to question anything from the validity of our knowledge to the truthfulness of our beliefs. This can go far beyond the Santa Claus syndrome (when we first discover there is no Santa Claus) to questioning many things we take for granted, such as "hard work leads to success" or that we will work in a single profession for our entire career.

# 8

# UNDERSTANDING THE ROLE OF KNOWLEDGE IN ORGANIZATIONS

## Executive Summary

This chapter examines the changing role of knowledge in organizations. The knowledge needs of businesses have changed significantly through the centuries. During the *Age of Arts and Crafts*, knowledge was handed down from master craftsmen to apprentices. During the *Machine Age* of the past two centuries, brilliantly designed systems and "scientific management" permitted mass production for global markets. Although business practices have tended to reflect the scientific thinking of their era, many current leaders remain entrenched in outdated mechanical paradigms. As the *Knowledge Era* (which dawned at the end of the 20th century) continues to emerge, the role of knowledge in business practices will become even more central. This chapter includes an interview with leading British consultant Colin Coulson-Thomas about why leaders should become "knowledge entrepreneurs." Knowledge leaders can integrate the best aspects of the Machine Age's *Brilliant Design strategy* and the Age of Arts and Crafts *Master Crafts strategy* to design a hybrid *Community Experiment strategy*, where employees constantly tinker with and improve well-designed work processes and systems. This strategy moves companies away from a dependency on embedded knowledge by targeting the capacity of the workforce to create new, pragmatic knowledge.

## A Look Back in Time

In this chapter, we will examine how knowledge has historically been viewed in work settings. While it is not the purpose of this book to explore either philosophy or science, it is instructive to note how the role of knowledge in organizations has usually mirrored its era's scientific advances. This understanding is important to knowledge leaders because most businesses now lag behind scientific thinking. The emerging Knowledge Era will help organizations incorporate the past century's scientific gains into improved business performance.

While businesspeople who wish to be practical may prefer focusing on how to best take action today, we argue that few things in business life are more practical than stepping back in time to hear the future's voice. That is, while the past does not directly predict the future, it does offer us glimpses of what has worked well in the past and which pitfalls we may need to avoid tomorrow.

## The Age of Arts and Crafts

Prior to the Age of Reason in Europe, knowledge usually referred to the kinds of know-how required for making things by hand. We refer to this knowledge era as *The Age of Arts and Crafts*, which lasted (in Europe) from roughly 1000 to 1750. These crafts revolved around fulfilling basic necessities for others, such as preparing food, building and construction activities, transportation, and agriculture. These, then, were the main areas that employed skilled workers. In this era, knowledge was integrated through intense practice of one's craft under the direction of an expert mentor or *master craftsman*. This was a highly inefficient way to produce goods, but it was viable then because most consumption was small scale—limited to one's own family, immediate community, and the few members of the ruling and emerging middle classes.

This was also a time of direct barter within communities—for example, a cobbler might exchange a pair of new shoes for fresh vegetables from a local farmer. The Age of Arts and Crafts was organized around guilds. Guilds are associations of craftspeople who owned their own business and who controlled the tools and materials they used in crafting their products. Guilds regulated the practice of each craft by governing the training of *apprentices*. The master craftsmen set the quality standards in their craft and the length of apprenticeship required for candidates to become midlevel *journeymen*. Among the first crafts to be organized in such a way was masonry. To give you an idea of how high the quality standards were in the Age of Arts and Crafts, masons were held accountable by penalty of death if they built a structure that fell on its dwellers.

By the start of the second century, craft guilds had spread throughout Europe. By the 14th century there were more than 50 different guilds in each of the major commercial centers of Europe. While guilds were the primary source of vocational training at that time in Europe, their usefulness began to diminish by the start of the 1700s when science, technology, and engineering all began to influence how products would be made. The noted historians, Will and Ariel Durant (1967), wrote of the demise of the craft guild movement:

The guilds were not competent to meet the demands of expanding markets at home and abroad. They had been instituted chiefly to supply the needs of a municipality and its environs; they were shackled by old regulations that discouraged invention, competition, and enterprise; they were not equipped to procure raw materials from distant sources or to acquire capital for enlarged production, or to calculate, obtain, or fill orders from abroad. Gradually, the guild masters were replaced by "projectors" (entrepreneurs) who knew how to raise money, to anticipate or create demand, to secure raw materials, and to organize machines and means to produce for markets in every quarter of the globe. (p. 670)

Although the longstanding tradition of arts and craftsmanship was eclipsed by the new Machine Age, small or specialized arts and crafts businesses (such as handcrafted Shaker furniture or expensive tailored clothes) have continued to operate alongside factories and "scientifically managed businesses" into the 21st century.

## THE MACHINE AGE

Not surprisingly, the mechanical era of industry followed directly on the heels of Europe's Age of Reason and the scientific breakthroughs of Descartes and Newton, who were pioneers in the use of rational reasoning and analysis. These thinking processes broke down anything complex into its smaller elements, thereby allowing greater control over the system as a whole. Two different types of knowledge rose to prominence during this time. *Know-how* became specialized and decentralized according to the principles of Max Weber's concept of the ideal *bureaucracy*, and *know-why* became centralized in the hands of system designers.

In the centuries that followed, advances in philosophy, science, and engineering expanded the range of the marketplace and thereby changed the face of the workplace and the role of knowledge. Craftsmanship was replaced by automation, and high-volume assembly lines in factories largely replaced the small craft shops by 1800. To raise efficiency, the work of craftsmen became divided into many specialized tasks that relatively unskilled people could easily learn and perform.

By 1755, the harnessing of various forms of power, such as steam for engines, enabled the large-scale mechanization of products in England. The era of improving productivity by mechanizing work reached America near the turn of the century as Eli Whitney designed the cotton gin for separating cottonseeds from cotton (1793). Years later, Whitney became a leading promoter of the new idea of mass-producing products through the rapid assembly of standardized parts. His most widely known application was in the production of firearms; he is credited with helping Samuel Colt open one of the world's first mass-production gun factories in Hartford, Connecticut.

It has been more than two centuries since Eli Whitney designed the *American System of Production* for goods in large quantities and at low cost. This brilliant innovation combined workers, machines, and processes into an integrated system that accomplished what none of its predecessors had been able to achieve. Namely, this was to establish low-cost, high-quality production of a somewhat techno-logically complex product. Whitney was criticized by British and French managers for allegedly taking the craftsmanship out of the production process. However, his system prevailed despite such dis-approval. Nearly a century after Whitney's innovation, Henry Ford took the same methodology to a new level when he mass-produced automobiles by standardizing parts and by staffing assembly lines with relatively unskilled, low-wage employees.

In the 20th century, and especially since the end of World War II, companies have faced an escalating demand to produce large volumes of low-priced products and services for the emerging mass-consumer societies. And at the end of the 20th century, emerging capitalist economies in countries such as China and former Eastern bloc members (Belarus, Czechoslovakia, Hungary, Poland, Romania, and Russia) joined the ranks of consumer-driven societies with free markets. Now, at the dawn of the 21st century, the pressure of global competition is greater than ever. Many corporations have responded by moving their manufacturing centers or customer service centers to lower-labor-cost nations where these new employees, working at a fraction of the expense, can quickly learn to play their respective roles in these machine systems.

## MACHINE AGE PRODUCTIVITY

The science of the Machine Age culminated in harnessing the power of steam, oil, electricity, and nuclear energy, and facilitated the mechanization of factories. Similar advances in transportation, communication, and computation all served to drive the companies of this era to previously unimagined heights of productivity.

The American system of production is one example of how knowledge applied from great inventors has led to the design of systems that reduced the need for labor, eliminated the need for labor altogether, or integrated labor into highly efficient systems. Here, training of workers to run these great machines became of critical importance. Pioneers such as Frederick Winslow Taylor, an inventive mechanical engineer, developed "scientific methods" for training workers so they could play their role in a high-speed interdependent system. This was a brilliant application of the current science because it allowed immigrants who had recently poured into the United States from all over the world to work side by side without needing to speak to or understand each other. However, because the tasks were tightly coupled, the risk of failure in such systems was very high. If any single worker failed to effectively perform his or her task, then all of the workers downstream on the line would be adversely affected. Elegant design and thorough training provided the critical elements of this system's success.

The Machine Age enabled consumer economies and societies to become well established around the world. The knowledge employed in creating brilliant system designs replaced the need for high levels of knowledge among individual employees—yet still yielded high levels of quality and productivity. Employees were considered extensions of the machine or system. Based on the enthusiasm of designers for the promise of such systems, the design process always started with the mechanical core of the system; human "components" were of secondary importance. Here, the chief knowledge activity of employees was to learn how to act in accord with the great machines they operated. In essence, the goal for workers was to become smoothly functioning cogs in a larger gear mechanism that could then act with even greater speed and precision.

Since machines cannot learn, organizational systems were designed for a specific purpose that the machines could fulfill very well. That is, these systems were highly functional, stable, and predictable. However, they had very low capacity for being able to adapt to changing circumstances. In this machine worldview, the main role of the system designers and controllers (managers) is to ensure that workers receive the knowledge they need to perform their specialized work flawlessly. An underlying and unstated assumption of this worldview is that the future is simply an extension of the present— that is, just more of the same. Ergo, adaptability is simply not an issue, and it is traded off for functionality and sustainability (that is, sustainability within a stable economic environment).

Unfortunately, the fact that the uniquely human capacity for adaptability is not incorporated into such systems means that if and when things do change, the organization is at high risk of failure. The real problem with mechanical approaches is that they encompass much more than the mechanization of work processes. Indeed, the ideal of Machine Age thinking was to transform *entire organizations* into highly efficient machines that were engineered to operate in sequential and deterministic ways. In the mechanical worldview still embraced by many business leaders, the ideal workplace remains much like highly automated assembly lines staffed with low-skill workers who do what the boss says and follow tight procedures to master their work tasks. These efficient workplaces produce large volumes of product at high speeds and low costs. Unfortunately, they do not allow people to think for themselves, which is a prerequisite for the development of knowledge.

Although knowledge was important during the prior two eras, its centrality will rise exponentially in the emerging Knowledge Era. In both the Machine and the Arts traditions, knowledge played critical roles, but these traditions required different types of knowledge that were employed in widely divergent ways. In Arts and Crafts systems, the knowledge of a master craftsman is passed down to apprentices and journeymen through years of training, on-the-job learning, and experience. These craftspeople are not only producers of products, they are also inventors and tinkerers who understand their product thoroughly. On the other hand, the Machine system of production relied on different kinds of knowledge: (1) engineering wizardry (the design of brilliant systems that integrated numerous complex subsystems into an efficient and reliable working whole) and (2) specific job knowledge (the training that allowed workers to quickly learn and execute activities that produced a large quantity of products in a short period of time).

In the new Knowledge Era, it will be vital for leaders to learn from the best and the worst experiences of these two prior eras, then use that knowledge to conceive of better ways to operate their businesses in today's highly competitive environment.

## THE EMERGING ERA OF KNOWLEDGE

The Knowledge Era began its entrance into organizational thinking just a few years before the dawn of the 21st century. One landmark event was when a consortium of U.S. companies started the "Initiative for Managing Knowledge Assets" (1989). Other important events in the development of the discipline of knowledge management include the publication of the book *The Knowledge Creating Company* by Ikujiro Nonaka and Hirotaka Takeuchi (1995); the start of Brian (Bo) Newman's Web-Based Knowledge Management Forum (1995); the publication of Karl Wiig's seminal article, "Knowledge Management: An Introduction and Perspective" in the first issue of *The Journal of Knowledge Management* (1997); and the founding of the first professional association of knowledge managers (Knowledge Management Consortium International [KMCI]) in 1998.

Unfortunately, although our current Knowledge Era is defined by thousands of scientific breakthroughs such as quantum physics, laser surgery, and photos being beamed back from Saturn, most organizational leaders still seem entrenched in outdated mechanical paradigms. The fact that so many corporate leaders are unwittingly trapped in the past century's scientific thinking makes for bad business decisions. As the famed economist John Maynard Keyes once observed, many self-proclaimed "practical" people claim that their thinking has not been influenced by the ideas of philosophers, but inevitably, these very same people became the "intellectual prisoners" of the discredited philosophers of a bygone era.

The fact that so many business leaders are still stuck in the thinking of the past Machine Age can be attributed to many factors. One is that they must constantly justify their decision-making rationale to numerous interested parties and stakeholders. For example, in the wake of corporate scandals (such as the much publicized difficulties in Enron and Arthur Anderson), there has been a backlash of increased public scrutiny and financial accountability. In this under-the-microscope environment, managers often find it difficult to try anything new. That is, it is hard for them to justify using anything but the already familiar, tried-and-true mechanical approaches.

Harvard Business School professor Clayton M. Christensen provides another reason in an interview with Walter Kiechel (2003), namely that most management reward systems are based on what economists call the "principal-agent" theory. This results in an incentive system that aligns executive income with the interests of stockholders—"so that what makes [the executives] rich makes the shareholders rich."

Other reasons for the slowness of corporate leaders to enter the Knowledge Era are detailed in the exclusive interview with Colin Coulson-Thomas that follows. Coulson-Thomas is an experienced chairman of award-winning companies, an active consultant on knowledge creation and exploitation, and author of *The Knowledge Entrepreneur* (Kogan Page, 2003). He has extensive hands-on experience helping more than 80 corporate boards build knowledge businesses. Thomas encourages leaders to be "knowledge entrepreneurs." He lays much of the blame for the slow entrance to the Knowledge Era on leaders who are unwilling to think for themselves and who therefore rely on consultants who "lead them by the nose" to purchase technological solutions and implement ineffective reorganizations.

---

## Becoming a Knowledge Entrepreneur
### An Interview with Colin Coulson-Thomas

*Knowledge managers often approach KM from a technical and systems perspective, but this leaves a leadership void in most organizations. Who are best suited to be the knowledge leaders of the future?*

Coulson-Thomas: Many management teams are missing exciting opportunities to transform corporate performance by better exploiting know-how and using knowledge-based job support tools to boost productivity. They are also forgoing unprecedented possibilities for generating additional revenues from exploiting existing know-how and creating and providing new knowledge-based offerings. A technological solution is not enough. People need to be inspired to create and exploit knowledge.

The most successful knowledge leaders of the future will be knowledge entrepreneurs, people who understand how to generate income and profit by creating and exploiting know-how. The people best suited to such a role will be those who understand how to create new knowledge-based offerings and activities and also how to exploit knowledge to increase the performance and productivity of existing operations, for

*Continued*

example, by equipping people with knowledge-based support tools that enable average operators to emulate the approaches and behaviors of more successful superstar colleagues.

*Many companies seem to prefer the technical route to doing KM that involves using hardware and software to create wide access databases, share knowledge, etc.—yet many of the elite companies, such as Toyota, Xerox, and 3M, approach knowledge from a completely different perspective that focuses on action learning, continuous improvement, and knowledge creation . . . things that are often taboo in many companies. How do you account for such differences, and what can you infer about how the non elite companies view knowledge?*

Coulson-Thomas: The approaches of many companies in the area of knowledge management reflect the advice they receive from consultants and what suppliers of technology chose to sell to them. Rather than think through themselves what is required, they end up being led by the nose by self-styled experts, whose main priority is selling the time of their consultants and securing software sales. This is why so much effort and money is spent on acquiring and installing technologies for capturing and sharing information and knowledge that may or may not be relevant to business development objectives, delivering greater customer and shareholder value, and securing market leadership. The emphasis is upon managing know-how that is in formats that can be handled by the technology being sold, rather than creating and exploiting the know-how required to compete and win.

Companies are adopting managerial rather than entrepreneurial approaches. The focus is upon managing what is currently known, rather than creating new information and knowledge-based services, tools, ventures, and businesses. Many knowledge management processes are missing explicit knowledge creation and exploitation stages.

*Why do so few companies see KM as being a route to innovation? Most companies seem to see KM more simply as a way to leverage existing knowledge so as to get greater impact from existing resources—why do you think this is the case?*

Coulson-Thomas: Many companies are led by insecure managers and cautious executives, rather than entrepreneurs. Their people copy and imitate others. They follow management fashions and fads, rather than think for themselves and develop their

*Continued*

own approaches. There are far more people drawing from the well of existing knowledge than there are replenishing the supply. Hence in many companies existing knowledge is being captured and shared, but the new knowledge required to develop fresh offerings, give customers new options, and provide additional choices is not being developed.

Knowledge entrepreneurship rather than the management of existing knowledge is required. Innovators are prepared to go out in front and explore, pioneer, and discover. Despite the pre-occupation with, and the focus upon, leveraging existing knowl-edge, the Managing Intellectual Capital to Grow Shareholder Value research project I led found that most companies only actively exploit a small proportion of the twenty or so major categories of intellectual capital examined by the project team.

Yet we stand at the threshold of a new management revolu-tion. There is simply enormous potential for knowledge entre-preneurship, performance improvement, and developing the additional knowledge needed to deliver greater customer and shareholder value. Most organizations and executives are barely scratching the surface. There is considerable scope for both improving the performance of existing operations and creating new knowledge-based products and services.

*Based on your experience as a leading consultant in the KM arena, what approaches to KM seem to be most popular and what are the strengths and weaknesses of these approaches?*

Coulson-Thomas: One popular approach seems to be to capture as much existing information and knowledge as possi-ble and make it available on a corporate intranet in the hope that this will encourage its sharing. It can lead to an extensive repository of knowledge that happens to be in formats that are easy for the technology provided by mainstream suppliers to handle. Maybe creating a latent potential for the beneficial use of what is stored—even though this might or might not be real-ized—could be regarded as an advantage. However, people can become overwhelmed by the sheer volume of information avail-able, while lacking what they need to be more effective in their jobs. More effort needs to be devoted to equipping key work groups with the information and knowledge they need, as and when it is required and providing people with the tools they require to effectively use and beneficially apply them.

*Continued*

We need to step up from information management to knowledge entrepreneurship. There is an urgent requirement for knowledge entrepreneurs who know how to acquire, develop, package, share, manage, and exploit information, knowledge and understanding and introduce related job support tools.

Just providing people with relevant knowledge may not be sufficient. They may also require tools to help them use and apply it. Practical knowledge-based tools can transform workgroup productivity by increasing understanding, communicating best practice, and sharing the essence of how superstars operate.

*Your approach to KM centers on an entrepreneurial view of KM as a tool for driving innovation, as opposed to the more conventional approach for capturing lessons learned, sharing best-practices, etc. What kind of successes have you seen with using your approach with your clients?*

Coulson-Thomas: Many conventional approaches lack entrepreneurial spirit, focus, and drive. The benefits of an entrepreneurial approach will depend upon the objectives of the particular project and the extent of entrepreneurial awareness and ambition in the boardroom. Some clients have transformed their prospects by exploiting particular categories of intellectual capital, for example, packaging their approaches and licensing them to others with greater resources and reach. Too many companies overlook opportunities under their noses. For example, there are over thirty different types of moneymaking offerings that could be provided by a training and development team.

In themselves, management approaches, methodologies, tools, and techniques and their enabling technologies tend to be neutral. How they are used, and for what purpose, determines whether they are vital and crucial or an irrelevant distraction. Identifying critical success factors for key activities such as winning business or building customer relationships and capturing how high performers operate can be particularly useful when developing support tools.

Pioneer clients have used knowledge-based support tools to transform business win rates, launch new products, and build supply chain quality. They can enable greater delegation and more bespoke responses in complex and regulated areas. In relation to winning business, returns of over 20 times an initial investment can be quickly achieved. Sales support tools have

*Continued*

> significantly increased business win rates, brought orders forward, and enabled dramatic reductions to be made in the number of specialist support staff required to accompany sales teams in the field. Experience suggests that winning is increasingly a matter of choice of approach. It is both easier and much more enjoyable than managing the consequences of failure.

With the help of knowledge leaders such as Colin Coulson-Thomas, many managers will transition successfully from Machine Age to Knowledge Era organizational approaches. Up to now, the links between a company's performance needs and popular knowledge-based approaches have appeared too fuzzy to justify their adoption. We believe that the shift to the Knowledge Era is on the verge of accelerating dramatically as evidence mounts about how elite companies, such as BP Amoco, Honda, 3M, and Toyota, have all employed knowledge-based approaches to deliver outstanding financial performance.

In our view, then, the question is not whether more organizations will shift to knowledge-based strategies—it is simply a matter of *when*. The logic of our argument is simple: Because knowledge-based approaches are extremely difficult for competitors to copy, they often provide a sustainable competitive advantage. A primary challenge facing prospective knowledge leaders right now is how to overcome the prevailing prejudice that knowledge is limited in its usefulness to product innovation, rather than also being vital to the improvement of traditional performance measures such as cost savings and waste reduction.

## THE CHALLENGE OF RECONCILING COMPETING FORCES

Despite the emergence of KM, learning and knowledge-based corporate strategies have lost their luster in the eyes of most corporate executives. Even though Peter Senge's (1990) *The Fifth Discipline* (which asserted that learning was the only form of sustainable competitive advantage) was an international best-seller, most executives still do not incorporate learning into their business strategies. This is actually no surprise, since learning-based initiatives are not easy to implement, can be complex to manage, and have uncertain payoffs. In contrast, more conventional management approaches provide reliable gains—up to a point. For many companies, these conventional tools are fine because they can increase the effectiveness of the current business strategies. However, the great limitation of such static approaches is that they are not built for adaptation (which will be increasingly important as market conditions continue to change). This is because all forms of adaptation—problem solving, continuous improvement, and innovation are based on human learning and knowledge creation.

An important issue for prospective knowledge leaders to address is whose knowledge matters most when it comes to business effectiveness—executives, managers, or workers? This question tends to divide companies into several major camps that differ in the emphasis and resources they would allocate to three basic elements that govern the role of knowledge in their organizations: (1) strategy formulation, (2) system design, and (3) operational work performance.

In the first competing camp are companies that invest heavily in (1) strategy formulation and (2) designing systems that require employees with low knowledge and need for learning. We call this the *Brilliant Design strategy*. For example, a company that seeks to be the low-price leader in a highly competitive consumer products market will invest heavily in designing and implementing sophisticated operating systems where employees are highly trained, low skilled, and low wage. Such configurations are highly functional and offer good timeliness, but they have virtually no adaptability and low-to-moderate levels of sustainability. Many airlines, general merchandise retail stores, and fast-food restaurants use this approach. The underlying assumption here is that a company with a winning plan designed by outstanding strategists will be so superior to its competitors that it will enjoy a long period of competitive advantage until that plan fades and needs to be replaced by a new brilliant strategy.

In the second major camp are companies that use simple strategies and systems, but invest heavily in their workforce. This approach brings together highly skilled, educated, or knowledgeable groups of people who may customize their work or produce high-value products and services. We refer to this approach as the *Master Craft strategy*. For example, a practice of brain surgeons would be such a group. These physicians have mastered their profession through many years of education, training, and apprenticeship. The role of managers in such groups is to run the business side of the organization at the behest and direction of the masters. Other examples of organizations with Master Craft strategies include manufacturers of top-of-the-line musical instruments, professional sports teams, or companies where highly skilled craftspeople play a critical role in attaining business success.

This strategy works whenever Master Craft people can perform specialized tasks or make radical process or product improvements that are difficult for their competitors to duplicate. Typically, Master Craft systems are designed loosely to give practitioners optimal freedom in expressing their craft and making professional judgments. Such systems also allow for high levels of independence, where the actions of individual practitioners have little impact on colleagues. The heavy investment in workers with particular knowledge-sets means that these organizations are highly specialized and may have difficulty transitioning to new products, services, or markets. These businesses are only sustainable as long as the economics of their industry support their high-priced, customized strategies.

In these two polar opposite systems, learning and knowledge play very different kinds of roles. The Master Craft system is labor inten-sive, whereas the Brilliant Design system uses minimal amounts of labor. Interestingly, both of these systems rely on large amounts of knowledge. In the Brilliant Design strategy, a great amount of knowl-edge goes into designing the system and implementing it. However, once the system is operating, much less knowledge is required to keep it functioning. The Master Craft system also relies on large amounts of knowledge, but most of it is acquired by the craftspeople prior to joining the organization.

Both of these systems rely heavily on *embedded knowledge*. For the Brilliant Design strategy, embedded knowledge is the know-how that is expressed in the way the system is designed, and it is manifested in the form of routines, processes, and technologies designed by engineers and inventors. For example, when carpenter's tape measure rules are manufactured, a key step in the process is to bake the metal of the tape rule at a high temperature prior to painting or labeling it with the demarcations for inches and feet. This is done to enhance the flexi-bility of the metal and to decrease the risk of breakage during use. The oven is part of the production process because, through experience and research, it was determined essential for extending the usable life of the tape rule. This is an illustration of how knowledge became embedded in organizational systems. In simpler terms, people learned the best way to do something, then made a habit of it by designing machines, systems, and processes that have that specific learning built into them.

In the case of Master Craft systems, embedded knowledge exists in the methods and techniques that are taught to apprentices by prior masters. Artisans such as potters, glassblowers, and weavers all use methods that have been passed on to them through generations. Oftentimes, family members specialized in a particular art or craft to ensure that this precious acquired knowledge was transferred to their children to enhance their chances for success. Indeed, craft trades such as Baker or (black)Smith identified generations of families—until many adopted the name of their trade.

Whereas, the Master Craft strategy is an *inside-out strategy*, the Brilliant Design strategy is an *outside-in strategy*. In the Master Craft strategy, the embedded or *known knowledge* comes from inside (the master craft artisan) and is handed down (outside) to the apprentice. In the Brilliant Design's outside-in strategy, the known knowledge is built into a system by its designers (comes from outside). Learning means that employees acquire this existing knowledge (bring it inside) and put it to work quickly and effectively. Knowledge, then, is the understanding needed to operate the system; it must be supplied to the employees by the designers or acquired by the employees as a requisite for their job. In the Brilliant Design setting, knowledge is an external resource (such as best practices) that is imported into the system to help activate it.

In an unfortunate and growing trend in Western countries, some desperate companies completely bypass the Brilliant Design and the Master Craft strategies in favor of hiring charismatic CEOs to solve their problems. Most often, these CEOs do not understand the company's culture or how it processes knowledge, because it often takes years to fully understand such matters. In lieu of developing a detailed feel for the subtleties of how a company operates, the new "hired gun" CEO makes radical changes to send a strong signal to investors and financial analysts that performance improvements are just around the corner. Rarely do such changes prove to be productive. Rather, they are rooted in a fantasy fiction scenario that is often reinforced by nervous boards of directors. As Harvard Business School professor Rakesh Khurana observed:

The problem is that the board's selection process is embedded within a larger system of analysts, institutional investors, etc. They also believe in fast results; they also make the attribution that if a firm is not doing well, it must be because of the CEO; and if it is doing well, it must be because of the CEO. They live in a society that has always treasured the image of a cowboy, the Lone Ranger, or Prince Valiant coming in to clean up the town or rescue the distressed. So, in many ways they are just as much embedded in this larger kind of cultural construct. (Lagace, 2002)

We contend that strong communities do not depend on strong leaders. Many companies undermine their own sustainability by under-investing in knowledge processing and community building activities while over-investing in charismatic CEOs. The result is that such organizations become collectively ineffective and dependent on such leaders to bail them out of trouble. Building a strong community that understands how to learn, experiment, and create knowledge is a critical function in order for businesses to become truly sustainable.

## THE COMMUNITY EXPERIMENT

A hybrid type of organization employs a knowledge strategy that we have labeled the *Community Experiment strategy*. This strategy moves companies away from a dependency on embedded knowledge by targeting the capacity of the firm's workforce to *create new knowledge*. Here, employees are encouraged to innovate and use their personal work experiences as the basis for creating new ways of looking at how things work. Employees in such companies are always experimenting with innovative ways to produce their product or service. System designs and strategies are viewed as only being rough templates that must be continually modified to reach their full potential. Such firms are highly adaptive, moderately functional, very sustainable, and more likely to move in timely ways—and are therefore most likely to be *FAST* companies. Two examples of Community Experiment companies are Toyota and 3M.

Community Experiment organizations build on the best traits of both the Brilliant Design strategy and the Master Craft strategy. Consequently, they have numerous strategic advantages. For example, in the Community Experiment, strategists have designed work processes and systems. However, here it is understood that the success of the design in achieving its purpose is not statically inherent in the design itself. Rather, the design's full potential will only be realized when the members of the community discover ways to modify it over time. This hybrid organization also calls on its people to be tinkerers and inventors, as in the Master Craft tradition, and to hand down their learning to peers and the next generation of workers.

In Community Experiment companies, work is not just the efficient delivery of a product or service. It is also an ongoing experiment to learn how things actually work best in practice. Innovation is not a discrete event. Rather, it is a continuous process of applying the scientific method to 1) derive new principles for guiding modifications to the system and 2) develop new methods for operating. In Community Experiment organizations, *everything* is continuously innovated: work processes and operational procedures, cycle-times, and product designs. Under these circumstances, the knowledge needed to help the system evolve is *unknown*, so employees create it by combining daily work experience with the process of experimentation. Knowledge, then, is regarded as being closely linked to the capacity of individuals and teams to learn from their own experiences.

In this approach, *knowledge is seen as arising through employees* as a consequence of their efforts to reflect, experiment, and discover new ways of seeing how things work in their jobs. Learning becomes a matter of *learning through action*, as opposed to a process of external discovery and inquiry. Because the experimenters are also the workers, innovations relate directly to their practical concerns. When successfully implemented, the Community Experiment strategy is geared to optimize efficiency, effectiveness—and innovation. We believe that, because the Community Experiment strategy incorporates some of the best traits of both the Brilliant Design and Master Craft strategies, it is an excellent business strategy for supporting employees in the development of new pragmatic knowledge for improved business performance and innovation.

In the next section of *Knowledge Leadership*, Part III, we will explore how knowledge leaders can develop pragmatic knowledge in their organizations, thereby providing them with significant competitive advantages for the future.

## REFERENCES

Durant, W., and Durant, A. (1967). *Rousseau and the Revolution.* New York: Simon & Schuster.

Kiechel, W. (2003). "Andy Grove on Confident Leaders," *Working Knowledge for Business Leaders,* Harvard Business School, Cambridge, MA.

Lagace, M. (2002). *The Irrational Quest for Charismatic CEOs,* Harvard Business School, *Working Knowledge for Business Leader,* Cambridge, MA, September 16. (http://hbswk.hbs.edu/item.jhtml?id=3526&t=leadership).

Nonaka, I., and Takeuchi, H. (1995). *The Knowledge Creating Company.* New York: Oxford University Press.

Senge, P. (1990). *The Fifth Discipline.* New York: Doubleday.

Wiig, K. (1997). "Knowledge Management: An Introduction and Perspective." *Journal of Knowledge Management,* vol. I, no.1.

# Part IV

# Developing Pragmatic Knowledge

# 9

# PUTTING ACTION INTO KNOWLEDGE

## Executive Summary

The field of KM has evolved with an emphasis on storing knowledge so that it can be reused at another place and time. The conventional wisdom holds that in order to store or move knowledge, it needs to be reduced to its basic, atomistic elements. The difficulty is that when knowledge is "atomized," we wind up with a very different sense of what is known. Moreover, this knowledge is not directly tied to action. Although the information-centric view of knowledge is attractive for organizations because it is simple and easy to use, it does not assure performance improvements nor is it very useful for solving complex problems. This chapter discusses how to "put action into knowledge" to create pragmatic knowledge. *Pragmatic knowledge* is high-quality, situation-specific knowledge that helps us understand *what* works, *why* it works, *how often*, and *under what circumstances*. It reveals relationships that leaders would otherwise not easily recognize. Although pragmatic knowledge is generally less manageable than "atomized" knowledge, it provides the basis for continuous improvement. *Acts of knowing* are a prerequisite to creating many kinds of knowledge that may prove to be useful at some point in the future. Seven acts of knowing are discussed in this chapter. Organizational knowledge is built on a shared understanding of which acts of knowing are potentially useful to improve performance.

Every time you take an action to achieve a goal, you gain new knowledge. If your actions are successful in helping you reach your goal, you learn from that experience about what works well in practice. If you are unsuccessful, you also learn from that experience—this time about what does *not* work well in practice. This chapter describes how you can put action into knowledge to create high-quality, pragmatic knowledge. Pragmatic knowledge is situation-specific knowledge that can help you understand *what* works, *why* it works, *how often*, and *under what circumstances*, thereby providing you with new understandings and revealing relationships that you might otherwise not have recognized.

## EXAMINING KNOWLEDGE IN A PRACTICAL LIGHT

Since the advent of KM, knowledge has progressively been defined in ways that are either academic or operational. In this book, we will avoid academic definitions because they offer little potential for adding insight to the questions we pose. On the other hand, KM's operational definition of knowledge appears to have more practical relevance to business managers. In fact, the field of KM has evolved with an emphasis on the importance of sharing, storing, leveraging, and cataloging knowledge so it can be reused at another place and time. To achieve the necessary universality, mobility, and storability of knowledge for use in KM systems, knowledge needs to be reduced to its basic, atomistic elements, in much the same way as ultra-small pieces of physical matter are defined in quantum physics.

We will look to the atom, the building block of life, as an instructive metaphor for understanding the difference between information and knowledge. (If you are a chemist or physicist, please forgive the technical liberties we have taken in this illustration.) Because information by itself is neutral, it can be compared to the zero-charged neutron in the atom's center (nucleus). Knowledge enhances the nucleus of information by adding the context (the positively charged proton in the atom's nucleus) and meaning (the outer moving/changing part of the atom, the electron) to create a "knowledge atom." In this metaphor, the data that make up information could be compared to the subatomic particles that compose the neutrally charged neutron of information. The following example illustrates how data can contribute to information, and possibly point to knowledge.

*Data*: Market research data show that ACME Corporation's market share was 12% during 2003.

*Context*: Analysis reveals that ACME's market share dropped by 2% in the first two quarters of 2004, while its closest competitor, Cajun Corporation, gained 3%.

*Meaning*: One possible conclusion that could be gained from combining these facts is that ACME is losing market share to Cajun. However, this is only one of many possible conclusions, or meanings, that could be ascribed to the information.

The realization that ACME has lost ground during the past quarter may be useful information to ACME's managers. Or this information could be entirely meaningless because it does not include contextual variables that may be important for interpretation.

Our point is not to debunk the value of information. Rather we want to emphasize that it is important not to confuse information with knowledge. The information just presented is not knowledge because it did not originate in, nor is it directly tied to, action. Clearly, it is better to make decisions on information plus reason, rather than on reason alone. Information can be used to lead to knowledge. Information can highlight potential relationships that can be explored, tested through action, and then used to form the basis for new knowledge. Decisions that are based on this kind of tested through-action knowledge will be most likely to produce the goals desired. However, it is also important to remember that because almost all knowledge is incomplete, it is not 100% reliable. Therefore knowledge is not the same as truth.

Within the field of KM, the prevailing thought is that knowledge can be managed when it is atomized, and there is general acceptance of the following three principles:

1. Data are statements of fact, measures of activity.
2. Information is data plus context.
3. Knowledge is information that is given meaning by circumstance.

The KM model places information at the heart of knowledge. The information-centric view of knowledge is attractive for organizations because it is simple and easy to use. Simplicity and ease of use are good things, but they do not assure performance improvements. Information has many characteristics that make it ideal for being managed, yet simultaneously it has significant limitations that may make it unsuitable for applications to knowledge-based activities.

To say that information is at the center of knowledge is to trivialize the role of knowledge in solving complex problems. It is like saying that the quality of the paints used by Monet is at the core of his masterpieces or that effective use of color will reliably produce high-quality art. Through the work of impressionist painters like

Monet, painting shifted from being an objective duplication of reality to a highly subjective and personalized interpretation of a given subject matter. While the art of painting can be reduced to simple technical considerations, such as drawing, composition, style, color, and texture, it can also be much more than that. Painting—like knowledge leadership—involves perception and interpretation. When leaders sift through large amounts of information, they act much like artists who deliberately draw attention to certain aspects of the viewing field at the exclusion of other aspects.

We are not saying that managers need to be the equivalent of impressionistic artists, or that it is insufficient to be technically competent in one's work. The point we wish to make is that every way we define and operationalize knowledge has both advantages and limitations. Atomizing knowledge, as is customary in most KM systems, severely limits the possible effective applications of this knowledge. It is a bit like focusing only on the beautifully colored dots in an impressionist painting and never stepping back to see the meaning that is contained in the whole picture.

The greatest mistake that aspiring knowledge leaders can make is to apply this narrow and specific type of knowledge to complex circumstances. While the KM approach is simple to learn and master, it is not effective in solving complex problems or serving as the basis of innovation. The major overlooked risk of the atomized information approach is that this information is ungrounded, not directly connected to action, does not include a validation process, lacks context, and neglects critical elements that define relevant circumstances. Consequently, there is a much higher probability that leaders who rely on it will reach seriously wrong conclusions.

Pragmatic knowledge addresses many of these limitations. Much of this chapter will be devoted to explaining pragmatic knowledge, its creation, and its application in organizations. Pragmatic knowledge also has its limitations. It is generally less manageable, at least in the conventional sense. However, when companies or their subunits are designed around pragmatic knowledge, it becomes much easier to use effectively—though it is not really accurate to say that pragmatic knowledge is "managed." Rather, pragmatic knowledge becomes the basis for continuous improvement and self-directed activity by employees. It may seem unbelievable to most managers that pragmatic knowledge systems could ever be used routinely in business. The good news is that, not only are companies already using the pragmatic knowledge approach—but they are doing so with outstanding success.

When knowledge is *managed* from a conventional perspective, there appears to be an inversely proportional relationship between its *load-bearing capacity* and its *manageability* (see Figure 9.1) The load-bearing capacity of knowledge can be thought of as a combination of the quantity and types of knowledge elements that it contains. Manageability is the ability of a KM system to share, store, and provide leaders and workers access to knowledge.

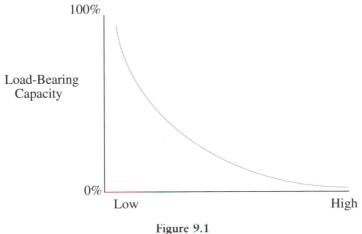

**Figure 9.1**
*Manageability*

It is important to note that Figure 9.1 applies only to cases where knowledge is managed in a conventional sense—that is, where there are systemic efforts to share knowledge on a large scale, store, and access it. When work systems are designed for high load-bearing pragmatic knowledge, the manageability tradeoffs become virtually irrelevant. But before we discuss how organizations develop pragmatic knowledge systems, let's first consider how pragmatic knowledge is created individually, by the process of learning through experience.

## ACTS OF KNOWING

Knowing is an active process of awareness that enables individuals to mentally construct a story in their minds that explains something relevant to the present action. When we know something, we pay attention to it, we recognize it—and sometimes we may actually understand it. Acts of knowing are a prerequisite to creating many kinds of knowledge that may prove to be useful at some point in the future. There are many ways of knowing, each of which provides special insights and has limitations. Among these ways of knowing are the following:

1. Acts of recognition
2. Acts of understanding how things work
3. Acts of understanding why things work
4. Acts of execution involving the performance of a series of sequential tasks or processes
5. Acts of logical inference through reasoning
6. Acts of performance—discovering things work well and reliably in certain cases
7. Acts of intuitive knowing

## Acts of Recognition

Upon hearing the meow of a cat, infants point to the animal and say the word "cat" or "kitty." This is an act of recognition. That is, they observe that the animal in their view meets certain standards of "catness" that define the identity of this creature. Cats make different sounds than dogs, including meowing and purring. They have whiskers that are more evident, frequently lick their own bodies, and scratch objects, such as furniture or trees with their claws. Similarly, managers may recognize a certain situation as being a "quality problem" or a "productivity problem." That is, they recognize the correspondence between the definition of certain kinds of problems and the facts or information they have observed. This process is similar to the way physicians make the diagnosis of an illness.

## Acts of Understanding How Things Work

Understanding *how* things work generally involves understanding the links between causes and their effects. For example, automobile mechanics understand that if the cylinders and pistons in an engine are corroded, the engine is likely to consume oil more rapidly. Mechanics may not be able to explain the physics or chemistry of the corrosion process, but they would likely understand how to repair the problem.

## Acts of Understanding Why Things Work

Understanding *why* things work as they do generally requires a level of knowing that goes beyond the simple mechanics of cause-

and-effect relationships—to knowing the general forces or principles that underlie those mechanics. Chemical engineers are likely to understand *why* motor oil with certain chemical properties burns more rapidly in a corroded engine. With this understanding they may be able to limit the severity of the oil consumption problem. They may not, however, understand *how* to fix the engine as well as the automobile mechanics.

## Acts of Execution

Knowing how to perform a particular task is an act of execution. For example, people may know how to check the voicemail function on their cell phone and successfully reply to a message. However, knowing how to respond to the cue that they have a voicemail message does not require them to understand how or why things work as they do. It only demands that they can precisely follow the steps to execute a particular sequence of acts to retrieve that message.

## Acts of Inferential Reasoning

There are types of knowing that arise through using accepted facts or assumptions to reach conclusions about other states of affairs through the use of deductive reasoning. For example, if you know that the speed limit where you are driving is 65 miles per hour, and you know that if you are caught speeding (again) you will lose your insurance, then you can conclude that if you are arrested for speeding you will be in serious trouble. This conclusion is reached through the use of deductive reasoning, which is simply applying general rules to specific circumstances.

## Acts of Performance

This type of knowing is perhaps the most pragmatic of all and deserves a more detailed explanation. Let us start with a situation where you are making an effort to solve a problem or achieve a goal. After diagnosing the problem or identifying the goal, you then make a decision and take action. After some period of time, the action you took produces effects. That is, there is some type of outcome that stems from your action.

Imagine that you are trying to reduce your body weight and your action was to increase your exercise and activity levels. A week later, you weigh yourself and discover that your weight has not gone down. Your belief is that this difference between the actual weight and your expectation simply reflects a time delay and that it may take longer for the improvements to show. After another week, much to your disappointment, you find that your weight has still not changed. You conclude that your increased activity level was not sufficient to burn the necessary calories to show up on the scale as lost weight. It could also be that you are not losing weight because you are increasing muscle mass, or that you need to perform other actions to lose weight—perhaps eat different kinds of foods or consume less food overall. The experience you gained in your first two weeks of exercising has helped you learn how reliably certain actions produce expected outcomes (total weight loss).

This type of knowing is very important because, it is not only pragmatic, in that it connects actions to goals and performance, but it also enables us to discover the level of effectiveness of our strategy. This type of knowing is often critical for corporate leaders who are concerned with performance enhancement.

## Acts of Intuitive Knowing

Such acts of knowing rely on the totality of human experience, such as intuition, gut feelings, or listening to an inner voice. Many great business leaders report relying heavily on their intuition (and many other leaders use their intuition quietly, but do not admit doing so because they fear being thought too far out of the box). This intuitive way of knowing uses all of the human senses, in addition to the logical part of the human mind. Science supports the extraordinary efficacy of this way of knowing. According to research by Tor Norretranders (1991), human beings receive 11,000,000 bits of data per second from our senses, yet we cognitively process a mere 16 bits of that data. A significant amount of the remaining data that has been filtered out by this screening process can be accessed intuitively—a mysterious, but highly useful knowledge process.

When Intel Corporation CEO Andy Grove (2003) was asked whether managers can be taught to draw on their own intuition in making decisions, he offered:

You can promote intuition. You can recognize the innate aptitude of people to grasp what cannot be spelled out and cannot be shown by data, to be in tune with those vague attributes on the other side of that vague valley. And put them in positions where they can act on their intuition. (p. 1)

Let us explore the process by which experience teaches us what actually might work in practice by looking at the observations and inferences of two workers in "Omega Financial Services."

## OMEGA FINANCIAL SERVICES

It is Monday morning at the office of Omega Financial Services, and you are en route to your next meeting. Though you are walking at a brisk pace, it seems this morning that your coworkers are moving even more quickly and that they are more focused than you. One of your coworkers, Jennifer, is walking in the same direction and at the same speed as you. She begins a conversation by observing, "Everyone appears so harried today. Don't you think so?"

You reply, "Yes, I know."

Jennifer continues, "Everyone here is so productive, our numbers must be going through the roof this quarter. Don't you think so?"

After pausing to ponder the question, you answer, "Hmmm, I don't have a clue about that, Jen. Those productivity numbers have always been a mystery to me."

What are you really saying to Jennifer when you affirm her observation that your coworkers are looking harried this morning?

To start with, you are referring to an experience that you both have had. Namely, it is the experience of walking among coworkers within the same office during the same period this morning. During this time, you have observed your coworkers' demeanors and you have reached a conclusion about their internal state (namely, that they appear to be busy and harried). In other words, they are moving more quickly or perhaps in a less social manner, and their facial expressions or body language suggest they are feeling stressed.

You have communicated to Jennifer that your observation has led to an interpretation and a possible explanation for what is happening with your coworkers. Saying, "I know," in this particular case denotes that there are general similarities between the observations, interpretations, and conclusions both you and Jennifer have made about your coworkers at a particular place and time.

But is this really *knowing*? What does it mean when we say that we *know* something? In this example, we are saying that, from our past experience of observing our coworkers at the office, we believe we know something to be true. However, believing that we know something to be true, knowing something, and having it be true are all very different things.

Many information-based approaches to knowledge are not really a process of knowing either. The preceding example is missing key ingredients whether you look at it from the perspective of either information-based knowledge or pragmatic knowledge. In the information-based approach, information is the result of data, and data are obtained via a process of measurement. There is no objective measurement process going on in this example, although a subjective or informal measurement process has occurred. The two observers, you and Jennifer, perhaps unknowingly, compared your observations of the pace of walking and body language/facial expressions today to some reference baseline of what seems normal in your mind. So compared to the baseline average of these factors in your memory, the observations on this specific day gave you reason to make the particular interpretation that people are more stressed than normal.

Is this what some KM experts refer to as "tacit knowledge"? No, tacit knowledge generally refers to uncodified or informal types of *know-how* (knowing what to do, how to perform a task, or what sequence of steps to take). There is not any know-how involved in this situation. Although the observations that you and Jennifer have made could be quite accurate and insightful, this kind of knowing is highly individualized and subjective because it is based largely on intuition and observation. However, this way of knowing is a good place to start our exploration. It is extremely useful when we are trying to define a situation that we know relatively little about. It helps us make sense of a situation long before we have taken any formal steps to discover how something actually works in practice. This sort of knowing is based on beliefs, reasoning, and perceptions that are disconnected from action, or action that has been disconnected from one's personal beliefs and reasoning processes.

Now let's say that you and Jennifer had a more objective measure of how busy and harried your coworkers were on this Monday morning. In fact, let's say that the two of you work Omega Financial Center's customer service office and that when clients are upset with the quality of their service experience, there is a toll-free number they call to file complaints. Could this be an indirect measure of whether the service center employees are feeling busy or harried? Trying to measure the emotional state of employees at a particular moment in time can be quite difficult. However, it is much easier to assess productivity by measuring calls serviced per day or some other output measure. However, we do not know whether there is a time lag between when people start feeling stressed and when the effects become noticeable in performance numbers. In reality, feeling stressed can cause productivity indices to actually rise (at first), as employees spend less time per call to compensate for the additional pressure they are experiencing.

Collecting data on numbers of complaints the department has received and changes in productivity could be useful as a starting point for developing an explanation about what employees are experiencing. However, at this point, it is not known whether your coworkers are actually experiencing anything out of the ordinary— or whether it is impacting their work performance. Based on the use of such measures, we still do not know if your coworkers are actually experiencing the stress you have attributed to them or whether this stress is causing their work performance to change. As this example illustrates, it is often extremely difficult to make the necessary causal connections among all the variables at play to develop a viable explanation of which causes are producing which effects.

If we knew the following facts, we could formulate a hypothesis about how things are working. This then would allow us to set up an experiment that could be periodically tested through actions we would take.

1. Employees appear to us, through observation, to look busier than normal and harried.
2. Complaints have increased dramatically over the past three days.
3. Productivity declined briefly, then increased suddenly during this period.
4. Time spent per call increased briefly during this period and then decreased dramatically.

With this information, what we really know are *clues* that could potentially help us understand a situation. We do not yet know *how or why* things are working as they are. This kind of knowing is of the information contained in certain facts and measurements. This information is necessary for developing an explanation of how things work and why—but it is not sufficient so that we can truly say we know what is causing performance to change over time. We can say we believe something is true, because of our understanding of what has happened when certain causes and effects occurred in certain circumstances. However, believing is not the same as knowing, and knowing something works is not the same thing as knowing something is true. (Unless, of course, that something works 100% of the time.)

When it comes to organizations, cause and effect are seldom just simple chains of means and ends. There is a third influence that mediates cause-effect relationships. It was described by Charles Sanders Peirce as being the force of *thirdness*. Thirdness may be thought of as the influence of other forces and elements in the organization on how various *causes* work to produce *effects* that we see as performance. For example, the time it takes a company to deliver its orders may have risen to one month from its customary 2-week time. The managers of the manufacturing department respond by adding 5 hours of mandatory overtime for all production employees to reduce the backlog of orders. What they did not anticipate was that orders would surge again—due to a new marketing campaign and a 20% increase in hiring of new salespeople (which was unknown to the manufacturing staff).

Even though a reasonable decision was made to increase worker overtime, it did not improve performance due to the outside influence of the marketing department's actions. The decision to increase overtime was an example of *firstness*, the impact of more hours of overtime worked on the order backlog was a case of the effects of *secondness*, and the marketing department's influence on performance was attributable to *thirdness*. The effect of this "thirdness" factor was to more than offset the impact of the mandatory overtime—and cause the shipping delay to increase to 6 weeks.

Most often, when we say that we "know" something, we are reflecting that we have inferred (based on our experience of having acted a specific way under given circumstances) that we can predict how something will occur. For example, we can say that we know from our own personal experience that when we ask customers in our fast-food restaurant the question, "Would you like fries with that burger?" 60% of the time they will answer yes. We also know that if we subsequently ask the question, "Would you like to super-size those fries?" from past experience, 40% of the people will answer yes. In other words, we can say that in certain circumstances, if we act in a particular way, we know with some assignable degree of confidence that an expected result is probable. Now, we may not always be able to pinpoint the probability down to a specific percentage, but we can say that we believe a certain outcome to probable, improbable, or impossible, based on past experiences. So our knowledge is derived through action and feedback. But what is it that we really know?

We can conclude that under certain circumstances, we can act a certain way and expect a particular outcome. We also can conclude that experience has taught us that what we know has some degree of *verity* because it has some degree of reliability in achieving the result we seek. When we speak of having *know-how*, we can say that, based on our past experience we believe this know-how will produce certain outcomes under certain circumstances. This kind of knowing is one step closer to the most practical kind of knowing—that is, pragmatic knowing.

## THE PRAGMATIC WAY OF KNOWING

The pragmatic way of knowing enables us to take a more holistic view of how our actions help us achieve our aims. If we know, based on thousands of repetitions of a certain action, that it always flawlessly produced the result we expected, then this action would become automatic as our way to achieve the expected outcome. On the other hand, if we know something never produces the expected result, not only are we going to abandon that particular action—we may change our minds about how things work in practice. Practical knowledge is not simply a tool for improving performance, it is one of the most powerful ways to leverage past experience for current problem-solving efforts. In their fictional book written for knowledge leaders, *Inside Knowledge*, Fearon and Cavaleri (2005) claim that pragmatic knowledge helps managers in managing risk, solving problems, improving performance, and heightening job satisfaction.

Knowing what works reliably in practice not only enables us to do a better job of choosing potential effective actions in the future, it also helps us clarify how things work and what might work well the next time. This kind of knowing is far more useful than simple know-how, because it helps us to personally understand the following:

- What works
- Why it works
- How often
- And under what circumstances

The pragmatic way of knowing enables us to discern relationships we would otherwise not easily recognize—that is, the relationship between how we view a situation, the rules we adopt to govern our actions, the actions we take, and how well our actions produce the desired effects. This type of thinking is the essence of the control process in most organizations. But unlike most control systems, pragmatic ways of knowing enable us to view situations differently each time we approach them—and therefore to formulate improved action strategies based on the lessons we learn from our experiences. Most important, this way of knowing is especially useful for creating new knowledge and improving the quality of existing knowledge.

Ultimately, the higher the quality of knowledge people have available, the greater the probability that their actions will be effective in achieving the desired results. After all, the purpose of knowledge is to inform action that is directed toward achieving performance. Charles Sanders Peirce, the "father" of pragmatism, spent most of his life trying to make discovery and the establishment of belief more scientific. Peirce was a strong believer in the value of the scientific method, and one of his greatest accomplishments was developing a scientific method for improving the quality of knowledge for action.

## KNOWLEDGE FOR ACTION

To transform "knowledge" so that it becomes highly mobile, sharable, and storable, most organizations fragment it in ways that separate it either from action or from beliefs about how things work in action. For example, some consultants argue that "best practices" are knowledge and that sharing best practices is a form of sharing knowledge. Unfortunately, best practices only engage people on the level of action, not on the level of belief about how things actually work in action. Unless leaders gain control over habitual ways of thinking and acting, there is no viable way to improve the quality of knowledge in their companies. That is, if people act on the basis of directive (authority) or routine, there will be no improvement process to raise the quality of knowledge. For improvement to happen, people must be engaged through knowledge at the level of belief and action (Figure 9.2).

Other KM methods (such as capturing lessons learned through post-project review or after-action analysis) deal with the level of action and knowledge but oftentimes do not deal explicitly with the area of belief and routine, even though they potentially could do so.

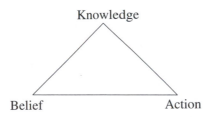

**Figure 9.2**
*Mediating Role of Knowledge*

As you can see, how we define knowledge often determines the effectiveness of our future actions.

At the end of the day, all action taken in organizations is purposeful. By purposeful, we mean that these actions are directed toward one or more of the following:

1. A goal or expected outcome
2. A desired state of affairs
3. A solution to a problem that has previously been defined
4. The realization of an identity

This is not to infer that all actions taken by individuals in organizations are directed toward the right goals or even the goals of the organization. (As some of our more jaded colleagues have asserted, many people are pragmatically pursuing personal goals that may have little in common with their organization's goals.)

There is little doubt that most leaders in organizations aspire to be pragmatic in the way they approach solving problems and act to improve performance. In Peirce's approach, to be *pragmatic* means to start by understanding causes and their effects. Peirce proposed that we become more pragmatic in our thinking by considering how our actions will affect the matters that concern us. Peirce's approach is similar to some aspects of *systems thinking*, particularly the organizational systems thinking that is an offshoot of Forrester's system dynamics. In systems thinking, cause-effect analysis is central to understanding how the underlying information feedback structures of systems can be explained as the source of much of their behavior (Senge, 1990). Firestone and McElroy (2003) have also identified problem solving as the basis for most knowledge-creating efforts. They cite Karl Popper's work in the science of discovery to explain that knowledge is created in the continuous process of problem solving. Here problem solving is described as being a continuous process because the act of solving problems creates new knowledge that helps us, in turn, to identify new problems. Firestone and McElroy (2003) observe that "new knowledge suggests new problems (P2), which, in turn trigger successive episodes of Popper's schema" (p. 38). (Figure 9.3). In this model, P2 represents the new or previously unknown emergent problem that arises after the initial problem, P1, has either been solved or modified.

The main advantage of the Popperian approach to knowledge is that it is anchored in action that is focused on problem solving and goal attainment—the two activities that are the essence of all managerial activity. Here, problem solving and the attainment of goals are processes that focus on the elimination of errors and the continuous improvement of an organization's quality of knowledge.

Since the 1970s, Argyris and Schon's (1978) model of Double Loop Learning has often been included as an example of a practical approach to knowledge. This model is anchored in decision making and provides a framework for explaining how the managerial action can be improved based on the feedback from results. Unfortunately, the model is so general and disconnected from normal managerial action that it does not stand well on its own. However, in combination with the Peircian and Popperian approaches, the Double Loop Learning model can be a useful tool for conceptualizing the development of knowledge in business.

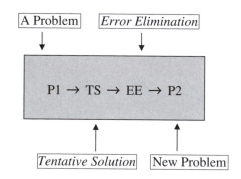

**Figure 9.3**
*Popper's Tetradic Schema: A Framework for Adaptation
From Firestone and McElroy (2003).*

## What Is Knowledge?

So what is knowledge? Most simply, *knowledge is the product of any act of knowing.* Knowledge is a stock of acts for taking effective action under various circumstances. Any of these acts may be used to achieve a desired result in a specific situation. Over time and through experience, these acts can be improved, combined with other acts, or even abandoned based on feedback indicating the effectiveness of prior actions.

Organizational knowledge is a shared understanding of which acts are potentially useful in any number of recurring situations. It may also be encoded in various structural artifacts commonly found in organizations, such as *processes, principles, procedures, programs,* and *policies* that guide action to solve problems, achieve goals, or secure a desired state of affairs (Figure 9.4).

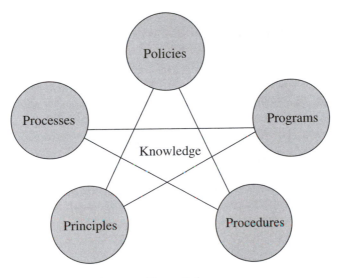

**Figure 9.4**
*The Five P's of Knowledge*

Both know-how and knowledge can be accumulated over time as the product of our purposeful goal-directed actions. Know-how usually results when we discover what works reliably well and are able to duplicate it over time. Through multiple cycles, past acts of knowing enable more facile actions to be taken in similar situations with a higher degree of effectiveness. The obvious limitation of know-how is that it does not involve the development of understandings, nor does it have the potential to significantly shift beliefs about how things work in practice. It is helpful, but not sufficient, for driving innovation. While know-how is valuable for some purposes, it has a relatively narrow scope of potential uses. When we consider the complex work that most business leaders do, it is transparent that acting reliably and effectively requires more than simple know-how. For leaders who want to act more effectively, solve complex problems, and promote innovation, moving from simple knowing to pragmatic knowledge is paramount (Figure 9.5).

**Figure 9.5**
*Knowledge as a Driver of Effective Action*

Knowledge influences the actions we take. Then, through the actions we take, we gain new knowledge. Most people take action to achieve a purpose, usually to reach a goal or desired state of affairs. When we act, we do so with the full expectation (or at least strong hope) that the effects of our actions will produce a performance that reaches our goals. Figure 9.6 demonstrates that the process of learning from experience is based on feedback received from taking action to achieve a goal. Both success and failure to achieve ideal results are potentially instructive to leaders. For example, if you reach your goal, it teaches you something about what works in practice. On the other hand, if you fail to meet your goal, it teaches you about what does not work well in practice; this feedback helps create new theories about what might work in the future, as you have eliminated at least one possible explanation of what would work.

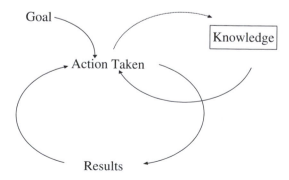

**Figure 9.6**
*Performance Feedback and Knowledge Creation*

## PRAGMATIC KNOWLEDGE

In the Machine Age, organizations and systems were designed to be machine-like. That is, they operated in highly structured and precise ways driven by basic rules that maximized efficiency and predictability. Here, problem solving was focused on finding and fixing the cause of every problem, then removing its symptoms via the fix. If you want to repair a machine, you need an "owner's manual" that explains how that machine operates. Once you know how the machine operates, you can repair it. The machine does not need to be improved because it was designed for optimal efficiency. The only intervention the machine needs is for you to do the necessary repairs when its parts fail.

The machine model is no longer appropriate for most organizations. These systems are so complex and dynamic that they rarely act in mechanical fashion, despite the fervent wishes of managers to the contrary. Owner's manuals are virtually useless now, and because things have become interconnected in ways the system designers never dreamed of—and "repairs" can create as many problems as they solve. Indeed, complex organizational problems not only resist simple repair efforts, they tend to morph into more complicated, less recognizable, subterranean problems that persist over time.

This new generation of organizational problems persist, in part, because they are not only complex but also ill defined and with unclear origins. The need to create new knowledge to address these challenges is growing as the lines between cause and effect become increasingly blurred by time delays, ambiguities, and perceptual distortions. Often, problems that were initially thought to be insignificant have become threatening to the system's survival. Such complexities apply not only to making good business decisions but also to finding solutions for increasingly complex social and political problems—everything from national healthcare policies, military strategies, education for our children, space shuttle missions, terrorist threats, and environmental issues.

Customized knowledge that is acquired over time and through experience is more useful than ever because organizational owner's manuals are no longer sufficient. When the manual can't tell us what to do, we need to discover it ourselves through some kind of scientific inquiry. We need to build on past knowing, know-how, and reflections to, in effect, write a new customized owner's manual that will enable us to solve the complex problems we face.

There are always those who argue that it is inefficient to spend time creating a new, customized owner's manual. Not surprisingly, these are likely to be the same people who argue that we should instead simplify, control, and reduce these complex problems to their most important components. The difficulty is that when you "atomize" knowledge, you end up with a very different sense of what the real problems are. Moreover, this process most often leads you into a series of moves to correct "the problem" that, in turn, usually makes the underlying and unrecognized problems even worse.

Knowledge that is pragmatic is situation specific because it draws on the lessons of our past experiences about how things have actually worked and employs the scientific method to discover what does work. It also explains *why* things work so we can change our beliefs about what will happen in the future as a result of our actions. This pragmatic knowledge can be defined as the knowing we have gained as a result of witnessing how our ways of defining situations, and the actions we took to achieve a particular outcome, enabled us to do what we expected.

In the next chapter, we will continue our discussion about how to transform learning and knowledge into pragmatic knowledge.

## References

Argyris, C., and Schon, D. (1978). *Organizational Learning*. Reading, MA: Addison-Wesley.

Fearon, D., and Cavaleri, S. (2005). *Inside Knowledge*. Milwaukee, WI: Quality Press.

Firestone, J., and McElroy, M. (2003). *Key Issues in the New Knowledge Management*. Burlington, MA: Butterworth-Heinemann.

Grove, A. (2003). In an interview with Kiechel, W., "Andy Grove on Confident Leaders," *Working Knowledge for Business Leaders*, April 14, Harvard Business School, Cambridge, MA, *http://hbswk.hbs.edu/item.jhtml?id=3419&t=innovation*.

Norretranders, T. (1991). *The User Illusion: Cutting Consciousness Down to Size*. Translated by Jonathan Sydenham, 1998. New York: Viking.

Senge, P. (1990). *The Fifth Discipline*. New York: Doubleday/Currency.

# 10

# LEARNING TO MAKE KNOWLEDGE PRAGMATIC

## Executive Summary

There are few ways of defining knowledge that are directly relevant to the interests of business leaders. However, performance driven pragmatic knowledge is effective for businesses because it (1) is tailored to a specific situation, (2) has context and performance targets, and (3) provides feedback from the results of actions. Over time, the quality of pragmatic knowledge continually improves because it helps us understand the reasons for gaps between expected and actual performance. It can be thought of as a triadic model that integrates (1) our diagnosis of the problem with (2) our expected results and (3) rules for action that have been developed from our prior experiences. Pragmatic knowledge provides us with a cache of *acts* that may potentially be used in a given situation. Acts are programs that govern behavior under specific circumstances; they define the situation, set performance targets, and direct the required action. Every bit of knowledge is a system composed of a *case*, a *rule*, and an expected *result*; taken together, we refer to this as a *knowledgeable act* (KA). KAs help us take effective action that is based on knowledge—rather than just based on reason, faith, or good guesses. The pragmatic approach links *action learning* with knowledge creation by uniting the inner and outer worlds of practitioners and by reconciling their objective and subjective perceptions (as described in our *Four Worlds Model of Pragmatic Knowledge*). Visionary knowledge leaders can use pragmatic knowledge to create KBOs with sustainable competitive advantages that are very difficult for competitors to duplicate.

It is amazing that not only has the word *knowledge* been defined in many different ways, but also that most of these definitions seem to hold little relevance to the concerns of business managers. For example, in their widely known book *The Knowledge-Creating Company*, Ikujiro Nonaka and Hirotaka Takeuchi (1995) defined knowledge as "a dynamic human process of justifying personal belief toward the ['truth']" (p. 58). While these authors have contributed significantly to the general understanding of how knowledge is created in organizations, it is our opinion that this definition focuses narrowly on elements of knowledge that hold less interest for leaders and managers.

Nonaka and Takeuchi see knowledge as a process of discovering the necessary evidence to reach a rationale for believing that something is true. While this definition may make theoretical sense, business practitioners are more concerned with whether an action will work reliably well in practice than with whether or not it is true. In other words, business practitioners seek to become more effective, not to discover an abstract truth. Nonaka and Takeuchi regard knowledge as a process, the result of the act of knowing. In our view, knowledge is formulated through a process that requires action, receipt of feedback from the effects of actions, learning, and reasoning.

The notion proposed by Nonaka and Takeuchi that knowledge is a means to *justify personal belief* misses the point that this is a secondary, rather than primary, interest of practitioners. While knowledge can confirm or invalidate the verity of our beliefs, practitioners are more interested in the power of knowledge to help them make their companies more effective and competitive. This is not to minimize the importance of aligning our beliefs about how things work in practice with how they actually do work. Beliefs are one of the most powerful controllers of how we look at things and how we act, yet they are also among the most difficult factors for us to control.

At the other extreme of knowledge definitions are the information based views popularized by the field of KM. Ironically, although the information-based view of knowledge is favored by some managers because it is thought to be utilitarian, it cannot provide sustainable competitive advantage to firms. This is because being innovative and solving problems require leaders to develop robust explanations of how things work in practice based on what has worked reliably well in the past.

The idea most popular among information technology professionals these days is that knowledge is "information with context." We consider this definition too vague and disconnected from performance to be of much value to practitioners. This definition emphasizes the aspect of knowledge that is focused on diagnosing a situation. Performance-driven knowledge must be tailored to a specific situation, as general knowledge is too broad to be practical. Information with context can help leaders reach conclusions about which actions may be most appropriate for them to take, but this definition of knowledge fails to consider the importance of the *effectiveness* of actions taken on the basis of this information. What is typically ignored when knowledge is viewed as being "information with context" is the way that *context* is interpreted. A more dynamic definition of knowledge includes continuous inquiry that is driven by the gap between expected and actual results (as measured by the feedback that enables leaders to see the differences between *performance targets and results*) (Figure 10.1).

As this figure illustrates, the information-based view of knowledge overlooks most of the factors that enable knowledge to be performance driven. This is not to say that the information-based view is wrong, rather that it is incomplete and disconnected from either performance or innovation.

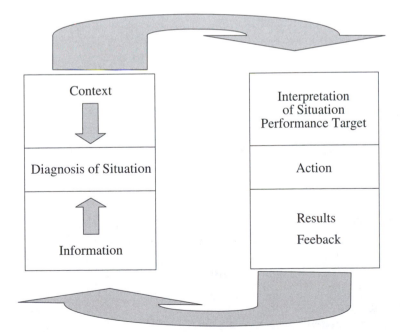

**Figure 10.1**
*The Role of Information in Knowledge*

Groff and Jones (2003) defined knowledge as "information combined with understanding and capability; it lives in the minds of people. Typically, knowledge provides a level of predictability that usually stems from the recognition of patterns" (p. 3). Such information-based views of knowledge are attractive to managers because they suit many needs of businesses: information can easily be compartmentalized, plus it is mobile and storable. However, not only does defining knowledge in this way disconnect it from performance, it also prevents people from seeing the critical cause-effect patterns that link their actions and the results of these actions. We believe that defining knowledge as being "information with knowledge" unnecessarily limits the richness of knowledge and its potential for enabling effective action. It is akin to saying the human eye is only for seeing and requires visual acuity, rather than that the human eye serves multiple other functions, such as motion detection, providing security from possible dangers or threats, and defining spatial relationships. In the first case, the eye is considered a passive receiver of information, while in the second case it is regarded as a perceptual tool that individuals use to assertively capture images of whatever they have judged to be important.

## Knowledge for Performance

While information, understanding, and capability are all necessary for using knowledge, they are not the same as knowledge, nor are they sufficient for employing knowledge in a pragmatic way. To serve the interests of today's managers and leaders, *knowledge must be pragmatic*. That is, knowledge must have the capability to explain the reasons for gaps between expected and actual performance. In short, pragmatic knowledge is performance based and focused on specific situations that are perceived as important to leaders and employees.

Pragmatic knowledge needs not only to provide the basis for incremental gains; it also needs to add to the effectiveness and innovativeness of all leaders who use it. Pragmatic knowledge is the product of a system that integrates human action, beliefs, past experiences, perception, and reasoning. Unfortunately, the process of knowledge management is too often conceived of as a mechanical system that can be deconstructed into its parts. In far too many organizations, knowledge is treated in a virtually *robotic* way, by which we mean that knowledge is viewed as being inanimate, an object, something apart from the employees, rather than as a direct mirror of human experience. The result is that employees wind up having a robot-to-machine relationship with knowledge.

In many respects, knowledge has become so disconnected from what we really believe about how things actually work in practice, that two opposing forms of knowledge have come to exist side-by-side in organizations. These are *artificial knowledge* (that is separate and distinct from what a person really believes) and *natural knowledge* (that accurately reflects what an individual believes about which actions are likely to work reliably well in practice). As you might guess, in many companies artificial knowledge dominates. Consequently, many managers find themselves trapped into using precisely the kind of knowledge that has the least potential for effective problem solving and innovation.

Natural knowledge forms the basis for pragmatic knowledge. Pragmatic knowledge flows from the human capacity to do the following:

- Evaluate the effectiveness of actions taken to achieve a goal or desired state.
- Align our beliefs about what works best in practice with our perceptions of situations.
- Integrate our diagnostic problem statements with the expected result(s) and the rules for action that are based on our prior experiences.

*Evaluating the effectiveness of actions taken to achieve a goal or desired state* provides us with a measure of the reliability of our success or failure. That is, achieving expected results tells us about the *quality* of our knowledge. For example, if we are successful in catching a fish with a particular lure once every thousand tries, and we estimate the average lure has one catch per hundred tries, then we can judge that not only is the performance of this particular lure ineffective, but our knowledge in selecting lures may be equally ineffective. The assumption is that if we knew precisely which lure was most likely to catch fish, we would select that type of lure over others. This takes us to our belief about what works best in practice. Do we believe that all lures are equally effective? Do we have a favorite lure that we keep using despite our experience? It may also be possible that we are doing something else wrong—such as fishing in locations where there are no fish. Clearly, we can ask the same pragmatic questions about our choice of fishing locations. Over time, this process helps us align our beliefs about what works best in practice with our perceptions of situations.

People define what they believe are problems by mentally constructing a problem statement in their minds. We refer to the problem statement as being the *knowledge diagnosis* or simply the *K-diagnosis*. K-diagnosis is very subjective; it is grounded in a process called *semiosis*—the process of analyzing the relationship among a sign, an object, and its meaning. Signs *represent* certain objects or events (they are not the object or the event itself). For example, a persistent cough may be a sign (a representation or symptom) that someone is ill (an event). Similarly, an increase in market share can be interpreted as a "sign" that the company is on the right track with regard to its marketing, product development, and strategy.

Pragmatic knowledge-creating processes reflect the fact that different people are likely to interpret the meaning of problem situations quite differently. That is, one leader will interpret the meaning of the same signs differently from a second leader, causing them to arrive at completely different diagnoses about what needs to be solved. (This constant interpretation of signs is vital to the "art" of knowledge leadership.) Over time, the quality of pragmatic knowledge continually improves as we accumulate performance-related information by observing the relationship between actions taken, results produced, and whether performance expectations were met. Therefore, pragmatic knowledge *integrates our diagnostic problem statements with the expected result(s) and the rules for action that are based on our prior experiences*. The rules for action that we may use are often stated as situational "if/then" statements. For example, we might follow a rule that states, "When someone is driving an automobile on a major multilane highway in an unfamiliar region and the fuel gauge indicates that the tank is empty, it is best to refuel at a service station on the highway and pay the higher price than to get off the highway and risk getting lost or running out of fuel.

In this view, knowledge is not only what enables us to take effective action, it is also created as a result of our actions—effective or not. Taking this pragmatic view, knowledge is composed of a set of rules for action that are intended to achieve an expected outcome in a diagnosed situation (Figure 10.2).

Let us take a look at how the Pragmatic Knowledge Triad might work in action by examining the fictional company known as Fountain of Youth Vitamins Corporation.

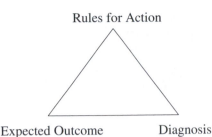

**Figure 10.2**
*The Pragmatic Knowledge Triad*

## THE PRAGMATIC KNOWLEDGE TRIAD IN ACTION

Tanya is a manager at a nutritional supplement company called Fountain of Youth Vitamins Corporation (FYVC). Approximately 80% of FYVC's sales are placed via telephone calls in response to its quarterly four-color catalog. Tanya diagnoses that the rate of customer retention is falling because the company has been experiencing problems with customer service as a result of extremely high turnover of service employees. Wages paid by this company are low because of intense competition and declining market share. The company is doing a good job of securing new customers, but its rate of customer retention is plummeting.

Tanya believes that the root cause of the customer retention problem is that the company is doing a poor job in selecting customer service representatives. Although wages are low, she argues, there are promotional opportunities that upwardly mobile employees would find attractive. However, FYVC recruiters in the human resources (HR) department have been focusing on filling staff slots based on the educational level, technical skills, and communication skills of candidates, without assessing their career aspirations. Consequently, many current employees want a low-stress job to supplement their spouses' income, and they are not attracted by the added responsibilities of a promotion or its higher pay rate.

*Tanya's Diagnosis*: The primary problem in FYVC's customer retention is the hiring criteria used by the HR department to recruit and select customer service representatives.

*Tanya's Action Rule*: Meet with the HR director and request a change in selection profile and recruitment policy.

*Tanya's Expected Result*: A 20% decline in turnover of customer service representatives within one year.

As the Fountain of Youth Vitamins Corporation case shows, it has yet to be proven whether Tanya's triadic knowledge works reliably well in practice. Since knowledge is not the same as truth, and all knowledge is not equally reliable at yielding expected results, only further experience will show whether Tanya's knowledge claim is actually valid and reliable. Pragmatic knowledge is based on several building blocks that, when effectively integrated, enable people to improve the quality of their knowledge so they become more effective in taking action. Unlike most approaches to knowledge, pragmatic knowledge is highly practical and useful to knowledge leaders because it focuses on action and performance.

## KEY ELEMENTS OF PRAGMATIC KNOWLEDGE

Many definitions of knowledge emphasize the importance of human reasoning processes but fail to include critical elements such as causal analysis and feedback. By *causal analysis* we mean the process of identifying chains of cause-effect relations that lead back from results to the actions that produced those results. In the context of pragmatic knowledge, the term *feedback* means a circular flow of information from person to action to results and back to that person, who can then use that knowledge to examine (and when necessary change) beliefs (Figure 10.3).

To enable knowledge to be performance driven, it is critical that all knowledge processes incorporate feedback on the effectiveness of results. Feedback is not just the measure of the result itself. For example, the results may be that product quality improved because defects were reduced from 5% to 2%. Feedback also includes an evaluation of whether the action was effective in producing the *expected result*. Figure 10.3 shows that there is usually a gap between actual and expected results. In the case of the preceding quality example, the expectation may have been that as a result of a new quality improvement, the rate of product defects would decline to 1%. Consequently, a drop in the defect rate to only 2% would be interpreted as an ineffective result. As Figure 10.3 illustrates, our beliefs about how things work in practice influence both the actions we take and the results we expect from those actions. Knowledge of the effectiveness of past results (from similar actions in like circumstances)

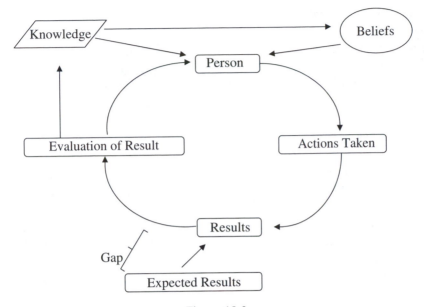

**Figure 10.3**
*Role of Feedback in Pragmatic Knowledge*

will help us reshape our beliefs by informing us about what really does work in practice.

Feedback from the effects of an action enables leaders to know whether that action produced the desired results and also to infer whether the knowledge and beliefs that served as the basis of that action are useful and accurate. In the pragmatic perspective, discovering truth is done through the process of analyzing both the effects of our actions and the means we used to achieve those results. In summary, pragmatic knowledge provides leaders with a radically honest, reality-tested approach to solving workplace problems.

By understanding how and why things work as they do in practice and by observing the effects of our actions, we can begin to establish a causal connection between our actions and their effects. The pragmatic approach to knowledge stands in sharp contrast to many philosophies that argue that what is true can be known simply by observation and reasoning. While at first glance this may seem to be a minor philosophical issue, it has become a major point of disagreement in the KM community. As we stated previously, leaders typically are less interested in determining absolute truth and more interested in discovering what actions will improve organizational performance. Pragmatic knowledge helps leaders determine which actions they will take, and that knowledge is in turn shaped by the results of those actions. The role of pragmatic knowledge *as both a cause and effect* produces an interesting dynamic tension between what we think we already know and the new lessons we learn that are at odds with our existing knowledge. This is a significant vital force that can lead us to the continuous improvement of knowledge over time.

Since knowledge is not the same as truth, it is imperfect. It does not enable us to take actions that will always be flawlessly effective in helping us achieve the results we seek. A common misconception is that when we have knowledge of something, that object of our attention is *fully known* to us. On the contrary, most knowledge provides us with only partial insight into what works reliably well in practice. Some knowledge, for example, may only be effective in helping us achieve our desired ends 30% of the time. In such cases, this knowledge may not offer an edge over simple guessing. However, if there are more than 100 possible alternative actions, and we know that this one action offers us a 30% probability of success, then that same knowledge may be very valuable to us—even if it is imperfect. Knowledge can be thought of as a repository of noted lessons from experience about what tends to work well under certain circumstances.

A more action-oriented definition is that *knowledge is a cache of acts that may potentially be used in a given situation.* An act is a program that governs behavior under specific circumstances. Acts contain three basic elements: they define the situation, set performance targets, and direct the required action. Found at the core of all acts are simple performance routines. A *routine* is a prescribed set of actions governed by an operative policy that is used to reach a specific performance target (Figure 10.4). Acts are evolved to fit each situation, so it is possible for different types of acts to fit different

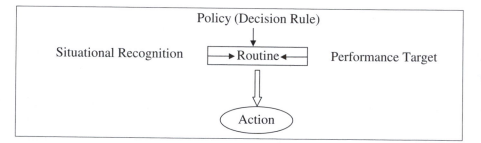

**Figure 10.4**
*Action-Oriented View of Knowledge*

circumstances. Because acts are situational, there is a perceptual element to their use. That is, knowledge leaders need to determine which act is appropriate for a given situation, then initiate a routine that fits that set of circumstances.

Many knowledge theorists would argue that, because circumstances are external, they should not be included within an act. Such an objectivist view discounts the role played by beliefs in governing people's perceptions. However, human perception is highly interpretive, and each person's perspective is determined by a host of factors, including one's own internal symbolic representations. In other words, we can only perceive those things that are familiar to us in some way. We filter out what we do not understand. Ultimately, our perceptions originate in our internal capacity for recognizing and interpreting symbols. In fact, situational representations located in a given act are the result of our internalization of some prior external phenomena.

Finally, performance targets are merely expected results that range from specific to general in scope. For example, we recognize a horse by its shape, distinctive sounds made, and style of movement. There is an intrinsic identity of "horseness" that, over time, we come to recognize and rely on—and that helps us decide how to act around horses. If we were walking along a country road and noticed a grassy area enclosed by a white wooden fence with several horse-like animals in the area, we might be drawn to take a closer look. However, if upon moving closer to the area we recognized the animals as being zebras, we might have a different reaction. And if we recognized these creatures as bears, we would most likely run away. The same sorts of interpretations based on knowledge, reasoning, and astute observation apply when leaders distinguish between "good employee" or "bad employee," or between a "marketing problem" and a "quality problem."

## ACTION LEARNING AND PRAGMATIC KNOWLEDGE

Lessons learned through experience enable a leader's cache of acts to accumulate as new acts evolve and others are modified. This is where *action learning* comes into play. Action learning is the process by which (1) individuals or groups reflect back on those actions they have taken and their effects, (2) new hypotheses are created to explain why those actions caused those effects, and (3) new actionable approaches are designed. In effect, action learning is the process that enables people to modify existing acts and create new ones. Action learning can be viewed as a reiterative cycle that involves both looking back on prior actions as well as looking forward to antici- pated acts. It also involves the process of making meaning from our past experiences, building new theories of practice, and acting exper- imentally to test new theories of how things work. What is being reflected on in the action-learning cycle includes the effectiveness of prior acts in producing desired results, the accuracy of how we have defined the problems we are trying to solve, the meaning of the feed- back we receive from performance and our speculations about whether the relationships we have observed will remain constant in the future.

Action learning uses the evidence of past experience to improve the quality of our theories about how things really work in practice by providing a basis for our comparing expected results with actual performance. Much in the same way as quality improvement methods use the performance feedback from measuring product quality to systematically improve causes of quality, the action-learn- ing cycle provides a scientific process for improving both the quality of our knowledge and our theories about how things really work in practice. In many respects, the action-learning cycle is a way of employing the scientific method of investigation to disconfirm or confirm the value of our theories of effective action. In more practi- cal terms, the action-learning cycle is intended to determine possible reasons why the prior actions and the decision rules that govern them were effective or not. Finally, the experimentation phase of the cycle means experimenting with new acts that we create as a result of our new or revised theories about how things work in practice. Figure 10.5 depicts the version of the action-learning cycle that has been popularized by Kolb, Rubin, and McIntyre (1984).

Taking a pragmatic view of knowledge requires that leaders design knowledge systems that integrate knowledge acts into a "triadic" system for achieving desired results. In this definition, every knowl- edge act is made of three elements: (1) a case, (2) a rule for action, and (3) an expected result. In other words, knowledge arises from

1. Recognizing recurring or similar situations (case)
2. Employing acts or routines for guiding action (rule)
3. Clearly defining statements of expected results

Taken together, a *case*, a *rule*, and an expected *result* constitute a *knowledgeable act* (KA). Another way to say this is that we are acting

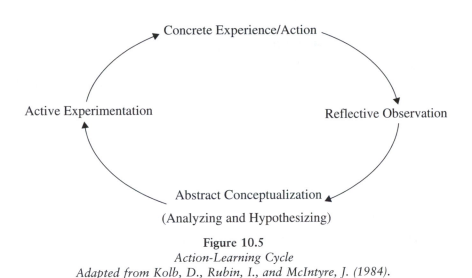

**Figure 10.5**
*Action-Learning Cycle*
*Adapted from Kolb, D., Rubin, I., and McIntyre, J. (1984).*

on the basis of knowledge, as opposed to other factors such as faith, guesswork, or a personal agenda. A KA allows us to perform more intelligently in a situation that we recognize as having certain characteristics, so we are more likely to achieve an expected result. If a knowledgeable act is successful in achieving the expected results, then we can say our action was effective. Knowing that our action was either effective or ineffective helps us refine our knowledge even further, so it is increasingly aligned with how things really work in practice. Pragmatic knowledge has several important attributes: it is a pool of potentially usable acts we can draw on under certain circumstances; it is also a set of acts that evolve over time through our experience, improvement efforts, and reasoning that enable other practitioners to use our acts or create new ones.

## KNOWLEDGE IS A REPOSITORY FOR KNOWLEDGEABLE ACTS

It is useful to think of knowledge as being similar to a bank where deposits are made. Instead of being stocked with monetary currency, the knowledge bank is filled with KAs that may be withdrawn at any time for use in taking action. Just as currency comes in many different denominations, such as $1, $20, and $100 bills, there are also many kinds of KAs in our knowledge bank—proven, disproved, and unproven ones—any of which may be called up for use in the future. The KAs may be further differentiated in terms of their proven degree of effectiveness in past experience, such as a KA that is effective 27% of the time. In other words, this bank contains all kinds of KAs with varying degrees of utility. Some of the KAs in this bank are old, some are new, and some may even be temporarily forgotten. A critical function in knowledge-creating systems is to track and measure the effectiveness of various KAs, then evaluate and code them for future use.

Knowledgeable acts are sets of rules for knowledgeable action that are contingent on (1) how we perceive a situation and (2) the results we expect from our actions. Each rule for knowledgeable action fits a specific situation and expected outcome. In such a pragmatic knowledge system, every problem situation refers to a set of rules for KAs. There are few acts that are guaranteed to work all of the time. Therefore, we propose that most KAs are only potentially effective for producing expected results. Very often KAs can be linked together to form "knowledge chains."

For example, leaders in a company may wish to improve long-term employee productivity by increasing the level of intrinsic work satisfaction and reducing burnout levels. Consequently, they may dedicate a quiet lounge where employees can take time out for creative thinking, reflection, or reviewing inspirational materials in a peaceful environment. Even though many companies practice continuous quality improvement and wish to be more innovative, few businesses organize themselves around the notion of achieving *continuous improvement in innovation*. Toyota is an example of one high-profile company that has proven it possible to do so. By combining KAs for continuous improvement *and* innovation, knowledge leaders can craft larger corporate acts for the purpose of continuously improving innovation within their organizations.

## REASONING FOR KNOWLEDGEABLE ACTS

By combining lessons learned from experience with various logical reasoning processes, new KAs can be created. Three basic forms of reasoning are *abduction*, *induction*, and *deduction*. Creating new knowledge to understand how things work is *abduction*. Inferring something is a dog because it barks and chases cars is *induction*. Putting the dog on a leash because you anticipate that it might get hurt if it chases cars is *deduction*. (Look to Appendix B for a more detailed description of these forms of reasoning.)

Such situation-specific decision rules are the essence of organizational knowledge. For example, a leader may reason that most employees enjoy offsite company meetings that combine social activity with business. This leader may also note that after such meetings, productivity tends to increase for about 3 months. The leader then reasons that it might be a good idea to plan three or four such social/business meetings per year. Over time, observations of whether these meetings produce the expected results will determine if the new policy (rule for action) will be modified. Learning through observing the effects of actions and discerning their relevance to knowledge is critical for all organizations. This process of discernment is neither simple nor mechanical; it relies on leaders' capacity to make meaningful judgments and also their openness to explore alternative interpretations. Allowing feedback to *wash over oneself* and to reflectively interpret the meaning of this feedback are inner "artful" skills that differentiate great leaders from good ones. Success in this domain requires that leaders be able to integrate their inner and outer worlds. (In Part II of *Knowledge Leadership*, we referred to the importance of this inner/outer integration during our discussion of Yogi and Commissar leaders.)

## LEADING AND LEARNING THROUGH THE FOUR WORLDS OF PRAGMATIC KNOWLEDGE

Over time, by paying attention to the effects produced by their actions, leaders will learn whether their action rules are effective. If the results do not meet their expectations, leaders can change their diagnosis, action rules, or expectations. Over a longer period of time, the lessons learned by leaders may cause them to reexamine their beliefs about how things work in practice. This gradual process of discovering what actions work best in practice is a form of action learning.

Action learning is the basis for the ideal of the *learning organization*, first popularized by Peter Senge (1990). Both action learning and organizational learning play essential roles in creating pragmatic knowledge, because they are both goal-driven and action-based. They also are of critical importance to the systemic process of knowledge management. Charles Peirce, and his protégé, John Dewey, were among the first to recognize the links between the processes of action learning and pragmatic knowledge creation.

Many theorists consider knowledge to be the product of action learning. However, the mechanics of how action learning can produce pragmatic knowledge have often been misconstrued. This misunderstanding can be traced to the father of American psychology, William James. James, who was also the founder of the Harvard psychology department, interpreted the writings of his mentor, Peirce, to mean that effective knowledge is merely contingent on learning whatever works reliably well, because that tells us what is true.

However, Peirce believed that we cannot accurately judge the value of our beliefs simply by knowing whether we have reliably achieved any expected outcome. If we infer from the success or failure of our actions that the means we used are correct, this need not necessarily suggest that the beliefs we hold in this respect are valid. That assumption would be an oversimplification because it ignores the important role of the third pragmatic force on shaping outcomes. If you recall, *thirdness* represents the impact of other system elements, processes, and natural laws on performance. Thirdness can be a "wild card" factor that influences our results by influencing the larger systems we operate within (this occurs via effects that we have not yet discovered and incorporated into our hypothesis of how things work in practice). Only through continuous experimentation, over time, can we begin to discern the degree of truthfulness of our beliefs. Peirce was of the opinion that it is extremely difficult to determine which actions will prove effective in yielding the desired outcome with perfect certainty. In life, there are relatively few things of which we can be absolutely sure—except for those forces that continually exert their influence on us in a way that cannot be denied.

However, James's interpretations of Peirce's pragmatic principles became quite popular. By the end of the 19th century, these simplifications overshadowed the more elegant theories of Peirce that held greater relevance for knowledge-creating processes. James's version of pragmatism emphasized the importance of learning what works in practice, while Peirce's work (and later Dewey's) was directed toward discovering what works in practice *and* understanding the cause-effect linkages that determine *how* and *why* certain actions produce certain results. Most important, however, was Peirce's notion that to be effective over the long run, it is critical to allow our knowledge of what works (and how and why it works) to inform our personal beliefs about what is possible in practice.

The key distinction is that Peirce's process of learning from experience unites (1) purposeful action, (2) attentiveness to the effects of those actions, and (3) analysis of the reasons for those effects with (4) one's perceptions and beliefs about how things actually work in practice. The significance of this pragmatic approach to linking action learning with knowledge creation is that it both unites the *inner* and *outer* worlds of practitioners, and reconciles their *objective* and *subjective* perceptions (Figure 10.6).

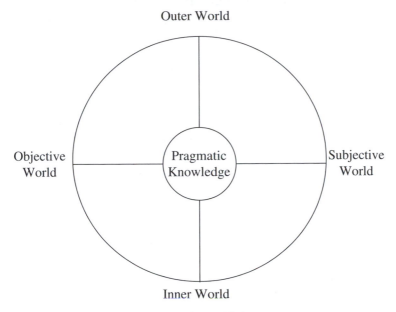

**Figure 10.6**
*The Four Worlds Model of Pragmatic Knowledge*

The Four Worlds Model underscores the need of knowledge leaders to integrate four different perspectives that are typically not easy to combine. We should note here that, to the orthodox pragmatist, the notions of outer world and objective experience have little meaning. In sharp contrast, the concepts of inner world and subjective experience have little interest to most business leaders. These divergent perspectives call to mind the ongoing debate between Yogis and Commissars. Commissars readily describe an outer and objective world that Yogis argue is a creation of the Commissars' imaginations. Meanwhile, Yogis focus on a subjective inner world that Commissars want no part of. The Four Worlds Model of Pragmatic Knowledge reflects a point of common ground that can help knowledge leaders mediate and balance the different worldviews of Yogis and Commissars.

The pragmatic approach proposes that—because the work of leaders is so complex, and it is difficult for them to decipher with certainty the true nature of problems, their causes, and effects—they can discover how things really work by carefully noting the effects of their actions in producing expected outcomes. As the model points out, some of these actions and effects will be transparent because they happen in a part of the four worlds where relationships can be seen objectively. For example, if gravity and centrifugal force operate with certainty and regularity, then hitting a golf ball in a certain way with a certain golf club will usually produce the same effect time after time.

However, leaders must process their experiences of the outer world to create meaning in their inner world. In some aspects of human experience, such as human relations, there are fewer regular laws that govern dynamics and behavior. As a result, the inner world of experience becomes even more significant to creating knowledge. Objective experiences normally exert themselves on us in undeniable ways. That is, when we feel rain fall on our head, there is little interpretation required to determine that it is, in fact, rain. For knowledge leaders, however, things are rarely that simple. Indeed, the work of leaders is normally colored with many subjective experiences where feedback and the meaning of our actions are filtered not only by our own beliefs, but also by circumstances (such as time delays between cause and effect), ambiguities in interpretation, and difficulties with measurement. When we create pragmatic knowledge using the Four Worlds Model, we are systematically trying to account for all of the sources of bias that would restrict or dilute the quality of our knowledge.

## The Emergence of Knowledge in Organizations

Interest in creating KBOs has grown dramatically as more leaders become aware of the potential of knowledge to drive innovation and improve performance. Yet most organizational efforts that are directed to becoming a KBO are woefully inadequate because they focus almost entirely on the technological, systems, and process side of the equation and virtually ignore the vital leadership and interpersonal KBO aspects. However, major cost reductions and performance increases have resulted from basic knowledge-based processes initiatives at companies such as BP Amoco and Buckman Labs, thereby demonstrating that even these rudimentary activities can be a good investment. However, relatively few companies have been able to master the four worlds approach to becoming a KBO.

Among the leading candidates for this honor are Toyota, 3M, Shell, and Xerox. All of these companies share the common denominator that they have created *balanced* systems where individual employees are actively engaged in action learning, experimentation, knowledge-creation, and innovation. While these organizations do rely on technology to support various knowledge-processing activities, technology is not at the center of their organizational knowledge system. The focus in these companies is to provide employees the freedom to actively learn from experience, experiment, and innovate by buffering them from excessively high demands for efficiency and productivity. The vast majority of business organizations are still built for efficiency and productivity. This makes them mechanical, precise, and programmed to produce the largest possible output at the minimal cost. As a result, such systems are rarely adaptive or innovative.

Interestingly, even though many corporate leaders speak about the importance of knowledge in helping their companies achieve success, rarely do they act as if knowledge was their chief imperative. KBOs are not only highly adaptive; they are also capable of being innovative in a wide variety of arenas, including cost reduction. KBOs rely on effective knowledge creation, pragmatic knowledge, and visionary knowledge leadership to create unique sustainable competitive advantages that are difficult for competitors to duplicate. Harvard Business School professor Stephen Spear (2004) observed in regard to Toyota's sustained competitive advantage:

If Toyota has been so widely studied and copied, why have so few companies been able to match its performance? . . . The problem is that most outsiders have focused on Toyota's tools and tactics—kanban pull systems, cords, production cells, and the like—and not on its basic set of operating principles. . . . These principles lead to ongoing improvements in reliability, flexibility, market share, and profitability. (p. 79)

It is our observation that KBOs have knowledge leadership and knowledge systems at all levels of the organization that reflect the outer/inner and subjective/objective knowledge balance illustrated in the Four Worlds Model of Pragmatic Knowledge.

## GROUNDING KNOWLEDGE IN PRACTICE

Effective knowledge creation in businesses can bring new understandings of how problems impede employee performance. Such knowledge may help reframe the way employees view problems or provide them with new rules for action learning. Pragmatic knowledge-creating activities have a more structured and task-specific focus than general action learning, because they include explicit consideration of expected performance outcomes. Pragmatic knowledge-creating activities focus on performance feedback, expectations, and beliefs about what works in practice, whereas action learning is typically less focused on results. Despite this difference, there is an important connection between these two approaches. Effective pragmatic knowledge-creating activities and action-learning processes both depend on demonstrated results to ground them in reality. Unlike other forms of learning that are rooted primarily in the use of reasoning, action-learning and pragmatic knowledge-creating activities rely on continuous efforts to validate the accuracy of mental models and beliefs through practice and the feedback of results (Figure 10.7).

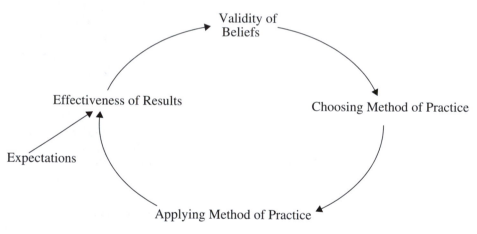

**Figure 10.7**
*Reality Testing in Pragmatic Knowledge Creation*

Achieving desired results is the standard by which the usefulness and validity of knowledge is assessed in both these approaches. From a systems perspective, these "cybernetic" processes are goal seeking and produce balancing loops that bring knowledge into alignment with beliefs, action, and results. There is a strong tradition of using models of continuous cycles that combine action, learning, and knowledge. For example, such action-learning cycles can be found in the writings of systems theorists A. E. Singer, Ackoff, and Churchman.

John Dewey underscored the relevance of action-learning theories to the processes of knowledge creation by noting that sense making requires the facility for being both active and passive—at different times. That is, people act upon the world, but then they *endure the consequences.* Knowledge arises when the beliefs that led to the actions are either validated or invalidated by experiencing their consequences. Action-learning theories posit that people learn most deeply through the experience of doing—as opposed to learning in classroom lectures or by reading books. This is because experiencing the consequences of our actions holds the potentiality to refine the accuracy of our beliefs. This type of learning—modifying our beliefs—is often viewed as the most profound type of learning anyone can experience.

*Action learning, then, is a dualistic process. We do something to the world and the world does something back to us.* More often than not, managers who are under pressure to perform (usually by invoking well-practiced routines without regard to their own beliefs about causality) emphasize the *doing* part rather than the *sense-making* part of the action-learning cycle. The action parts of the cycle are doing and experimenting, whereas the sense-making parts are reflecting and hypothesizing. The essence of learning through experience is to do the following:

1. Take intentional action.
2. Mentally capture what was done, what happened, and in what context.
3. Develop a possible explanation for why things turned out as they did.
4. Formulate this explanation as a new hypothesis about how things really work.
5. Experiment by trying new actions that you expect will be effective in yielding desired goals—and learn if the system really functions as you expect it to work.

The key point we are making here is that action learning is not about learning new information from sources outside of your own experience. Rather, action learning is the ability to draw new, and potentially unexpected, meaning from your experience. Ideally, action learning enables people to first change their minds about how things really work causally, develop new knowledge claims about how cause and effect actually function in any given situation, and then act differently, according to these new understandings. We may think of leadership itself as an act of knowing what to do under a wide array of circumstances—and why. Ideally, the cycle of managing is itself completed when, upon reflection, we learn what works best for the next time.

In action learning, the quality of knowledge claims is improved over time through a variety of processes including dialogue, planning, and collaboration. Organizational learning may be understood as *a collective form of action learning* that emphasizes the value of social interaction in surfacing and exploring one's own beliefs, mental models, and shared beliefs. Organizational action-learning strategies address a blind spot in every person's learning processes—namely, it is exceedingly difficult to recognize what Senge (1990) called "the incoherencies and incompleteness" of our own mental models. With organizational learning, coworkers provide mirrors for each other that can help them overcome the paradigm blindness that results from unseen perceptual filters.

Organizational action learning enables people, through social action, to effectively provide another form of grounding in reality—namely, the social reality that in pragmatic knowledge-creating activities is associated with *communities of practice*. From an action-learning perspective, people may learn directly from the feedback resulting from their actions—or they may test the validity of their ideas in the social reality of their community. As Chris Argyris (1993) noted:

Seeking truth is an ongoing activity—never fully achieved, always approximated. It has always been regarded as the ultimate purpose of research. The major test of how well we are doing in seeking truth (small t) is to formulate statements of truth as hypotheses and then strive to disconfirm them, not simply confirm them. (p. 284)

Interestingly, leaders who engage in pragmatic knowledge-creating activities grow to appreciate Karl Popper's notion that it is equally important to *disconfirm* their hypotheses about what works best in practice as it is to confirm them.

In most complex workplaces it is virtually impossible for leaders to continually increase their effectiveness without relying on an ongoing process of continuous improvement of the quality of their knowledge. The pragmatic model of knowledge processing is the perfect model for such purposes because it is a performance-driven model that operates on the premise of continuous improvement. The strong link between pragmatic knowledge and continuous quality improvement processes is not surprising. According to Fearon and Cavaleri (2005), W. Edwards Deming (the father of the quality movement) was a protégé of Walter Shewhart of Bell Labs (who was heavily influenced by the writings of Harvard resident pragmatist C. I. Lewis). In turn, C. I. Lewis was mentored by some of the great pragmatists of all time—William James and Josiah Royce—both of whom were protégés of Charles Sanders Peirce.

In the next chapter, we will discuss how knowledge leaders can develop pragmatic knowledge as part of their on-going knowledge processing efforts.

## References

Argyris, C. (1993). *Knowledge for Action*. San Francisco: Jossey-Bass.

Fearon, D., and Cavaleri, S. (2005). *Inside Knowledge*. Milwaukee, WI: Quality Press.

Groff, T., and Jones, T. (2003). *Introduction to Knowledge Management*. Burlington, MA: Butterworth-Heinemann.

Kolb, D. A., Rubin, I. M., and McIntyre, J. M. (1984). *Organizational Psychology: An Experiential Approach to Organizational Behavior* (4th ed.). Englewood Cliffs, NJ: Prentice Hall.

Nonaka, I., and Takeuchi, II. (1995). *The Knowledge-Creating Company*. New York: Oxford University Press.

Senge, P. (1990). *The Fifth Discipline*. New York: Doubleday.

Spear, S. (2004, May). "Learning to Lead at Toyota." *Harvard Business Review*, 78–86.

Wiener, P. (1958). *Peirce's Philosophical Perspectives*. New York: Dover Publications.

# 11

# LEADING KNOWLEDGE PROCESSING

## Executive Summary

Most companies focus on extracting productivity from existing resources. However, *extractive* operational strategies eventually cause an organization to become depleted or "anemic" because little has been reinvested to renew or sustain it. Moreover, as KBOs increasingly dominate industries, firms that rely on extractive strategies will increasingly be at a competitive disadvantage. Unfortunately, most of what passes for knowledge in organizations is really unproved *knowledge claims*. The role of knowledge claims becomes more important in a business's higher complexity areas where the validity of knowledge is of greater importance. The quality of this knowledge can be improved through *knowledge processing*. Knowledge processing is a human social process that involves the production, evaluation, integration, and control of how knowledge is created and used. Because high-quality knowledge is the precursor to all effective business processes, one of the most significant functions in organizations is to improve the quality of knowledge or create new, higher-quality knowledge. At the core of knowledge processing is the *Knowledge Quality Improvement Process* (KQIP), a continuous process that extends the viable *life* of knowledge by prolonging its usefulness. The core process that drives KQIP is based on a model known as the *Knowledge Life Cycle model* (KLC). Inserting a KQIP process into key areas where there appears to be a potentially attractive return on investment is a good way for knowledge leaders to do *target knowledge processing* (TKP), which enables organizations to mitigate unfavorable risks, solve resistant problems, or take advantage of emerging opportunities.

There are at least five basic ways to target knowledge-processing systems; these are explained in this chapter. Knowledge leaders can use KQIP, KLC, and TKP to increase the number of knowledge claims and to install processes for improving the quality of knowledge claims throughout their organizations.

The notion that organizations are held together by the glue of common beliefs, values, identity, or knowledge is still a controversial notion in many academic and business circles. To many corporate leaders, the process of management is about progressively gaining ever-tighter control over the factors of production, namely *soft assets* (people) and *hard assets* (finances, buildings, and equipment). In such companies, the order of the day is to ensure full compliance with their brilliant system design. This strategy, while appearing to be the best way to extract productivity from the organization's resources, is, by its very nature, self-limiting. That is, any system that relies exclusively on an *extractive* operational philosophy eventually collapses upon itself because little has been reinvested to renew, energize, or sustain it.

Some leaders may argue that an extractive approach is necessary because financial analysts and investors demand high returns, at any cost, and there is no way to produce these outcomes while still operating businesses in a balanced way. The expression "pay me now, or pay me later . . . but you *will* pay me" seems to apply here. There is no avoiding the ultimate collapse of such a system. All that can be done is to defer that collapse and then seek to cover up the final demise through mergers and acquisitions in the name of a great *strategic fit* between the two businesses. As the number of KBOs increases and their success enables them to dominate industries, the laggards who employ exclusively extractive strategies will be naturally selected out of the marketplace.

Those who continue to lead their companies toward becoming a KBO have already accepted the premise that knowledge is the product of learning and knowing—and that there is no learning without risk. Even more important, knowledge leaders usually come to realize that the kinds of knowledge with the highest value are often the most difficult to create. What is more commonly agreed on in the knowledge community is that there are many different kinds of knowledge—and that some types are more likely than others to be valued in organizations. Specifically, systemic *objective* knowledge tends to be valued more highly in businesses than individual *subjective* interpretations of experience.

For example, statistically refined market research reveals that TAB Software's market share has declined by 4% in the past year. Moreover, data analysis hints that this decline is highly correlated with a 23% increase in the number of delayed shipments. These two factors suggest to the management team that delivery delays are causing orders to drop, and that they should increase production capacity ASAP.

This objective knowledge claim is more likely to be valued than the knowledge gained by one of TAB Software's field sales representatives during a recent emotionally charged conversation with a disgruntled customer. Her interpretation was that this particular customer not only was dissatisfied with the company's shipping delays, but that he also felt strongly that the company was being unresponsive to his needs. As a result, he was starting to interview alternative vendors.

The sales representative's (subjective) knowledge claim is that TAB Software must act immediately to retain customers by working with them to jointly plan their purchasing needs and have earlier notice of incoming orders. Both claims made by the management team (objective) and the sales representative (subjective) are unproven. After all, they are only *knowledge claims*. Knowledge that has yet to be proven to be reliable or valid is referred to as a knowledge claim. Knowledge claims are assertions—hypotheses—that declare that a specific action will lead to a particular outcome. For example, if we state that you will become a great leader by reading this book, that statement is a knowledge claim.

Most of what passes for knowledge in organizations is really just a set of knowledge claims that have yet to be proven effective in achieving desired results. Although businesses tend to prefer objective knowledge claims over subjective knowledge claims, at the end of the workday, they are all still only knowledge *claims*. So how are knowledge leaders to proceed in the face of such uncertainty? It is unreasonable to suggest that a company should wait on decisions or action until the relevant knowledge claims are proven or disproved. What knowledge leaders need to do is to institute mechanisms by which knowledge claims are formed, shared, tested, and evaluated in an ongoing way. This will put the company ahead of the game—so its knowledge claims can evolve to the point of real usefulness. In most organizations, such knowledge-creating processes are either nonexistent or buried by more powerful political and cultural processes.

Such political circumstances restrict the potential for groups to improve the quality of their knowledge by systematically processing it. The act of processing knowledge promotes its refinement in ways that raise its quality and make it more valuable to the organization. This is critical because effective action can only be reliably taken on the basis of high-quality knowledge. Unfortunately, some leaders operate under the delusion that their intelligence is sufficient to create a performance level that would sustain a *FAST* KBO. Collectively, the four dimensions of *FAST* (being functional, adaptive, sustainable, and timely) set a gold standard for business strategies. Organizational knowledge is a critical element for businesses that want to become *FAST* KBOs. Once leaders accept that knowledge is necessary to become a *FAST* company, they will need to determine what kind of *knowledge mix* will be aligned, first with the organization's identity, and then with its strategy. It will also be important for knowledge leaders to distinguish when the organization should engage in wide-scale knowledge processing and when it is not necessary to do so.

While knowledge processing can be costly and time consuming, it also reduces risks and improves effectiveness. However, making investments in an organization's knowledge-processing capacity should not be taken lightly, because there are no guarantees that the knowledge sought will be created—or that it will reliably produce the desired results. However, it is critical for knowledge leaders to realize that certain kinds of performance outcomes are virtually unattainable without effective knowledge processing. As you will read later in this chapter, there are situations where knowledge processing is superfluous, yet there are other situations where a failure to engage in knowledge processing is foolhardy, to say the least. The importance of knowledge claims for business performance depends on the types of knowledge in question and the complexity of the problems to be faced.

## COMPLEXITY AND KNOWLEDGE CLAIMS

Different types of knowledge are often found in organizations. These include *procedural knowledge, declarative knowledge, actionable knowledge, and pragmatic knowledge.* Knowledge claims do not have much relevance to the simplest kind of knowledge (procedural knowledge), because it is generally regarded as having a very high rate of reliability. Procedural knowledge is used mainly to solve relatively routine problems or to complete simple tasks. Let us assume for the moment that we work in a fast-food restaurant and that we discover how to produce optimal quality burgers in a speedy manner and at low cost. Ordinarily, when it comes to knowledge claims we would say "case closed" and not give the matter any further consideration. Clearly, the role of knowledge claims becomes more significant in the higher-complexity areas of an organization.

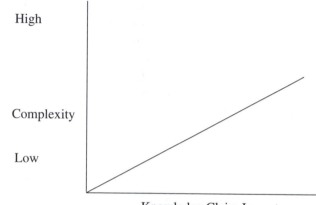

**Figure 11.1**
*Relationship of Complexity to Importance in Knowledge Claims*

As shown in Figure 11.1, it becomes increasingly important to have a greater number of *competing knowledge claims* as the level of complexity rises. The reasons for this are simple. The higher the complexity, the fewer existing proven reliable answers, and the greater the uncertainty as to the correct decision or solution. A knowledge claim is an expression of belief stated in the form of an actionable proposition. For example, a leader might propose to his or her employees: "If we outsource our information technology functions, we will be able to reduce costs by 27% and quality will only drop by 4%, so we will be much better off in the long run." The verity of this statement will remain unknown until it is actually tested. However, whether this strategy is eventually implemented will depend on how well it fares against other competing knowledge claims.

Even in businesses that appear to have low complexity, challenges can surface that are difficult to resolve without the benefit of knowledge. For example, while you might think a fast-food restaurant is an operation with very low complexity, this is not necessarily the case. There are many factors in this industry that may cause higher levels of complexity to arise. For example, there may be shortages of qualified employees, intense price-driven competition, and emerging competition from substitute products. Managers in such environments often harbor the illusion that its relatively routine technology defines the entire organization as being of low complexity. In fact, technology is only one of many ways to address the problems posed by complexity.

One of the main challenges for fast-food restaurants is to discover ways to serve low-cost food of acceptable quality. The technology and operating system of the fast-food restaurant themselves represent existing knowledge claims. For example, the choice to cook burgers by microwaving them, then searing them over an open flame broiler, as opposed to frying or steaming them, reflects a yet-to-be-proven claim that this is the best way to prepare burgers. Outside of the organization's operating system, there are even more significant claims that are embedded in the company's knowledge system.

Another knowledge claim in fast-food restaurants is reflected in the scope of its menu—that is, the types of food offered to customers reflect knowledge claims about what constitutes a good menu for this particular company. Competing knowledge claims would include questions such as should McDonald's sell submarine sandwiches like those marketed by Subway franchises? Should Burger King sell Mexican-style foods?

Leaders may choose among competing knowledge claims based on strategic or operational decisions. In this process however, they need to continually align the organization's tasks, operations, strategies and identity in order to achieve the necessary synergy for success.

Organizational identity is the preeminent factor that knowledge leaders need to match with knowledge processes. One of the most common traps that leaders fall into is to start their knowledge initiatives by aligning them first with the firm's *strategy*. The problem is that strategy is not an enduring characteristic of an organization. In American companies, general business strategies tend to be more a reflection of the firm's current leaders than the organization's more enduring identity. Creating knowledge alignments that are not based on the identity of the organization can produce all sorts of unintended problems because knowledge processes become slaves to changing strategies. Therefore, it is vital that leaders design knowledge strategies so that they are congruent with the traditions, legacy, values, and collective understanding of what the company is all about.

A case study of Great Northern Technologies will be presented in the next section of this book to explain what can go wrong when knowledge strategies are aligned solely with business strategies, instead of with the more essential corporate identity. A common example of a knowledge strategy gone awry is when a new leader overlays a brilliant design on a company that has an identity as an industry innovator and a culture that is characterized by openness, respect for individuals, and inclusiveness in knowledge processing. This new leader's strategy will likely fail due to its misalignment between identity, business strategy, and knowledge strategy.

We propose that leaders must assess the knowledge needs of their business by surveying the complexity and knowledge claims at every level of the company. Most important, knowledge leaders must be able to determine not only the types of learning that are needed, but also the scope of knowledge processing and consensus that is required to successfully implement all necessary strategies.

## What Is Knowledge Processing?

McElroy (2003) defines knowledge processing as "a set of social processes through which people in organizations create and integrate their knowledge" (p. 54). Knowledge processing, then, is fundamentally a human social process that involves the production, evaluation, integration, and control of how knowledge is created and used in organizations. If high-quality knowledge is the precursor to all effective business processes, then one of the most significant functions in organizations is to create effective knowledge. Knowledge leaders base their business processes on valid knowledge that produces reliable outcomes. Unfortunately, it is more common for leaders to design business processes based on vague impressions of how things work, long-established traditions, case studies, fond hopes, accepted practices, or political agendas.

Knowledge processes are composed of a series of activities that facilitate the evolution of knowledge toward greater reliability in producing desired results. Knowledge processes are not the same as KM processes, nor are they business processes, rather they are the operations required in any human social system to discover, create, refine, share, and evaluate knowledge for action. *One way to think of knowledge processes is that they are the product of a continuous quality improvement effort that creates higher-quality knowledge for use throughout an organization.*

Ideally, knowledge enables employees to take actions that always create the expected result. Unfortunately, this is rarely the case. In fact, the collective level of knowledge in many companies does not enable workers to successfully perform more than routine tasks with a high degree of reliability. Organizational complexity can be determined by a wide variety of factors, such as technologies, the type of workforce, its environment, and intensity of competition. While there may be a general level of complexity that defines an organization as a whole, there are also likely to be different types of complexity in different functions or parts of any company.

Business can deal with such complexity in a variety of ways. Probably the most common approach to complexity is to try to reduce it by means of brilliant design strategies such as job simplification, automation, and tight procedures. Other companies may seek instead to absorb complexity by developing more sophisticated knowledge. This latter strategy enables companies to draw on the collective insights of its employees to actually exploit complexity through innovation. This has the advantage of transforming the problem of complexity into a potential competitive advantage. Although it is much easier and less risky to execute the brilliant design strategy, the effect is that the company will remain dependent on its ability to adjust to continued complexity. On the other hand, the business that rises to a higher knowledge threshold will gradually move toward independence from the complexity.

Examples of the benefits of this meet-the-complexity strategy are to be found at 3M, BMW, Harley-Davidson, Rockwell Collins, and Teknion. As these and other elite organizations demonstrate, becoming a KBO can provide a significant financial return. For example, Rockwell Collins, a relatively conservative company with a tradition of being slow to change, was able to become one of the simplest types of knowledge-based organizations—a learning organization. In his book *Built to Learn*, Rockwell's Director of Learning and Development, Cliff Purington (2003) reported:

The impact of this learning organization process has been unparalleled. Within three years of implementing our strategic plan at Rockwell Collins, we saved the company $23 million on training expenditures while expanding the training offerings by 400%. If we can make this happen at Rockwell Collins using this process, it can be done at any company regardless of the size, culture, or industry. (p. 8)

During the Machine Age, having relatively low levels of collective knowledge did not pose a problem because organizations were designed to filter out complexity. These systems relied on top managers to make knowledgeable, effective decisions that would be executed by rank-and-file workers. However, the circumstances that enabled this strategy to be effective in the Machine Age no longer exist. Unfortunately, rather than recognize and accept this fact, many leaders are simply pushing harder on their system—which is a bit like pushing a rope uphill. The unhappy result is that such managers often unwittingly contribute to an organizational death spiral. That is, faced with declining growth prospects as a result of prior disinvestments in knowledge processes and innovation, they cut staff and capacity further in hopes that the business will become smaller but profitable. Inevitably, these managers discover one day that the company has lost its distinctiveness and has become easy prey for predators, such as copycat competitors and price cutters.

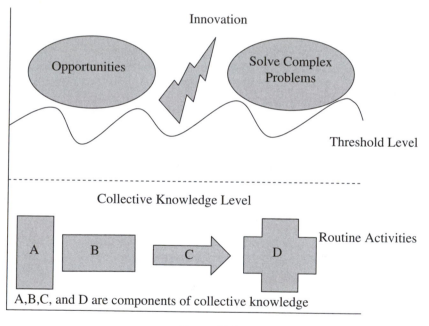

**Figure 11.2**
*Collective Knowledge Threshold*

Ideally, a company should invest in *broad-scale knowledge processing* to continually raise its collective knowledge threshold (Figure 11.2). This would enable it to take advantage of new opportunities, solve relatively complex problems, and innovate effectively. Realistically, however, most businesses have neither the expertise nor sufficient slack resources to engage in broad-scale knowledge processing.

Under such circumstances, it becomes critical for knowledge leaders to engage in *targeted knowledge processing*—that is, to focus in those high leverage areas where the investments are likely to make the most sense given the risk-reward tradeoffs of innovating, solving complex problems, and taking advantage of new opportunities.

## THE KNOWLEDGE PROCESSING ENGINE

While the form knowledge processing takes in any company can differ based on that organization's needs and capabilities, the goals of knowledge processing are always the same, that is, to do the following:

- Increase the effectiveness of knowledge in enabling human action.
- Refine, test, and evaluate knowledge by subjecting it to the tests of experience and scrutiny of a community of practitioners.
- Differentiate between the levels of effectiveness and reliability of various knowledge claims over time to expedite the process of choosing knowledge for action (Figure 11.3).

In Figure 11.3, it is unlikely that managers would be assigned to simply read books as a way to increase their managerial capacity, because that method alone is four times less effective in producing the expected result than the integrated method shown at the top. Not only is knowledge processing a way to continuously improve the quality of knowledge for use in an organization, it also provides a classification system that allows for the differentiation of grades of knowledge, based on effectiveness.

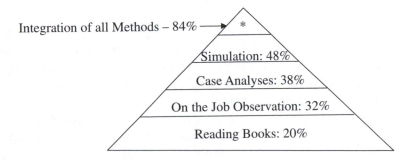

**Figure 11.3**
*Knowledge Claims for Effectiveness of Management Education Methods*

At the core of the knowledge-processing engine is what we refer to as the *Knowledge Quality Improvement Process* (KQIP). This continuous process is intended to extend the viable *life* of knowledge by prolonging it usefulness. Ordinarily, in situations defined by high complexity, there is a relatively high rate of knowledge failure. There are no guarantees regarding the life span of knowledge, because the assumptions on which that knowledge is based may be flawed.

The KQIP system acts in the same way as any quality control system. If it determines that a certain type of knowledge is defective, it could relegate that knowledge to the disproved knowledge waste bin. Alternatively, KQIP could modify this knowledge or combine it with other knowledge to form new knowledge. The core process that is the engine for KQIP is based on a model known as the *Knowledge Life Cycle model* (KLC). The KLC modle which was developed in the late 1990s by several members of the Knowledge Management Consortium International (KMCI), a Washington, D.C., based think tank depicts the process by which knowledge is created, evaluated, and distributed in organizations. (Steve Cavaleri served as president of KMCI from 2000 to 2002 and was one of the co-developers of the KLC modle (Figure 11.4).

In the KLC model, the utility of a knowledge claim is evaluated by an ongoing process of scrutiny, testing, and validation through experience. Once knowledge claim evaluation is done, then KM efforts shift toward sharing and distributing these knowledge claims. As Figure 11.4 on the following page illustrates, the recursive nature of this process, over time, sets the stage for both single-loop and double-loop learning processes, as well as for integration with existing processes. In the KLC model, knowledge processes are regarded as the primary basis for all knowledge process. That is, before any process is adopted as a business process, it is developed through a cycle where its underlying logic is first proposed, then scrutinized and studied prior to its implementation.

Typically, much of the work of the KLC is done by communities of practice in organizations. Each community of practice should decide how it will perform the basic KLC functions by employing the organizational processes that are best suited to its organization's culture and operating environment.

For example, in some companies it might be more compatible with the organization's cultural values to have a community of practice evaluate knowledge than to have managers directly involved in that process. In other organizations, the opposite might be true. There are both advantages and disadvantages to having informal groups

The Knowledge Life Cycle (KLC)

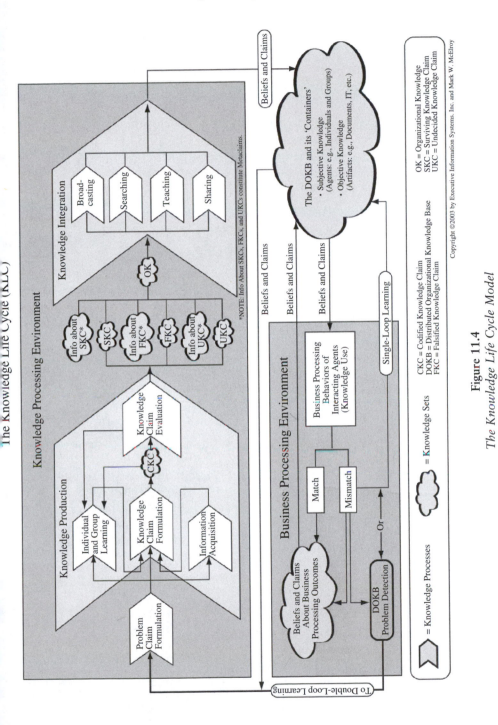

*NOTE: Info About SKCs, FKCs, and UKCs constitute Metaclaims.

OK = Organizational Knowledge
SKC = Surviving Knowledge Claim
UKC = Undecided Knowledge Claim

CKC = Codified Knowledge Claim
DOKB = Distributed Organizational Knowledge Base
FKC = Falsified Knowledge Claim

Copyright ©2003 by Executive Information Systems, Inc. and Mark W. McElroy

**Figure 11.4**
*The Knowledge Life Cycle Model*

perform KLC functions. In some cases, it is necessary to conduct more formal KLC functions through a project or task team. Let us take the example of an automobile redesign team that is using a concurrent engineering system where the team is composed of one person from each of the primary business functional areas (marketing, finance, engineering, research and development, and human resources). If leaders determine that the collective knowledge about this project has not yet risen to the threshold where it can address major challenges, they may want to add a KQIP process to the project. Inserting a KQIP process into key areas where there appears to be a potentially attractive return on investment is a good way for knowledge leaders to do *targeted knowledge processing.*

## Targeted Knowledge Processing

Targeted knowledge processing (TKP) enables organizations to ascend to the requisite threshold to mitigate unfavorable risks, solve resistant problems, or take advantage of emerging opportunities. More specifically, there are common business situations that are best addressed with particular types of knowledge-processing approaches. We alluded to the issue of complexity earlier in this chapter. The easiest way to think about the relationship between complexity and knowledge is that *the effectiveness of the knowledge must be greater than the complexity of the problem addressed by that knowledge.* This principle is similar to Ashby's *law of requite variety.* This law is one of the central precepts found in the body of knowledge known as *general systems theory.* It also recalls Einstein's famous observation that a problem can never be solved by the same kind of thinking that created it in the first place. From a knowledge leader's perspective, the quality of knowledge must be higher than the complexity of a problem in order for it to succeed in solving that problem.

A second consideration that must be addressed by TKP efforts is that of work interdependence. People who have little need for cooperation on work processes can have a different kind of knowledge than their coworkers, with little consequence. However, when there is a high level of interdependence required among employees to complete their projects, there must be a correspondingly high level of uniformity in their knowledge. Moreover, the new knowledge they create must be able to solve their various interests equally well. Here, it makes more sense to link KQIP functions to organizational learning, KD, or KM initiatives. Similarly, in some organizational situations there is a need for more variety in types of knowledge available, whereas other settings need a higher level of agreement. For example, the development of new drugs in the pharmaceutical industry depends on an innovation process. Innovation normally benefits in the early stages from greater variety of knowledge, yet requires a higher level of consensus in the latter stages (Figure 11.5).

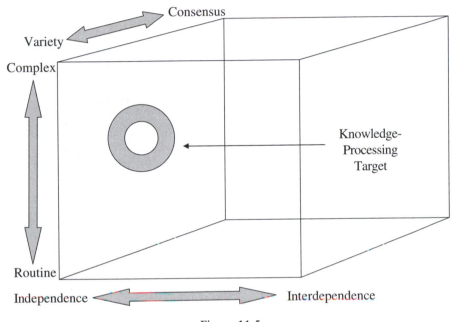

**Figure 11.5**
*Targeted Knowledge-Processing System*

There are at least five basic ways to target knowledge-processing systems. These include the Knowledge Life Cycle (KLC) as an adjunct to:

1. The work of a task or process group
2. An organizational learning or KD initiative
3. Project management processes
4. A KM initiative
5. The development of a community of practice or inquiry

The process of implementing a KLC system to improve the quality of knowledge in an organization can be as simple or complex as suits the purpose. That is, a simple process may produce the necessary results for reaching the threshold level required to solve the problems or take advantage of the desired opportunities. More complexity in a KLC is not always better. In a now famous study at the British petroleum company BP Amoco, a simple KM program was able to result in significant cost reductions.

Key elements to targeting a KLC system are as follows:

1. Assure that the corporate culture supports employees in openly making knowledge claims.
2. Focus on the positive aspects of the improvement process, rather than creating an environment that is based on criticism.
3. Use the KLC to develop a collective mindset where knowledge workers view their work as being an ongoing experiment.
4. Organize knowledge-process teams that consider ways to improve company-wide processes.
5. Develop policies that support the formation of self-organizing communities of practice. These informal groups often play a key role in the knowledge evaluation and integration functions of the KLC.

Since a KLC system is essentially a human social process, about *80% of all funding for KLC initiatives should be allocated directly toward human investments, while 20% should be invested in support technologies.* There is a strong tendency among managers to overlook the role of self-organizing human social interactions in knowledge processes. Instead, leaders typically rush to automate primitive knowledge processes. This can create significant unintended consequences by overlaying sophisticated technologies on rudimentary processes—thereby increasing the complexity of work and injuring performance. Any efforts to automate faulty processes are likely to fail. We have noticed that, even when businesses do recognize knowledge processes, there is a seductive tendency to "reengineer" them in the same manner as business process reengineering. Clearly, a reengineering approach is not appropriate for knowledge processing.

Optimally, KLC systems can provide the missing link that connects action learning, organizational learning, knowledge processing, and knowledge creation in organizations. The KLC framework need not be complex. Indeed, it can develop a few basic functions that promote learning from experience, capturing lessons learned, formulating and evaluating knowledge claims, and sharing knowledge. Although organizational learning has developed a somewhat tarnished reputation as being disconnected from the structure of work processes, KLC provides a framework that gives enough structure to organizational learning processes so that they can become more practical and therefore a better investment for companies. While there may be some domains of practice that can operate effectively without the benefits of organizational learning, it should not be dismissed as superfluous. Indeed, one of the main premises behind the notion of targeted knowledge systems is that leaders can choose which of many possible knowledge-based activities make the most sense for their organization, given its identity and strategic direction.

## ORGANIZATIONAL LEARNING IN KNOWLEDGE PROCESSING

Organizational learning is a collective process of inquiry and experimentation that uses groups as a forum to help employees draw new meanings from their past experiences. Knowledge is assumed to be the product of organizational learning processes, but most organizational learning processes to date have not been aligned with knowledge processes in a way that is pragmatic. The ideal of becoming a *learning organization* should still be considered an important vision for most companies. However, the methods for realizing this vision have typically been so vague that many managers consider it more of an intellectual exercise than a way to contribute to business performance. For example, Peter Senge (1990) envisioned a learning organization as being one that is "continually expanding its capacity to create its future" (p. 3). Pedler, Burgoyne, and Boydell (1991) saw a learning company as being a type of organization that is capable of facilitating the learning of all its members so as to be able to continually transform itself. Finally, Skyrme (2003) defined learning organizations as being those "organizations that have in place systems, mechanisms and processes, that are used to continually enhance their capabilities and those who work with it or for it, to achieve sustainable objectives—for themselves and the communities in which they participate" (p. 1).

All these definitions focus on the capability of organizational learning to promote greater adaptability through generative learning. However, these efforts have had limited usefulness because they are neither pragmatic nor explicitly considerate of the role of knowledge. Some experts explain such shortcomings by arguing that it is assumed that organizational learning is for action and that such learning automatically produces knowledge. However, this rationale is very misleading.

We assert that organizational learning processes must themselves be structured in a way that is pragmatic if they are to produce pragmatic knowledge. The simplest way to achieve this is to integrate organizational learning processes with the KLC system. Chris Argyris (1993) pointed to the importance of the connection between action learning and knowledge when he observed:

> Knowledge that is actionable, regardless of its content, contains causal claims. It says, if you act in such and such a way, the following will likely occur. That means actionable knowledge is produced in the form of if-then propositions that can be stored in and retrieved from the actor's mind under conditions of everyday life. (p. 2)

Firestone and McElroy (2003) wrote in similar vein about the KLC involving efforts to evaluate the truthfulness of knowledge claims. Similarly, Chris Argyris speaks of the need to detect and correct errors in causal claims.

The common thread in these approaches is unmistakable: They highlight the importance of leaders (1) increasing the number of knowledge claims and (2) installing processes for improving the quality of these knowledge claims. Both Argyris and Firestone/McElroy emphasized creating processes for evaluating the efficacy of knowledge claims by comparing actual results with expected results. Firestone and McElroy identified 24 different types of knowledge claims, including causal claims. They proposed that the validity of knowledge claims should be tested by applying success criteria that consider performance factors, such as the following:

1. Identifying improvements in cycle time without degradation in quality (efficiency)
2. Increase in production of surviving knowledge claims that are relevant to the problems motivating the knowledge life cycle (effectiveness)
3. Increase in production of surviving knowledge claims that are successful in use (effectiveness)
4. Increase in production of surviving knowledge claims of sufficient scope to handle problems motivating the knowledge life cycles of the enterprise (effectiveness)

By contrast, Argyris (1993) proposed several methods for testing the validity of causal claims. These include (1) showing causal or action maps that illustrate cause-effect linkages to organization members and then asking them to point out which features are incorrect and explaining why they disagree and (2) asking managers to make predictions based on their causal claims and then seeking to disconfirm them.

From a pragmatic view, causal claims or knowledge claims are important mirrors of one's beliefs about how and why things work as they do in practice. Determining whether a specific action works reliably well in practice is an important step in determining the validity of both the actions taken and the beliefs that underlie them. According to Charles Sanders Peirce, *the merits of one's beliefs are best judged by looking at the effectiveness of the results they produce.*[1]

According to this perspective, the importance of feedback about the effectiveness of prior actions is not so much to validate the knowledge used in obtaining these results as it is to clarify one's beliefs about how and why things work as they do. Senge (1990) referred to this process of belief clarification as "enriching one's mental model." In many respects, this process of testing, evaluating, and validating knowledge claims is strikingly similar to what Forrester (1965), Senge (1990), and Sterman (2000) have advocated in relation to systems thinking and modeling. As Senge noted:

Systems thinking forms a rich language for describing a vast array of interrelationships and patterns of change. Ultimately, it simplifies life by helping us see the deeper patterns lying behind the events and details. (p. 73)

In effect, this view of systems modeling is designed to surface causal claims and connect them within a coherent whole. The validity of systems models can be judged by their ability to provide managers with insights that enable them to predict actual patterns of performance. Alternately, computer simulations can be used to determine whether a model composed of causal claims produces the expected kinds of behavior.

What differs markedly among the disciplines of organizational learning, KM, systems thinking, and pragmatic philosophies is what is done with information regarding the validity of causal and knowledge claims. In pragmatist philosophy, especially the Peircian version, learning, knowledge, and action can never be separated from each other. As Potter (1996) noted:

Pragmatism is a doctrine of logic. It is a logical method helping us to know what we think and believe. The meaning of our thought is to be interpreted in terms of our willingness to act upon that thought; it is to be interpreted in terms of its conceived consequences. Peirce, then, sees a connection between good thinking and good doing. (p. 51)

Here we see that both learning and causal analysis are the concerns of knowledge for action. Pragmatic learning and knowledge cannot be separated, either in terms of individual or organizational practices. *Not surprisingly, total quality management, knowledge processing, knowledge management, action learning, and organization learning all are rooted in the work of the early 20th century pragmatists.* The intellectual lineage of all these fields can be traced directly from Charles Sanders Peirce, William James, John Dewey, C. I. Lewis, and E. A. Singer (all of whom were connected with pragmatism at Harvard) to renowned systems theorists (Russell Ackoff and C. West Churchman), to the founders of TQM (Walter Shewhart and W. Edwards Deming), to action-learning gurus (such as Donald Schon of MIT). In essence then, many of the most critical management philosophies of the late 20th century can be traced to the foundational precepts of pragmatism.

In the next section of *Knowledge Leadership (Part III)*, we will examine how pragmatic knowledge can become the foundation on which knowledge leaders build *FAST* KBOs.

# REFERENCES

Argyris, C. (1993). *Knowledge for Action.* San Franscisco, CA: Jossey-Bass. "Management." Accessed in August from www.strategy-partners.com. In Awad, E., and Ghaziri, H. *Knowledge Management*, Upper Saddle River, N. J., Pearson-Prentice-Hall.

Campbell, D. T., and Stanley, J. C. (1963). *Experimental and Quasi-experimental Design for Research.* Skokie, IL: Rand McNally.

Firestone, J., and McElroy, M. (2003). *Key Issues in the New Knowledge Management.* Boston: Butterworth-Heinemann.

Forrester, J. (1961). *Industrial Dynamics.* Portland, OR: Productivity Press.

McElroy, M. (2003). *The New Knowledge Management.* Boston: Butterworth-Heinemann.

Pedlar, M., Burgoyne, J., and Boydell, T. (1991). *The Learning Company.* London: McGraw-Hill.

Potter, V. (1996). *Peirce's Philosophical Perspectives.* New York: Fordham University Press.

Purington, C., and Butler, C. (2003). *Built to Learn.* New York: AMACOM.

Senge, P. (1990). *The Fifth Discipline.* New York: Doubleday/Currency.

Skyrme, D. (2003). Accessed in November from www.skyrme.com/insights/3lrnorg.htm.

Sterman, J. (2000). *Business Dynamics*. New York: Irwin-McGraw-Hill.

## NOTE

1. Charles Sanders Peirce advised: "Consider what effects, that might conceivably have practical bearings, we conceive the object of our conception to have. Then, our conception of these effects is the whole of our conception of the object" (Potter, 1996, p. 51).

# Part V

# Leading *FAST* Knowledge-Based Organizations (KBOs)

# 12

# DEVELOPING *FAST* KBOs

## Executive Summary

This chapter addresses what it means to become a knowledge leader capable of developing a *FAST* knowledge-based organization (KBO). Many companies have designated leaders, known as chief knowledge officers (CKOs), who typically focus on *managing* knowledge via the core KM functions. However, KM systems rarely meet the first three of our four *FAST* criteria. Most KM approaches operate with relatively high levels of speed and predictability—making them *timely*. Despite this last advantage, unless KM is quickly delivering *pragmatic* knowledge, it will not provide competitive advantage. One of the most glaring weaknesses of the whole KM movement has been to overlook the importance of personal knowledge development (KD). Knowledge leadership is the process of using personal influence to support KD processes and integrate them with KM initiatives to achieve an envisioned future. Effective knowledge leadership leads to the creation of pragmatic knowledge. Pragmatic knowledge is the ultimate knowledge for action because it is continually customized and upgraded based on the effectiveness of actions in producing expected results. Although pragmatic knowledge has its intellectual roots in America, it now flourishes primarily in Eastern businesses. This chapter ends with a description of how pragmatic knowledge has helped Toyota become a *FAST* KBO with astounding financial performance.

## DRILLING FOR KNOWLEDGE?

How can knowledge leaders create *FAST*, more pragmatic KBOs? To reiterate, *FAST* organizations use four basic criteria to evaluate all of their strategic initiatives:

1. Is the initiative *functional*—that is, is there strong reason to believe the initiative has a high probability of fulfilling its goal, mission, or purpose?
2. Is it *adaptive*—will it enable the organization to better adapt to changing market, economic, or other circumstances?
3. Is it *sustainable*? That is, does the initiative have the energy, resources, and design to operate at the desired level on a continued basis?
4. Is it *timely*? Will the initiative provide the promised deliverable on time? And, is this the most appropriate initiative at this time?

To answer these questions, we must first examine the conventional process of KM and differentiate it from the emerging role of knowledge leadership. While KM means many different things to different people, there are some common threads that unite most KM approaches. For example, many corporations around the world have CKOs, who are mainly concerned with designing and implementing systems to *manage* knowledge. The vast majority of these managers focus on gathering, distributing, housing, and leveraging information they consider relevant to knowledge, lessons learned, and best practices. The professional and trade journals are filled with examples of "successful" knowledge managers. Many CKOs consider their main role to be making certain that the requisite knowledge is available and applied appropriately to support the organization's strategy. Their leadership role is usually to advocate for the importance of knowledge in fulfilling the company's mission. CKOs are also the primary architects of the organization's knowledge systems. While they may not actually design these systems themselves, they choose which consultants to hire and which technologies to purchase, and they also make key staffing assignments.

CKOs often regard the most critical KM function to be the distribution of important knowledge throughout the organization to other employees. This approach requires CKOs to ensure that sufficient information is available both on people's desktops and in central storehouses, as well as to provide technology that enables employees to perform the conventional core KM functions. These core KM functions, known as the "5 Cs," are as follows:

1. *Collaborate* with peers in real-time projects through the use of virtual technologies.
2. *Capture* key lessons learned by reviewing past projects as keys to success.
3. *Collect* the most important lessons learned and collate them in order of value.
4. *Codify* knowledge by formalizing operating principles or best practices.
5. *Connect* employees to sources of knowledge, such as storehouses, via technology.

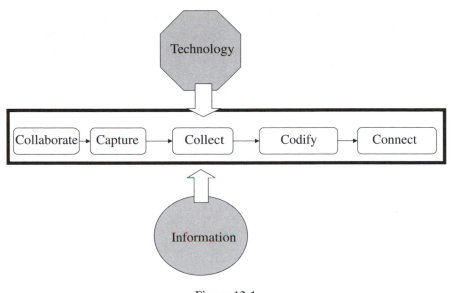

**Figure 12.1**
*Conventional KM Framework*

As shown in Figure 12.1, these functions are integrated through the use of technology and are used in combination with information. While many KM approaches treat knowledge and information as being virtual surrogates for each other, a more accurate description of their relationship is that information is often the precursor to creating new knowledge.

In some respects, the conventional KM model is similar to an agricultural model, where the *harvesting* of important knowledge gained over the course of projects can be compared to the process of reaping crops on a farm. The *connect* function, then, is like a marketplace that provides a centralized location where consumers (in this case, consumers of knowledge) can come together with suppliers (in this case, suppliers of knowledge). An example of the connect function is the KM process known as *expertise profiling*. The way organizations handle expertise-profiling processes can range from creating so-called Yellow Pages directories to using computer profiling systems that connect consumers (people seeking knowledge they need to solve a particular problem) with suppliers (people within the organization who are likely to possess that knowledge). The connect function in KM initiatives is generally to distribute knowledge through various organizational pipelines, such as e-mail, providing access to knowledge warehouses, corporate intranets, and holding storytelling sessions.

The purpose of KM according to the conventional 5-C approach depicted in Figure 12.1, is to leverage existing untapped intellectual assets. In other words, this KM process is based on an *economic resource utilization model*. This model is built on the economic theory that views managers' prime responsibility to be increasing their firms' efficiency. Here, intellectual assets are considered a "sunk cost"—an investment that has already been paid for. Therefore, the costs associated with extracting value from this asset are marginal and, hence, very attractive financially. Seen from this perspective, KM is an effort to "squeeze more juice from the lemon" by maximizing the utilization of a previously overlooked asset—namely, human knowledge.

In the conventional KM framework, the term *knowledge leader* is usually synonymous with CKO. In firms driven by the economic utilization model of KM, the prime responsibility of the CKO is to oversee the design and implementation of systems that fully exploit knowledge from existing intellectual assets. This is an attractive financial proposition for companies that view the vast majority of knowledge as being tacit, dormant, or unused. This perspective of knowledge can be compared to executives in a major oil company who discover a new drilling technology that will enable them to extract millions of square miles worth of untapped oil reserves at a modest cost. Clearly, these executives would regard this discovery as a major business boon.

The main difference between what actually happens in most organizations and our oil-drilling example is that the quality of the "oil" buried beneath the surface is significantly different at each company. Those companies with effective knowledge processes are likely to be resting atop relatively high-quality knowledge with rich potential for enabling effective action. On the other hand, their competitors may own inferior "oil assets" that hold much lower potential for driving effective action throughout their organizations in the future (Figure 12.2).

**Figure 12.2**
*The Oil-Drilling KM Approach*

We certainly understand the economic utilization approach to KM. After all, what is not to like about getting something for next to free? Indeed, as a matter of principle, it is desirable for businesses to operate more efficiently and achieve higher performance at little or no extra cost. This economic model has allowed Western companies to grow and prosper by utilizing their "human resources" in various productions and operations. In this economic definition, human resources are fully utilized when they produce valued outputs 100% of their work time.

If this model sounds too good to be true, that's probably because it is. While the economic utilization approach may incrementally raise employee performance or increase the overall knowledge waterline within a company, this strategy has serious limitations. Undoubtedly, effectively employing conventional KM can provide a business with a temporary edge over competitors who do not value knowledge at all. However, there are still many unanswered questions about the efficacy of conventional KM approaches. McElroy (2003), Firestone and McElroy (2003), and Wiig (2004) have already convincingly challenged many of the premises of the conventional KM approach. For example, Karl Wiig, considered by many to be the father of KM, has underscored the importance of creating knowledge that enhances an organization's *effectiveness*. According to Wiig, effectiveness is the result of being able to discern which, of all available options, are most likely to enable the company to achieve its large and small aims. Wiig observed that:

Overall enterprise performance—the degree to which enterprise objectives are fulfilled—is determined by the effectiveness of countless separate actions performed by individuals and groups—that is, how well regular situations and difficult challenges are handled. (p. 33)

There are many unanswered questions about the quality of knowledge in most organizations. Is it pragmatic? Is it reliably effective at producing the expected outcomes? Are the processes being used to create new knowledge capable of reliably improving the quality of knowledge?

## MOVING CLOSER TO *FAST* KBOs

To evaluate the potential value of conventional KM approaches, we will use the following criteria:

- Is the approach *FAST*?
- Is the approach targeted to desired performance?
- Is the approach pragmatic?

Using these criteria, we can more easily see that, while most conventional KM approaches have clear benefits to organizations, they also have limitations. First, we must question the *functionality* of traditional KM. Does it function reliably to produce the desired performance? In our view, although conventional KM has the capacity to capture lessons learned and share best practices, it rarely functions to improve organizational performance. This is because performance-driven continuous improvement processes are not built into KM systems.

Does conventional KM enhance an organization's capacity to *adapt*? The answer is largely no. Although KM can be used as part of a full knowledge strategy to support adaptation, KM by itself is not designed to perform such a function. However, in firms where customer and supplier information are widely shared, KM can support the development of an effective response to change. The problem with KM is that adaptive processes rely on the capacity for the "three Is"—*interpretation, intimacy, and innovation*. Most conventional KM systems are not designed to facilitate the creation of new interpretations of complex situations, intimate knowledge of relevant environmental features, or innovation. In summary, the vast majority of KM systems do not function well in facilitating organizational adaptation.

Noted complexity theorist John Holland (1995) defined adaptation as a process that occurs as a result of experience, whereby an organism "fits itself to its environment" in order to "make better use of its environment for its own ends." A more self-organizing view of adaptation can be found in the writings of biologists Humberto Maturana and Francisco Varela (1987). They defined adaptation as a *mutual process of structural change that occurs as both the environment and organism adjust to each other*. This alignment results from the organism's internal programming, which causes it to respond to certain external cues and ignore others. Adaptability, then, is the capacity of an organism (in this case, an organization) to align its structure to an environment because it suits the organism's ends and its own internal coding. Adaptability, then, means that an organization is capable of changing in ways that remain congruent with its "internal coding"—its core values and identity.

For example, the Scottish soccer team Glasgow Celtic is unlikely to adapt to economic difficulties by switching into the business of manufacturing soccer balls, because it defines itself a football club that is in the business of playing soccer. Shifts in the economic environment that a manufacturer would recognize and need to adapt to are meaningless to a soccer team. In a similar vein, a maple tree would recognize different environmental cues than a cactus. But the maple tree will not become a cactus during a dry season, nor will a cactus switch to a maple during a cold season. Their core genetic material keeps their identity intact as they adapt. Organizations have much to learn about successful adaptation and survival from living organisms. For example, an "international petroleum company" needs to first enlarge its identity to being an "international energy company" if it is to successfully expand into the market of alternative fuels. The point is that all successful adaptation moves from the organism's identity outward.

Next we ask: Is the conventional KM model *sustainable*, does it significantly contribute to the sustainability of the organization? The answer to this question is usually "no—because extractive economic models are, by their very design, unsustainable. They are not built to replenish resources. In other words, new organizational knowledge must be created to replenish the knowledge that is being harvested or mined. In most companies, leaders do not realize this principle. For example, if a rare mineral was suddenly discovered to be a miraculous cure for cancer and heart disease, the world's supplies would dwindle quickly. Unless someone discovers a method for creating more, once it's gone—it's gone. Ordinarily, sustainability requires that anything that is extracted and consumed must be replaced in order to maintain equilibrium. This is the ecological principle behind reforestation and crop rotation. Some people argue that sharing knowledge actually makes it worth more—and can even generate more knowledge. There is an element of truth to this view. However, it only works this way if the knowledge being shared is already of high quality. Little is gained by sharing poor-quality knowledge—in fact, it may even hurt performance. Remember, knowledge is not the same as truth. Much of what passes for knowledge in organizations is poor-quality knowledge—that is, knowledge claims that have *not* been proven to be reliably effective.

While using knowledge does not deplete it in the same way as oil or mineral resources can be depleted, what is not sustainable in conventional KM is its reliance on knowledge that is obsolete, of poor quality, or not pragmatic as a business strategy. This statement may seem paradoxical and requires some explanation. Generally it is a good idea to base business strategies on knowledge. The problem is that, in most organizations, knowledge can only help us understand what actions have worked well *in the past*. In some respects, this kind of knowledge is similar to artifacts that have been unearthed by anthropologists digging through the ruins of an ancient city. These artifacts help us understand what life was like in a bygone era and appreciate ancient people's beliefs and values. In most cases, KM unearths knowledge as relatively raw nuggets—lessons learned that have been captured from experience. Generally, when these lessons learned are first brought to light, relatively little is known about their verity or reliability in helping employees act in more effective ways.

Unless companies have processes in place to refine this knowledge and evaluate its usefulness, odds are that it is probably of lower quality than is desirable. This is one of the major problems that results from the *knowledge as information* perspective. Conventional KM views knowledge and information in compartmentalized ways that are essentially disconnected from action, performance, and effectiveness. The tendency here is to view all information as being potentially usable, then flood employees throughout the organization with information that has little practical value. Employees can drown in this information overload. In fact, heavy reliance on leveraging low-quality, outdated knowledge may have a self-reinforcing negative effect.

While the process of performing conventional KM may itself be sustainable, there is nothing designed into the KM process to assure that the quality of knowledge is continuously improving or to create practical new knowledge that would be effective in getting desired results. While some KM advocates argue that the process of *corroboration* is performance driven, we believe that in the vast majority of cases, corroboration merely determines the integrity and credibility of that knowledge, rather than validate its effectiveness in producing expected results.

And lastly we ask: Is KM typically *timely*? The good news about conventional KM systems is that they usually meet the fourth *FAST* criterion. That is, they usually are very timely. Particularly if KM systems are well designed and have good technology, they tend to operate with relatively high levels of speed and predictability. However despite this advantage of timeliness, unless KM is quickly delivering *pragmatic* knowledge to its destination, it will not be supporting a company's competitive advantage.

## WHEN IS KNOWLEDGE PRAGMATIC?

The greatest weakness of conventional KM approaches is that they are generally not pragmatic. It is virtually impossible for them to target specific types of knowledge to particular tasks or problems in organizations. Pragmatic knowledge is created via a process that continually improves the quality of knowledge that fits *specific* situations. It also addresses how these situations are being defined and examines the meaning we give to them.

*Pragmatic knowledge is the ultimate knowledge for action— because it is continually being customized and upgraded based on the effectiveness of actions taken in producing the expected results.* Although the knowledge typically found in conventional KM systems is often based in experience (such as lessons learned), once this knowledge is passed on, it is usually viewed out of context. For example, the recipients of this knowledge rarely know how the original situation was defined, how effective this knowledge was in accomplishing its purpose, or whether this knowledge-in-use is being monitored to improve its future use.

Many variations of KM can be found in business practice. These range from storytelling, to measuring intellectual capital, to document management. As a result, it is difficult to generalize about KM as a field of practice. In fact, one problem that continues to plague this discipline is the lack of agreement over core definitions and terms. That said, the focus of most KM approaches is on the *management* aspects of the knowledge process. This causes KM designers to focus more on systems and processes and less on the self-organizing, knowledge-creating, and innovating aspects of KM.

KM systems usually are helpful for sharing knowledge and creating a knowledge-rich work context. Knowledge leaders must fully understand and appreciate both KM's potential and limitations. Knowledge leadership, therefore, includes KM but must go beyond it to embrace the interpersonal, self-organizing, and *knowledge-developing* (KD) aspects of knowledge in organizations. In contrast to KM, KD is an *inside-out* process that requires leadership through visioning, coaching, and mentoring. When employees are in a knowledge-rich KM environment without leadership or a pragmatic process of knowledge creation, the necessary dynamic tension is absent, and knowledge processes tend to stagnate.

Virtually anyone in an organization can become a knowledge leader as long as he or she understands the interplay between KM and KD (the interpersonal side of knowledge processing and knowledge creation). Unfortunately, in most organizations, KD is usually misunderstood or underemphasized. KD relies on achieving an alignment between the power of leaders and the personal learning and knowledge-creation efforts of individual employees.

Indeed one of the most glaring weaknesses of the whole KM movement has been to overlook the importance of personal knowledge development. Unless individuals have the skill and capacity for developing knowledge from their own experience, it will be virtually impossible for them to effectively participate in a meaningful way in KM initiatives. While a few KM experts, such as Steve Barth, have developed tools for personal knowledge management, relatively little attention has been paid to developing KD processes.

Many KM practitioners wrongly assume that employees can automatically learn from experience and that they therefore can create knowledge based on those lessons learned. This is an unwarranted assumption, as traditional business structures and public education systems have handicapped people's knowledge-creating capacities to the point that many of us have become *chronically unknowledgeable*. This learning handicap is evident in many employees' inability to engage in critical thinking and solve complex problems that require specific ad hoc knowledge gleaned from situations.

*Knowledge leadership is the process of using personal influence to support knowledge-development processes and integrate them with knowledge-management initiatives to achieve an envisioned future.* (Figure 12.3). This envisioned future involves ideals for both optimum performance and knowledge mix. When knowledge leadership is done effectively, it leads to the creation of pragmatic knowledge.

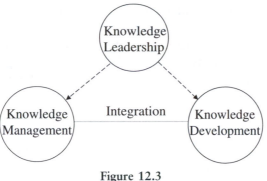

**Figure 12.3**
*Knowledge Leadership*

## PRAGMATIC ORGANIZATIONAL KNOWLEDGE

Many companies have been reluctant to invest scarce resources in becoming a so-called "learning organization" because the process is perceived as too complex and slow. However, many companies across the world are thriving while becoming learning organizations. For example, we have noticed in our recent trips to Ireland and the Netherlands, that many European companies are increasingly emphasizing the role knowledge plays in their success. Perhaps the greatest concentration of knowledge-based companies, per capita, can be found in The Netherlands, where well-known knowledge-intensive companies, such as Unilever, Royal Dutch Shell, and ABN AMRO operate. To the north, household names, such as cell phone manufacturers, Nokia and Ericsson set the pace for knowledge-intensive companies. In the U.K. well known firms, such as BP Amoco, Rolls Royce, and the BBC have all embraced the drive to become more knowledge-focused in their approach to operating their companies. Throughout the center of Europe, one can find knowledge-based companies in France, Germany and Italy–including AirBus and Schlumberger in France, Siemens, Volkswagen, and Boehringer Ingelheim in Germany and Benetton in Italy. Finally, but not least, Spain has embraced the importance of knowledge on a national level with new institution of new government policies to suppor the development of a knowledge-based *society*. Leading Spanish knowledge-based companies include Telefonica Moviles, and Irizar. At first blush, it seems ironic that learning and pragmatic knowledge management approaches, developed largely in the United States, have become so much more popular in other parts of the world. However we believe there are many cultural and historical reasons for this phenomenon. In particular, the strength of the pragmatic knowledge approach in Asia is not surprising when we realize that many Asian companies, such as Canon, Honda, Kao, Ricoh, Samsung, Sony, and Toyota, still attribute their roots in management theory to the work of W. Edwards Deming, considered by many to be the father of the quality movement. These companies are indeed fortunate because their leaders were not indoctrinated with the legacies of Frederick Winslow Taylor's *scientific management* approach, as happened in the United States. During the 1960s and 1970s, the human relations movement in America attempted to balance the still prevalent "scientific management" theories originally espoused by Taylor in the early 1900s. The irony is that Taylor's approach was based on a very narrow definition of science that is more applicable to Taylor's original occupation—mechanical engineering. Taylor's management theory, therefore, could more aptly be called *organizational engineering.*

Taylor's basic idea was to revolutionize the management process by introducing efficiency principles that had grown popular in engineering circles. Unfortunately, these ideas were largely disconnected from the best scientific thinking even of that time. The legacy of Taylorism is still with us today, resulting in the highly ironic situation that truly scientific views of knowledge are considered by many leaders to be impractical. In contrast, the Industrial Revolution never fully emerged in Japan until the rebuilding after World War II. Japanese managers at that time were open to learning Deming's pragmatic ideas because they had not already invested heavily in the American business practice of scientific management.

W. Edwards Deming learned quality improvement principles from Walter Shewhart of Bell Labs, who developed them based on his study of the writings of the pragmatist C. I. Lewis. Lewis learned the tenets of philosophical pragmatism under the noted William James and Josiah Royce—and also had numerous conversations with the founder of pragmatism, Charles Sanders Peirce. The discussions with Peirce greatly influenced Lewis's thinking on the origins of knowledge and spurred him to write one of his greatest books, *The Pragmatic Element in Knowledge.* In this book, Lewis extended his theories of the workings of pragmatism to include the concept of "a priori" in his theory of knowledge. *A priori* assumptions and judgments are based exclusively on reasoning—without the aid of supportive evidence gained from experience.

Taking the lead of both Peirce and Royce, Lewis identified three elements in knowledge that can be only be separated by the process of analysis:

1. The element of experience that is known to an individual
2. The structure of concepts by which an individual interprets the meaning of what he or she has observed and experienced
3. That person's act of interpreting what was observed and experienced by means of applying those relevant concepts

Lewis envisioned a process where people construct meaning based on the concepts they employ to make sense of their own experience. He regarded these concepts as being only experimental—that is, subject to revision based on feedback from actions that would be taken at some future time. Chris Argyris refers to these concepts as being *theories of action*, while Peter Senge calls them *mental models*. Regardless of what we call these devices, they are artificial objects, lenses if you will, that we use for sense making. They are experimental in that they enable us to create new meanings based on our past and future experiences. At many of the well-known Japanese companies, all of the philosophical theories listed here became operational through the mechanism of Walter Shewhart's PDCA cycle (plan, do, check, act) for continuous improvement. In fact, *the PDCA cycle is a formula for creating pragmatic learning and knowledge.*

At Toyota for example, the PDCA cycle occurs at every level of the organization, from individuals up through groups. These ongoing processes measure how well performance stacks up against goals, and corrective action is taken whenever there is a performance gap (Figure 12.4). In such companies, continuous improvement cycles operate simultaneously at all levels of the organization including within projects, groups, divisions, and between the company and partner companies in the supply chain.

The tension between the ideal and actual states of performance, and between execution and innovation, drives the continuous learning cycles that lead to knowledge at all levels of the organization. The types of knowledge that emerge from improvement processes are usually actionable and, at times, pragmatic. Process-oriented companies that employ such an approach generally move slowly, since they tend to carefully analyze each step before acting. However, it appears that such firms achieve higher levels of *effectiveness* than swift-acting competitors and that their strong improvement processes limit the harmful impact of errors. This is not to imply that there are not advantages to being a rapid-moving company when it comes to securing first-mover advantage in the marketplace and reducing cycle times for model revisions. Interestingly, in reality, there are certain paradoxes here. We have noticed that KBOs appear to have the

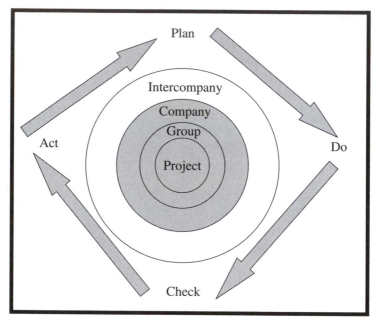

**Figure 12.4**
*Multilevel Improvement Cycles*
*Adapted from Liker (2004)*

ability to take quick and effective action in today's market. We believe this results from their decades of planning and learning that have accumulated as robust knowledge.

## DESIGNING A KNOWLEDGE MIX

There is probably not an organization in the world that would not be happy to have all positions within the organization filled with employees who possess increasingly higher levels of knowledge over time. The problem for most leaders is that each type of employee in the company is faced with different challenges, and it is extremely inefficient and unproductive to distribute the same kinds of knowledge to all employees. One solution to the problem posed by employees having different knowledge needs is for leaders to design a *knowledge mix* that will address the various needs throughout the organization.

One of the central functions of knowledge leaders is to create a knowledge mix that mirrors the identity, strategy, and performance needs of their organizations. A knowledge mix is an amalgam of the various types of knowledge that are available and that can be used to address the performance needs of an organization. A knowledge mix is composed of four types of knowledge: (1) procedural knowledge, (2) declarative knowledge, (3) action knowledge, and (4) pragmatic knowledge.

Ideally, an organization's knowledge mix should be closely aligned with its business strategy and the nature of the opportunities it seeks. Most leaders try to achieve a tight alignment between their company's knowledge mix and desired performance outcomes by relying on standard managerial methods of analysis. However, because knowledge is essentially the product of human social systems, typical control-oriented methods of management are less likely to prove effective. This is where the art of leadership comes to the foreground as the prospective knowledge leader encourages employees to engage in knowledge development as part of drawing them toward an ideal vision of the organization's future. According to Bob Buckman (2004), former CEO of Buckman Labs, "If you want culture change in a department, the head of that department has to lead it. If you want culture change in an organization, then the head of that organization has to lead it. Everybody watches the boss" (pp. 45–46).

A number of leading companies are demonstrating that there is much more to effectively using knowledge for organizational performance than relying on simple information technologies and standard KM formulas (such as sharing best practices, getting the right knowledge to the right people at the right time, and leveraging intellectual capital). Some of these businesses can be found on the list of finalists for the Most Admired Knowledge Enterprises Award (MAKE) (Table 12.1).

**Table 12.1**
*2003 Global Most Admired Knowledge Enterprises*

| | |
|---|---|
| ■ Accenture | ■ McKinsey & Company |
| ■ Amazon.com | ■ Microsoft |
| ■ BP | ■ Nokia |
| ■ Buckman Laboratories | ■ PricewaterhouseCoopers |
| ■ Canon | ■ Royal Dutch/Shell |
| ■ Ernst & Young | ■ Siemens |
| ■ General Electric | ■ 3M |
| ■ Hewlett-Packard | ■ Toyota Motor |
| ■ IBM | ■ World Bank |
| ■ Infosys Technologies | ■ Xerox |

## Pragmatic Knowledge at Toyota

The advent of the 21st century is generally regarded as the turning point from the Machine Age to the Knowledge Era. The introduction of workplaces populated mainly by knowledge workers has not only raised optimism regarding the potential for performance gains from effective use of knowledge, it has also turned many traditional "laws" of managing and leading completely upside down. We must emphasize again that to be effective in this new breed of enterprise, knowledge leaders will not only need to understand knowledge, they will also have to redefine the principles of leading and managing.

There are many riddles and paradoxes for knowledge leaders that are waiting to be solved. Many of these answers will require paradigms that differ from those used by traditional leaders. What we do know for certain is that 21st century KBOs cannot be managed by applying the principles of industrial management and leadership. There are numerous examples to help make this point, but perhaps one of the most startling is that of the Japanese automobile manufacturer Toyota.

There can be little doubt of Toyota's long-term success—as measured by a wide variety of metrics, including standard financial performance measures. For example, let's look at Toyota's *market capitalization value*—a measure of the total value of its common stock as determined by the amount investors are willing to pay based on current stock market valuations. This value indicates that although Toyota is only the fourth largest automaker in the world, *its market capitalization of $105 billion is worth more than that of Chrysler, Ford, and General Motors combined*!

Moreover, Toyota consistently manufactures products of higher quality, with less time to develop new models, and at higher profits by employing a knowledge-based approach. Many of the principles that Toyota adheres to steadfastly would be considered heresy in traditional organizations. For example, while it is a common management convention that there is a tradeoff between efficiency and knowledge-creating processes, Toyota proves this idea wrong by getting *both* high-quality knowledge and efficiency. Toyota appears to have discovered a number of truths that would be considered counterintuitive—or impossible—by most business leaders.

Jeffrey Liker (2003), a professor at the University of Michigan, has discovered the following beliefs to be pervasive at Toyota:

- Often the best thing you can do is to idle a machine and stop producing parts.
- It may not be a priority to keep workers busy making parts as quickly as possible.
- It is best to selectively use information technology and often to use manual processes even when automation is available and would seem to justify its cost in reducing headcount.
- Without *hansei* (reflection) it is impossible to have *kaizen* (continuous improvement).

Liker (2003) observed that Toyota stands out among all the world-class institutions he has studied:

I believe Toyota is the best learning organization. The reason is that it sees standardization and innovation as two sides of the same coin, melding them in a way that creates great continuity. . . . This is the foundation for the Toyota Way of learning, standardization *punctuated* by innovation, which gets translated into new standards. (p. 251)

Let us take the process of *reflection* as an example of the differences between the paradigms of traditional versus knowledge-based leadership. A colleague of ours asked a visiting professor from Japan who was touring the United States what he observed as the major differences between the management of American and Japanese companies. After pausing to think, the professor replied, "In America, a worker who is observed looking out a window is reprimanded for not being productive. In Japan, the same worker is praised for being productive."

This little story illustrates a critical difference between leading for efficiency versus leading for innovation. In the machine model, requiring workers to engage in continuous action is viewed as being the most productive use of human resources. In the knowledge-based view, performance outcomes result when individuals gain knowledge by learning from experience. In this second case, the improvement process is regarded as having sufficient untapped potential for greater yield that it can justify employees investing time in discovering it.

In the Machine Age management model, the role of improvement is reserved largely for experts. The workforce is considered one of the resources that is "consumed" by the production process. As college students still learn in Economics 101, the point of optimal efficiency is where the difference between resource consumption, cost, and output is the greatest. In this view, the primary source of efficiency is the design of the operating system. The workers' primary role in Machine Age systems is to operate in a reliable, efficient manner so that things run without delay or stoppage.

In sharp contrast, KBOs consider workers as the primary creators of knowledge and innovation. Their activities generate value for customers and revenue for the company in a wide variety of ways—reducing waste, improving processes, increasing efficiency, tinkering with product redesign, and creating new products or services as other sources of organizational revenue. According to this scenario, wages paid to workers, time devoted to reflection, training, and measurement are all viewed as being worthwhile investments in a creative, wealth-generating process.

Essentially, what is regarded as being static and inert in the Machine Age model is seen as dynamic and organic in the knowledge-based paradigm. This paradigm difference is similar to how conventional allopathic medicine and osteopathy view the human cranium. In allopathic medicine, the human skull is viewed as being fixed in form at the time of birth. On the other hand, osteopathic physician Dr. William Garner Sutherland discovered in 1899 that the skull contains bevels much like the gills of a fish—it is flexible. Much of the osteopathic practice of cranial manipulation is based on the use of techniques that exploit the flexible properties of the skull to increase circulation of cerebrospinal fluids that nourish and cleanse the brain and nervous system. Similarly, from a knowledge-based perspective, both workers and an organization's operating systems are viewed as being dynamic and containing large reserves of untapped potential for creating value.

There are no guarantees that every worker, process, and system can be fully activated in ways that contribute to an organization becoming more knowledge based, but there is little doubt that most workers have capabilities for participating in knowledge-based initiatives that far exceed those required by Machine Age models. The path to becoming a pragmatic KBO demands a significant culture shift in most companies. Corporate leaders will need to realize that, while Tayloristic systems gain organizational control, they also severely damage knowledge-creating capabilities. The shift from Tayloristic systems to pragmatic systems will require organizations to make a gradual transformation from an environment of control to one of experimentation.

Pragmatic KBOs are driven by continuous experimentation at every level of the company. Harvard Business School's Stephen Spear

(2004) viewed this change as requiring a qualitative shift in the thinking of leaders. Referencing Toyota, he observed:

It is one thing to realize that the Toyota Production System (TPS) is a system of nested experiments through which operations are continually improved. It is another to have an organization in which employees and managers at all levels in all functions are able to live those principles and teach others to apply them. Decoding the DNA of Toyota doesn't mean that you can replicate it. (p. 80)

For knowledge leaders to emulate the way Toyota and other pragmatic KBOs operate will require a major shift of mind. First, the idea that leaders, managers, and workers can learn or create knowledge without opportunity for reflection and experimentation must be abandoned. Second, all organization members must become skilled at *both* inner and outer knowledge-creating activities. That is, leaders and workers should learn how to design experiments for individuals and groups, and they also must learn how to use those results as surprising facts to disconfirm or support their own beliefs about how things work in practice.

In the next chapter we will discuss how knowledge leaders can ensure the success of knowledge initiatives within the context of their company's existing management systems—which are typically designed to guarantee organizational structure and control, rather than learning and knowledge development.

## REFERENCES

Buckman, R. (2004). *Building a Knowledge-Driven Organization*. New York: McGraw-Hill.

Firestone, J., and McElroy, M. (2003). *Key Issues in the New Knowledge Management*. Burlington, MA: Butterworth-Heinemann (KMCI Press).

Holland, J. (1995). *Hidden Order: How Adaptation Builds Complexity*. Reading, MA: Perseus Books.

Liker, J. (2004). *The Toyota Way*. New York: McGraw-Hill.

Maturana, H., and Varela, F. (1987). *The Tree of Knowledge*. Boston, MA: Shamabala.

McElroy, M. (2003). *The New Knowledge Management*. Burlington, MA: Butterworth-Heinemann (KMCI Press).

Spear, S. (2004, May). "Learning to Lead at Toyota." *Harvard Business Review*, 78–86.

Wiig, K. (2004). *People-Focused Knowledge Management*. Burlington, MA: Butterworth-Heinemann.

# 13

# LEARNING FROM EXPERIENCE: A CASE OF MISTAKEN IDENTITY

## Executive Summary

Knowledge leaders must operate effectively within the context of existing management systems so that they can leverage them to support knowledge initiatives. A *management system* consists of interconnected and interactive management tools, functions, and processes that collectively have the effect of influencing performance as if they were acting as a single entity. There is a natural tension between management systems and the knowledge development process. Management systems are designed to provide structure and control in organizations (external focus), whereas KD has an *inner focus* on creating and improving the quality of knowledge. This chapter examines in depth "A Case of Mistaken Identity"—a real-life story that illustrates the importance of taking an organization's identity into consideration before initiating any changes in strategy. Knowing the identity of a business clarifies what leaders can let go of without significant loss (much like excess fat) and what is vital to organizational success (much like healthy muscle/organs/bone). Organizational identity must be built into an organization's strategies and knowledge initiatives. The case study of GNT also points out natural tensions between corporate *explorers* (who focus on *effectiveness—doing the right things)* and *settlers* (who focus on *efficiency—doing things right*). It is our contention that most organizations fail because they are doing the wrong things quite efficiently.

Those who argue for the importance of leadership in organizations often deal with the subject as if it existed *outside* the context of management processes. In reality, knowledge leaders must operate effectively within the context of management systems so that they can leverage them to support rather than thwart their knowledge initiatives.

A *management system* consists of interconnected and interactive management tools, functions, and processes that collectively have the effect of influencing performance as if they were acting as a single entity. There is a natural tension, and sometimes an incompatibility, between management systems and the process of knowledge development. Management systems, including KM, are designed to provide structure and control in organizations (external focus), whereas KD has an *inner focus* on the creation of personal knowledge. Clearly, the creative forces that produce innovation typically have difficulty flowing easily through the restrictive channels of traditionally designed management systems.

Does this antagonistic relationship between KM and KD sound familiar? It should—because it is much like the dynamic tension between the Yogi and the Commissar. In many ways, the Yogi is the personification of knowledge developers, while the Commissar represents knowledge managers. As we underscored in Part II of *Knowledge Leadership*, the dilemma of the Yogi and the Commissar (much like the dilemma of knowledge developers and knowledge managers) is that each is incomplete without the other, yet they tend to repel each other like oil and water. Is this mutual repulsion a *fait accompli* for businesses that seek to integrate knowledge leadership processes with management systems? Clearly, if we believed that this unfortunate destiny was predetermined, we would not have bothered to write this book. We are encouraged that many companies appear to be well on their way to integrating these two seemingly irreconcilable forces.

Managers usually seek to bring order to chaos by reducing the amount of variation within their companies. In this way, they succeed in achieving greater stability and predictability. Knowledge developers, in contrast, experiment to discover what innovations can improve their organization's performance. These two forces—management and development—are the yin and the yang of organizational life, and *both* are necessary for knowledge leadership.

Many well-established corporations have focused on instituting management controls because they find themselves at such a cost disadvantage to businesses with cheaper labor supply in locales such as China, Mexico, and Poland. Yet pursuing such a management strategy inevitably results in a downward spiral: it shifts the burden for generating profits increasingly *away* from new sources of revenue and *toward* endless cycles of cost reductions. A major problem with reiterative cost cutting is that it often means losing experienced employees, and with them, much of the knowledge that could be turned into innovations.

Once the flow of new innovations slows to a trickle, it is exceedingly challenging for organizations to get the wellspring flowing again. A conversation we had with two business executives reflects the typical dynamic that unfolds when companies rely on cost-cutting measures to save themselves. These two managers recounted how, 5 years before, the former CEO of the company took steps to reduce costs by cutting most of the sources of innovation within the company. At first, it appeared that the strategy had worked. The company's stock price jumped to an all-time high, and the board of directors and some employees viewed the CEO as a hero. However, the two executives believed that the stock price was not an accurate reflection of the company's health. The result seemed too good to be true, and they were quite skeptical. As it turned out, they were right: a few short years later, the company's stock had dropped to a 25-year low. Shares of the company's common stock had plummeted to only 10% of their high price just two years earlier (Figure 13.1).

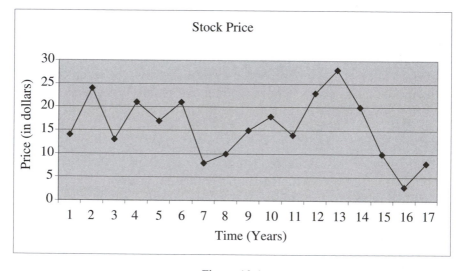

**Figure 13.1**
*Stock Price Changes*

The CEO's strategy began to take a damaging long-term toll on the company's workforce and performance. Many of the company's veteran top managers, who had been comfortable with the innovative culture developed by its founder, left in dismay as the new CEO force-fed a new culture that was foreign to them. The CEO was convinced that profits would rise dramatically once his new strategy to create a high-performing, low-cost, market-driven organization took effect. Instead, chaos and uncertainty reigned as senior managers were replaced with executives who did not understand the organization's culture, operations, or customers. The effects of this shakeup rippled through the company like an earthquake and its aftershocks, leaving disaster in its wake.

During this same time period, the company's two most heavily invested new product development efforts failed to even reach the market. The first product did not even make it out the front door. It was pulled when potential customers resisted the idea of the new technology, even though it was technically superior to the existing platform within the industry. The second product failed just as miserably. Its development process was overseen, at different times, by at least three different vice presidents. The purchasing and manufacturing departments ordered large quantities of custom parts in anticipation of the ramp-up that would be needed after introduction of this new product. Stunningly, the second product ended up coming to the market too late—and at a cost that exceeded the product's selling price! The company took a major financial hit to charge off costs for both failed projects. Morale at the company sunk to an all-time low.

Eventually, as his losses mounted, the CEO resigned under pressure after negotiating a very sizable severance package. The legacy he left behind was the transformation of a previously agile knowledge-creating company with a strong history and a great future into a cost-driven money machine that had unsuccessfully mortgaged its future.

Unfortunately, this kind of business story has become all too common as many executives try to implement simplistic strategies that ignore a company's core—its identity, culture, and legacy. The problem with simple cost-cutting strategies is that this sharp scalpel often surgically removes the very knowledge and innovation from an organization that are vital to its long-term success. The fatal miscalculation by this new CEO was that many of the company's senior executives loved working in an innovative environment where they could try out ideas that would not be tolerated in a more traditional corporation. The loss of so many members of the top management team through resignation and retirement was a fatal brain drain for the company. The knowledge loss of so many senior managers was multiplied when they were replaced by people handpicked by the CEO for their outstanding accomplishments in *other* industries. By the time these new managers got up to speed and began to understand the nuances of this unfamiliar business, the company was on the verge of collapse. Under such circumstances, how can anyone be surprised if the patient dies on the operating table?

An understanding of what is vital to an organization requires that you know the organization's identity—these are the core components of it, what is most essential to it, why it is in business, what has made it successful to date, and what sets its brand apart from competitors. Identity is where knowledge leaders need to begin in the creation of *FAST* KBOs. (In the final chapter of this book, we introduce a unique methodology [5-*Point Dynamic Mapping*®] that will help you design knowledge and other change initiatives that are fully aligned with your company's identity.) Knowing the core identity of a business clarifies what leaders can let go of without significant loss (much like excess fat) and what is vital to organizational success (much like healthy muscle/organs/bone). A common, everyday way to think about clarifying organizational identity is that it is similar to cleaning out your closets by eliminating the clothes that do not fit your tastes or lifestyle. That makes sense. Throwing out your most expensive custom-tailored suits does not.

The Case of Mistaken Identity that follows provides additional details of the corporate decline we have been describing here. In particular, it illustrates why it is so important to take an organization's identity into consideration before initiating any changes. This case (in which all names are changed) representative of many business stories we have witnessed in recent years.

## A Case of Mistaken Identity: Trouble at Great Northeast Technologies

Heinz Bremmer, a brilliant engineer, started Great Northeast Technologies (GNT) during the late 1960s as a company that specialized in producing machine tools for manufacturing companies. Bremmer was known as a prolific inventor. He was a genius when it came to transforming conventional manufacturing technologies into high-tech machines by automating the equipment. He held numerous patents for developing innovative equipment that had revolutionized several industries. To launch GNT, Bremmer brought together an excellent management team—a core group of like-minded engineers and scientists—who believed firmly in his vision of a technology-driven company that could grow by automating the manufacturing processes. Under Bremmer's leadership for 30 years, GNT became the dominant manufacturer of automation for a number of diverse industries, including publishing and healthcare.

GNT had a work hard/play hard culture where engineers, scientists, and inventors ruled the management team. In its early days, the company lived a new-product-to-new-product existence, where growth relied on innovation. Since its business did not involve frequent repeat sales, GNT found that once an industry had been automated with its products, it became necessary to grow by leap-frogging from one industry to the next. Gus Webber, president of GNT's publishing products division, called it "riding the thermals." Webber, who was an accomplished glider pilot, compared GNT's leap-frogging strategy to the way glider pilots catch and ride a column of warm rising air—much as hawks glide at high altitudes on summer mornings when the warming earth creates these thermals. Webber described GNT as a great place to work if you loved to be creative and think outside the box.

GNT's stock price reflected the feast-or-famine nature of its business, fluctuating between $22 and $28 per share during the 1980s and early 1990s. Although GNT was not a darling of Wall Street, it grew steadily. Eventually, it employed more than 5,000 employees worldwide. It seemed that GNT had found a formula for reliable, though not spectacular, growth.

Then everything changed radically. In 1997, Heinz Bremmer suffered a debilitating heart attack at the age of 64. He was hospitalized for several months, then died suddenly at home during his recuperation. GNT, reeling from this devastating blow, found itself directionless without its founder and creative genius. During Bremer's hospitalization and recuperation, GNT ran under the direction of its longtime chief legal counsel, Gordon Gaston. Gaston had been with GNT since the beginning and had been a longtime, trusted friend of Heinz Bremmer. He led the search committee to find a replacement—if that were possible—for a man who had become a legend in his own time. After a lengthy search, GNT announced in May 1999 that its new CEO would be Paul Taylor. Taylor was an engineer with an MBA degree. He had risen during the mid-1990s to be a division president at the international Global Electronics Corporation. Taylor seemed to have the perfect blend of technical expertise and business acumen to fill Heinz Bremmer's large shoes.

However, upon arriving at GNT, one of Taylor's first strategic decisions was to change the direction of the organization. He enjoyed using baseball terminology, saying that "it was too risky to always be looking to hit home runs." He proposed instead that GNT become a company that would make a living by hitting more singles and fewer home runs. This meant that under Taylor's direction, research and development (R&D) and innovation would play a much smaller role at GNT than it had in the past. He decided that GNT was to become a more traditional production-oriented firm. Taylor shocked many longtime GNT managers with his plans to restructure the company. He started by eliminating "unneeded" R&D positions and other "excess waste" in the system. Next, the company trimmed its "fat" by laying off employees and reengineering processes. Profits soared. Numerous Wall Street analysts, who were impressed by Taylor's authoritative direction, endorsed the changes. GNT's stock price rose to an all-time high of $38 per share by the year 2000.

Unfortunately, less than a year later, GNT was in complete chaos. The majority of GNT's longtime senior executives and managers had quit or taken early retirement, creating an enormous brain drain by taking their "intellectual capital" with them. Working under Heinz Bremmer had been fun and a meaningful challenge for them. It just wasn't the same working for Paul Taylor. The harder Taylor pushed to transform GNT into his image of a cost-driven model of manufacturing efficiency, the more GNT employees resisted.

GNT's longtime identity had been based on combining great science and engineering to create innovative products. Taylor's hard-driving strategy of improving production efficiency and profits in any manner possible—whether it fit with GNT's identity or not—put the organization into a tailspin. The temporary forward momentum that had driven up GNT's stock price soon came to a grinding halt. A virtual mutiny among GNT's remaining managers was in the making.

In September 2001, local newspapers reported that Paul Taylor had unexpectedly resigned to "pursue other career options." Knowing that he had lost the support and confidence of GNT's managers and employees, Taylor saw the handwriting on the wall: there no longer was sufficient support within the company to implement his initiatives. In November it was announced that Wayne Daggett, a young vice president at GNT, would be named as the new president of GNT. Surprisingly, Daggett had only several years experience with GNT and never even knew Heinz Bremmer. Many observers asked what would become of GNT's beleaguered culture of rapid scientific innovation under the leadership of a new president from the financial side of the operation.

By March 2002, GNT's stock price had sunk to a new low of $3.12 per share. Much of the decline in the price could be attributed to the slumping economy and the post–national crisis (9/11) economic decline. However, GNT's common stock was now far below every critic's worst predictions. By May of 2002, GNT's remaining R&D staff had been centralized into a new division of the company that was charged with developing products for new markets. This innovation crew started afresh with few resources and even less support from GNT's top management. However, many members of this crew were the remaining true believers in Bremmer's broad-based organization-wide innovation approach, and they hoped that they would now have the chance to prove their worth by saving the company from further deterioration.

By fall of 2002, the leaders of the new innovation division realized that they were canoeing upstream without a paddle. One of the heads of this division described the organization's conflict as follows: "It resembles a civil war or a religious persecution. I believe that the basis for the conflict arises from culture, style, methodology, and risk. We explorers are considered by the others to be the high rollers, big risk takers, and the home-run hitters. On the other hand, the settlers, as they are known here, are satisfied (to extend the baseball metaphor) with hitting singles. Settlers think of risk as being a four-letter word." The question for GNT at this crisis point was: Could explorers and settlers peacefully coexist in an organization that was once led and dominated by explorers but was now being led and dominated by settlers?

## AN ANALYSIS OF GNT'S PROBLEMS

First, it is important to translate the metaphors used by GNT's staff into direct operational terms. *Explorers* are defined here as people who identify and develop new processes, products, and problem-solving innovations that focus on *effectiveness*. Effectiveness means *doing the right things*. Effectiveness is the result of creating new knowledge and applying it to practice in an ill-defined situation. *Settlers* are defined here as people who focus on exploiting existing products/markets through *efficiency*. Efficiency means *doing things right*—it is mainly driven by precisely applying existing knowledge to a known situation.

We would like to underscore that most organizations fail due to ineffectiveness, not inefficiency. *In other words, most organizations fail because they are doing the wrong things quite efficiently.* They have not deliberately crafted a strategy that supports their identity—one that would allow them to become more effective by building on their strongest qualities (for example, the factors that set them apart in their market). Instead, most companies avoid dealing with the complexities of creating internal growth by further exploiting existing products/markets or by acquiring existing firms in desirable markets.

## A STRATEGIC VIEW

Any debate over the relative merits of the respective roles of explorers and settlers is misplaced. It is like asking the question, which does one need more—hands or feet? Clearly, the answer is that *both* settlers and explorers are necessary for the sustainable performance of the company. However, a key question remains: How will the business create new growth opportunities?

At the simplest level, there are two approaches to organizational growth—that is, *internal-* or *external*-oriented growth strategies. Internal growth strategies can include (1) *market development* (seeking new market segments), (2) *deeper market penetration* in existing markets to increase market share, and (3) *applications development* (such as creating products that supply needed disposable products, like film for a camera).

Decisions about corporate growth strategies often depend on the traditions and norms to which people have become accustomed. Many companies continue to deal with future growth opportunities by emphasizing settlement activities (production and efficiency) and avoiding exploratory activities. Unfortunately, as organizations become larger and increasingly risk averse, they tend to lose their agility and increasingly rely on growing through acquisition and strategic partnerships, such as joint ventures.

Once a firm has embarked on a settlement-oriented strategy, it is difficult to turn back or even coexist with exploratory strategies. This is because managers start viewing exploratory activities as unnecessary costs that detract from the firm's production efficiency. In other words, market penetration and development, as well as acquisition and joint ventures, are considered acceptable substitutes for exploratory activity. While growth is an indispensable component of an organization's long-term health and success, exploration is still regarded by most traditionally managed companies as a highly inefficient means to that end.

One thing is certain: organizational performance that is exclusively driven by such "settlement" activities is unsustainable. It is better for business viability to include a mix of both growth strategies. Possible corporate growth activities include a full spectrum of options that range from avoiding exploratory activity altogether (settlement activity supplemented with growth through acquisitions) all the way to what is referred to by William Miller and Langdon Morris (2002) as *fourth-generation R&D*—where exploratory innovation activity is paramount, decentralized, and widely spread throughout a company.

Happily, there are many successful international companies that are demonstrating the viability of achieving business growth by risking exploration and innovation. Oftentimes these companies have developed a strong culture based on a clear sense of identity that supports innovation. In Japan, corporate identity is considered to be a critical factor that executives must understand in order to manage effectively. In the United States there is a greater spirit of individualism that dominates corporate cultures. Indeed, American companies tend to place a much greater emphasis on attracting star executives who have a proven track record of high performance elsewhere. The high salaries of top executives in North American can be attributed in part to the bidding wars between companies who are competing to attract these high-profile managers. In Japan, such bidding wars are unnecessary because executives tend to commit to their companies for life. Moreover, their managers have relatively less influence than their American counterparts because changes in Japanese companies are determined not by force of individual will, but more by the collective will of employees, in harmony with the existing corporate culture.

## ORGANIZATIONAL SELF-IMAGE

The idea of self-image, self-concept, and self-identity all are well known within the field of psychology. Self-image is one's mental notion of one's own physical, emotional, and thinking attributes, such as attitudes, beliefs, and values. Self-image is learned through experience, and it is related to the cultural norms that the person most values. In a similar vein, an organization's self-image is the shared or collective notion of what its members perceive its identity to be. Organizational self-image is often difficult for people to construct in their minds because it is not associated with a specific face, body, style of speaking, and other symbols that more clearly define an individual's identity. Nonetheless, there are many artifacts and symbols that reflect an organization's identity: for example, what the company values, why it is in business, what traits and core competencies set it apart from its competitors, what kind of working culture it has, how employees are treated, what activities and behaviors are rewarded and which are punished, how the organization competes, which markets it competes within, and how willingly its leaders take risks.

The challenge for a knowledge leader is to help the company consciously refine and redefine its identity while simultaneously helping it adapt within a changing environment. Intel CEO Andrew Grove (2004) has compared the process of transforming organizational identity to jumping from one mountain peak to another through a "valley of death." Guiding a company through identity shifts requires leaders with great self-confidence and considerable respect for and understanding of the company's identity. The discussion that follows is a brief summary of the successful identity shaping (and reshaping) that Grove has done at Intel.

---

## Transforming Intel's Identity

Since the early 1980s, Andrew Grove has led Intel through two major transformations that were driven by a radical transformation of the company's strategy and its identity. Intel's core business, since the early 1980s, was in manufacturing computer memory chips for PCs. By the mid-1980s, Intel was faced with the onslaught of cutthroat pricing from Japanese chip makers. Despite Intel's best efforts to reduce costs and differentiate its product through heavy R&D spending, Intel's future looked bleak. At this point, Grove decided to transform Intel into a leading manufacturer of microprocessors for PCs. Opting to take a $173 million write-off to withdraw from the memory chip business, he launched the transition for Intel to become a microprocessor manufacturer. The company enjoyed spectacular success with establishing its brand name and image ("Intel Inside") in this emerging market. By 2001, over 80% of PCs contained Intel microprocessors. By the late 1990s, the PC market began to mature and sales started to level off as most households already owned at least one PC. To continue its outstanding growth, by 1998 Grove started leading Intel to the next mountain peak. This time Grove sought to define Intel as a component supplier to the industries being driven by the Internet. At this point, Intel launched a major new effort that expanded its capacity to serve industries that were bound to the Internet's burgeoning growth. Grove's initiatives to move Intel into closer alignment with Internet-related industries included creating Intel's Internet Health Day, a ground-breaking conference where 400 physicians and healthcare industry leaders explored how consumers, using their home PCs and the Internet, can improve their access to health information, products, and services. Intel's cosponsors were the American Medical Association and the American Academy of Pediatrics.

Seivert and colleagues (1996) described how vital identity is to the process of learning, adaptation, and survival in both organizations and living organisms. Their definition of organizational identity is an organic one, based on biologists Humberto Maturana and Francisco Varela's (1987) groundbreaking work on self-organizing systems. In their writings, these two noted biologists describe a process known as *autopoiesis* that drives the evolutionary development of self-organization by continually referencing that system's identity. According to Maturana and Varela, any autonomous system adapts to changes around it by learning. (Here, *learning* means making adjustments to its structure so that it successfully maintains its identity while responding to environmental pressures.)

Many of the most serious chronic problems in organizations can be traced to a lack of clarity about identity among leaders and executives. In many cases, a well-defined organizational identity may never have been formulated. Problems with confused identity are most visible in mergers and takeovers, where either or both parties are unclear as to the identity of the new organization. In American businesses, identity is viewed very differently than it is in Asian companies. For example, at Toyota, the thought of bringing in a top executive from outside the company is incomprehensible, while in American companies it is quite common. At Toyota it is believed that leaders must deeply understand the Toyota culture and demonstrate that they fully appreciate how to operate within its subtleties. Second, they need to fully comprehend the details of the operation so that they can make decisions with confidence. In contrast, American CEOs are expected to be strong leaders who shape the organization's way of doing things to fit their own individual vision of the future.

Andrew Grove (2003) offered a more balanced view of this leadership challenge when he argued that it is easier to get the support of an organization's members for your initiatives if you have been there a long time and employees believe that "this is your baby—that what you're interested in is in the interest of the organization," and also that your life "is interwoven with the company" (p. 1). Clearly, as the preceding example illustrates, this thoughtful approach to deliberately crafting corporate identity has worked wonders at Intel.

In some companies, the organization's identity is carefully shaped over many years and its preservation is viewed as being a collective responsibility that takes precedence over the vision of any one leader. Here, identity is built into and perceived by the organization's strategies. In some businesses, however, identity is closely controlled and guarded by a select few who "inform" other members of the organization what their core values and beliefs will be. Here, an organization's identity can morph frequently, with changing leaders and their changing strategies. The issue of identity is particularly relevant to an organization's knowledge-processing activities because exclusivity in defining identity, shaping culture, and controlling power will dramatically limit the types of knowledge-creating strategies that are viable in that organization. Another way to view organizational identity and knowledge strategies is through the lens of systems thinking.

## A Systems Thinking View

As companies rely increasingly on production efficiency to increase short-term returns, what Peter Senge (1990) has called a "shifting the burden" syndrome takes over and governs future performance dynamics. This is partly because an agile, exploration-driven strategy requires either a powerful visionary leader or a highly cohesive team that is strongly committed to achieving a common vision. A production-efficiency-driven strategy is much easier to implement. However, it offers fewer long-term strategic advantages. It is easy to see how a company can slip into the "nonknowledge" trap of becoming an efficient machine rather than an innovation-driven company. Innovation requires the creation of new knowledge, whereas efficiency results from applying old knowledge with precision. Understandably, as corporate profits slip and a sense of desperation grows, leaders tend to favor short-term expediency over fundamental solutions. A vicious downward cycle begins because fundamental solutions are perceived as being too slow in producing desired effects, too speculative, and relatively uncontrollable.

In Figure 13.2, the *problem symptom* that most managers usually address in these difficult circumstances is that of declining profits. The *symptomatic solution* (one that addresses only the symptoms of the problem and not its underlying cause) is the manager's decision to focus on reducing costs and increasing efficiency. The improved results and attention directed to cost-cutting obscure the manager's view of a subtle but more *fundamental solution* to increase the rate of innovation. Due to normal time delays between investments in innovation and the realization of results, this fundamental solution will take some time, and the outcome of this strategy is more uncertain.

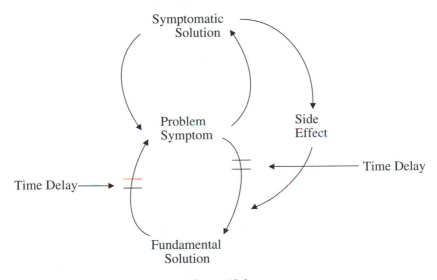

**Figure 13.2**
*Shifting the Burden Syndrome*

The unintended, and often unseen, side effect of the symptomatic solution is a reduction in the company's innovation capacity. Given declining profits, many managers consider it impractical and untimely to fund innovation activities. Unfortunately, under these deteriorating conditions the organization's capacity for innovation continues to atrophy. It becomes increasingly impractical to initiate an innovation strategy at any point in the future because the barriers have become greater than ever. These barriers to innovation are both *systemic* and *nonsystemic*. Systemic barriers to innovation include uncertain performance outcomes, difficulty controlling the process, and relatively long payback periods on funds invested. The nonsystematic barriers include the loss of organizational memory and expertise about how to effectively perform innovation as top talent and experienced employees jump ship or are forced out. This makes innovation an even more unattractive option to worried executives.

In the "shifting the burden" syndrome, the burden for keeping the company afloat typically has been shifted to a symptomatic solution that is not sustainable because—unless the company has a distinctive competency in being a low-cost leader—competitors will easily find similar ways to reduce costs. In truth, the long-term sustainability of a business depends *both* on the ability of the business to continue doing what it already does well (exploitation) and its ability to find a new supply of things to do well (exploration). Interestingly, in the long run, both activities are interdependent and contingent on each other for success. That is, exploration of new products/markets and exploitation of existing products/markets have a reinforcing relationship. Unfortunately, the reinforcing relationships between the processes of exploration and exploitation typically have extremely long time delays, and this commonly results in misperception of dynamics and a missing of potential leverage points. Exploitation capitalizes on *what already is*—it depends on a system stock with definable limits (for example, limits to potential market size or limits to potential customer spending). Exploration capitalizes on *what could be*. Both exploration and exploitation, by themselves, are not self-sustaining strategies.

All sustainable businesses require the ability to both *create* opportunities and to *capitalize* on them. Thus, businesses need to keep a dynamic balance between create/explore activities *and* exploit/capitalize activities. An over-reliance on capitalizing (exploitative) activity to increase short-term returns produces a dependence on those activities as it simultaneously reduces the company's exploratory (creative) capacity. The long-term cumulative effect of shifting the burden is that as exploratory capacity and breakthroughs decline, a significant shift occurs in the mental model of executives. They no longer understand the interdependence of these activities. Instead, they start to see exploratory activities as costly and unpredictable, particularly when they compare them to the short-term gains of exploitative activities.

Settlement-oriented activities, over time, deplete the stock of existing customers. The level of the stock declines in response to usage, competitive effects, influences of substitute products, and product life cycle maturation. New stocks must be created to ensure future growth. How that is done is a function of corporate strategy. Can explorers and settlers coexist? Yes, they probably can. The only requirement for them to do so is that the firm fulfill the functions of both growth and utilization. If the corporate strategy focuses only on nonexploratory approaches to growth, then explorers will be viewed as expendable.

So now we can return to the question with which we began: Can explorers and settlers coexist in an organization that was once led and dominated by explorers, but is now led and dominated by settlers?

First, note it has been 40 years since GNT was founded. Its problems did not occur overnight. Solving its current problems requires some people to stay for a long time. Only then can corporate leaders have a complete perspective—that is, know what things were like near the beginning, how they are now, and understand how they got to be this way. From this longer view, we can see that explorers become less prevalent over time at GNT, and settlers become more numerous. In the beginning, the company was composed largely of explorers—we will refer to them from this point forward as *developers*. Then, these developers migrated to the company's production function rather than leave the company. These same developers also comprised all the producers when GNT's production first began. Slowly, as the developers invented new products, the company hired more producers from the outside. So the company is still populated by many people who are either developers or who have been developers in the past. However, as the company continues to succeed, the ratio of developers to producers drops markedly. Figure 13.3 depicts how the relative ratio of developers to producers shifts over time in the firm.

As the ratio of developers to producers declines, the developers' influence on decision making decreases, and the influence of the newly hired producers increases. The longest-term developers remember when their group dominated decisions, and naturally they want to return to that level of influence. The outside-hired producers can't remember any value for the developers; they're too new to the company. So the problem is more about the declining prevalence of a group of people within a company than it is about survival of the fittest.

There are plenty of successful companies where firms have remained successful by having a large part of their activity devoted to exploration: Bausch & Lomb, Kodak, and Xerox, to name a few. But in many other cases, businesses have a natural technology cycle. Compaq eats DEC, HP eats Compaq, and so on. Then leaders have a completely new set of very complex problems that result from trying to integrate two diverse cultures—with distinctly different identities—into one. What about companies that don't settle for a

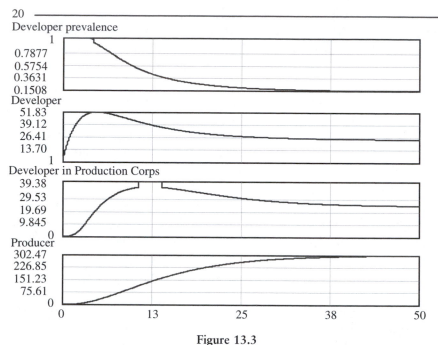

**Figure 13.3**
*Shifting Ratios of Developers to Producers*
*Developed by James P. Thompson (2004), Global Prospectus Corp,*
*jim@globalprospectus.com*

settlement growth strategy? IBM and 3M are two examples from disparate industries. They continually reinvent themselves. So returning to GNT: Is it inevitable that GNT fades away? No. But the chances of the older developers (explorers) ever regaining their collective voice within the company are small—unless the producers (settlers) realize that great opportunities lie in knowledge development for future innovative products.

## REFLECTIONS ON GNT

Replacing a legendary founder and corporate CEO is *always* a monumental task. To preserve the identity and long-term success of any organization requires thoughtful, proactive succession planning—and particularly in the case of such a charismatic leader. When the GNT board of directors were suddenly thrown into searching for a replacement for Heinz Bremmer, they did not take GNT's identity into consideration. Their ideal candidate was an experienced executive from a well-established firm who could introduce to GNT the strategies and processes of large corporations. Rather than build on the unique corporate identity and culture that Heinz Bremmer had developed at GNT, the search committee assumed that GNT's relatively small size was a negative feature. Like so many smaller and medium-sized companies, the board members wanted to play in the big leagues, so they hired a CEO who they thought could get them there. Ultimately, however, GNT's longtime, well-established identity and corporate culture were the hidden forces that forced a stalemate and precipitated Paul Taylor's resignation.

The first mistake Taylor made was that he failed to assess GNT's identity and culture of innovation. He completely underestimated its strength. In fact, aside from GNT's fine reputation in the marketplace, its greatest asset was its storehouse of intellectual capital that included proprietary processes, patents, and a dedicated workforce of scientists and engineers. Ironically, Taylor viewed GNT as being asset poor, as opposed to understanding that, from a knowledge standpoint, it was asset rich. Taylor's second mistake was to overlay a strategy of efficient production without innovation on a corporate culture that had long been focused on effective innovation and product development. Taylor's third mistake was to mortgage the company's future by undermining its potential for continued learning. He reduced staff to temporarily boost profits. This cost-cutting measure removed any slack from the system that could have enabled employees to learn from experience, as they had been doing all along. Instead, it forced employees into a mode of efficient, but mindless, production. Although GNT had many elements of a KBO already baked into it, its potential for success was systematically deconstructed under Taylor's direction. Sadly, Taylor was only doing what most managers have been trained to do. He was simply implementing the prevailing management paradigms that are still rooted in outdated science (and very little art).

In the next chapter of *Knowledge Leadership,* we will discuss how knowledge leaders can address the significant challenge of balancing knowledge and management systems in their organizations.

## REFERENCES

Grove, A. (2003). In an interview with Kiechel, W., "Andy Grove on Confident Leaders," *Working Knowledge for Business Leaders*, April 14, Harvard Business School, Cambridge, MA, http://hbswk.hbs.edu/item.jhtml?id=3419&t=innovation.

Maturana, H., and Varela, F. (1987). *The Tree of Knowledge.* Boston, MA: Shambala.

Miller, W., and Morris, L. (2002). *Fourth Generation R&D.* New York: John Wiley & Sons.

Seivert, S., Pattakos, A., Reed, F., and Cavaleri, S. (1996). "Learning from the Core." In Cavaleri, S., and Fearon, D. (1996). *Managing in Organizations That Learn.* Cambridge, MA: Blackwell Business Books.

Senge, P. (1990). *The Fifth Discipline.* New York: Doubleday/Currency.

# 14

# BALANCING KNOWLEDGE AND MANAGEMENT SYSTEMS

## Executive Summary

Management systems serve a different purpose than knowledge does. The purpose of management systems is *instrumental*—(simply, to get the work done) rather than *experimental*. Knowledge leadership is largely an indirect *experimental* process that operates on *instrumental* processes. It is our contention that instrumental management processes should be the product of (experimental) knowledge processes. In this chapter we describe the *Knowledge Leadership Life Cycle*, that shows how responsibility for redesigning an organization's systems shifts over time from people with outside knowledge to people with inside knowledge (which is generally more pragmatic and of higher quality). Knowledge leadership needs to become the *central function in both management systems and knowledge management systems*. Experimentation and performance are mirror images of the instrumental and experimental functions. In concurrent learning systems, *the same people* do the work of exploitation and exploration. By filling a dual role (leading people to a vision and being a system designer), a knowledge leader will move to the center of both general management systems and KM systems. A tool for accomplishing this is the *Policy Synchronization Method*. The basic elements of a management system are composed of the essential managerial tools of any business, for example, culture, leadership, infrastructure (rules and procedures), strategy, and structure. Leadership is the managerial tool that unifies and integrates the other elements of a management system.

As we mentioned in the previous chapter, knowledge leadership is not practiced in a vacuum. Rather, it occurs within the rich context of a management system. To reiterate, a *management system* consists of interconnected and interactive management tools, functions, and processes that collectively have the effect of influencing performance as if they were acting as a single entity. Clearly, practicing any knowledge-based activity, such as KM, knowledge processing, and KD cannot be separated from the larger context of the organization's existing management processes. The explanation for this is simple. Most companies are designed around the myriad management processes that are necessary to convert labor, information, raw materials, and technology into some sort of value-added product or service. For example, a furniture manufacturer combines wood, fabric, and metal (such as brackets and screws) into furniture. A system of management processes integrates the organization's resources so that they are all aligned to achieve a particular set of goals. Within this context, knowledge is generally viewed as a means to facilitate greater efficiency or effectiveness in these other processes. Knowledge is the product of reflective action, experimentation, reasoning, and social interaction in organizations. It arises from doing work that is interwoven into the management systems.

Management processes and systems serve a different purpose than knowledge does. The purpose of management systems is *instrumental*, rather than *experimental*. By instrumental, we mean that they are a means to achieve an end, simply, they are designed to get the work done. On the other hand, when something is experimental, it is intended to test or discover a principle through action. You may ask: Is leadership instrumental? Of course it is, but it operates in a much more indirect manner than management processes and systems. As we can now see, knowledge leadership is largely an indirect *experimental* process that operates on *instrumental* processes. In most traditional businesses, direct instrumental processes are typically valued as being more fundamentally important than indirect experimental processes. This prevailing business attitude is a significant challenge for knowledge leaders. Must knowledge always play second fiddle to instrumental processes? In a practical sense, this is largely a political issue in most organizations. McElroy (2003) has made a convincing argument that *instrumental processes should be the product of knowledge processes*. This raises a fascinating chicken-and-egg question. On the basis of what knowledge should a company design its first operating system? Operating systems include any process directly associated with providing a product or service.

Undoubtedly, the original design of an organization's operating system should come from the best source of knowledge available at the time (this source of knowledge may be the company founder, expert consultants, or employees with special expertise). What is critical for the evolution of the system is that the initial "brilliant design" of the operating system be viewed as only the first step in a long continual process of system redesign and improvement. Over time, as more knowledge is developed, the redesign process should gradually shift from the original system designers toward knowledge leaders, and it should increasingly mirror the insights that employees have gained through operational experience. Here now, we see that a *knowledge leadership life cycle* model emerges in which the responsibility for redesigning and improving an organization's systems gradually shifts over time from people with outside knowledge to people with inside knowledge of the system. Figure 14.1 depicts the pattern by which this shift most often occurs.

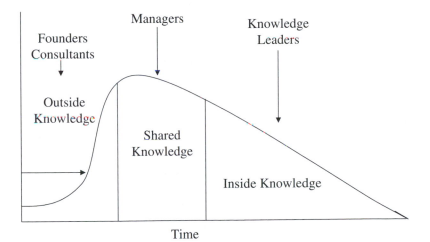

**Figure 14.1**
*Knowledge Leadership Life Cycle*

As Figure 14.1 illustrates, there is a gradual shift in the way the system is redesigned and improved from first relying on founders and expert consultants, then relying on managers, and over time relying on internal knowledge leaders. It is a key point to note that knowledge leaders create an experimental process by which operating employees can participate in ongoing improvement efforts. The goal of the knowledge leadership cycle is to continually improve the quality of knowledge used both for the operation *and* the redesign of the system. Essentially, this later knowledge is qualitatively different that the knowledge used in the earlier design and operation of the system. The major difference is that the latter is based on outside knowledge, whereas the knowledge used for the ongoing design efforts is what Fearon and Cavaleri (2005) termed "inside knowledge." They proposed that inside knowledge is generally more pragmatic than outside knowledge, and thus of higher quality.

## Improving Knowledge Quality

Most leaders recognize that a company's strategy, structure, and technology influence how knowledge is used within that organization. Interestingly, knowledge leadership can also influence the operation of an organization's management system by providing a flow of new knowledge to leaders who can, in turn, use these insights to improve the management system and overall performance. We argue that knowledge leadership should be the *central function in both management systems and KM systems*. Knowledge leaders are responsible for obtaining or developing knowledge that defines situations and creates a vision that is compelling to followers. In both management systems and KM systems, the knowledge leadership function is similar to the role of the composer and conductor of a symphony.

A composer creates music by combining melody, harmony, and rhythm into an integrated whole. The symphony conductor facilitates performance of this music by interpreting the composition, coordinating practices with the musicians, inspiring them to give a great performance, then keeping all the moving parts together during opening night. The musical composition, when completed, is a fixed piece. It is performed in a relatively similar manner whether the Berlin, London, New York, or Tokyo Philharmonic Orchestra is performing.

Much as with a finished composition, traditional management systems are not usually thought of as works in progress. And just as no mechanism is in place to redesign compositions based on how the musicians think it should be performed, few companies ask employees for their opinions on how the management systems should "perform." This is where KM and KD part company. At KBOs, there are continuous processes in place to *reinvent the means* by which performance is achieved. Here the human experience of performing is used to provide a foundation for reconsidering (1) how the performance should be done and (2) what means should be used to best achieve the envisioned performance.

The challenge for knowledge leaders is that the experimental processes within a business must somehow peacefully coexist with the performance-driven processes. More than a century ago, Charles Sanders Peirce recognized this dynamic tension between the two opposing forces of experimentation (inquiry) and performance. As noted in Figure 14.2, these two forces are mirror images of the instrumental and experimental functions. Balance is achieved when management systems operate in whatever way managers, leaders, and employees consider ideal. When they do not operate in this manner, then doubt arises, which sets off a process of inquiry and experimentation—until a new resolution is achieved that works well enough in practice to assuage the irritation of doubt.

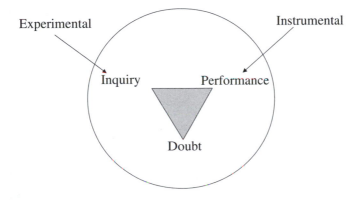

**Figure 14.2**
*Balancing Forces: Inquiry and Performance*

As Peter Senge (1990a) stated, "Nothing undermines openness more surely than certainty. Once we feel as if we have 'the answer,' all motivation to question our thinking disappears" (p. 281). In Peirce's model, people tend to stay in a performing mode as long as their actions produce the expected results. If he were still alive, he might argue that as long as you continue to double your return on investment each year by investing in the stock market, then you will continue to invest in the same way. However, if you perceive that your actions are no longer reliable in producing the outcomes you seek, then you are likely to shift to an inquiry mode (to dampen your growing irritation of doubt over how things are really working in practice). If you begin losing confidence in your investment strategy, you may address this gnawing feeling of doubt by researching other investment strategies. Or you may simply modify your current strategy and experiment with some variations to it. If your inquiry produces a new, more effective investment strategy, or if it produces an explanation about why your current strategy was less effective than you had hoped, then you are likely to shift back to a performing mode. In organizations, the same performance-inquiry dynamics hold true. However, these dynamics are more complex, due to the effects of time delays between inquiry and the implementation of new strategies or solutions (Figure 14.3).

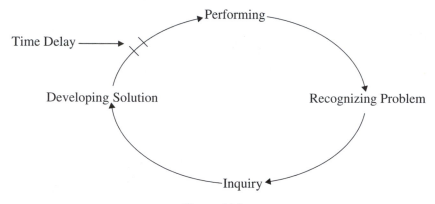

**Figure 14.3**
*Performance-Inquiry Loop*

In most companies, not only are there long delays between inquiry efforts and restoration of performance, but often there are also serious disconnects between problem recognition and the start of inquiry processes. The reason for this disconnect is that many corporations rely on brilliant design strategies and do not have ongoing inquiry efforts, such as KD systems, in place. Even businesses with ongoing knowledge-creating, organizational learning, or performance improvement processes in place can experience long delays in getting their processes aligned with problems. This, in part, explains why a new generation of organizations has arisen that engages in *parallel processing* where inquiry and performance systems operate simultaneously. This is one of the reasons that Toyota's system of continuous experimentation and improvement, coupled with organizational learning, has proven so powerful.

Charles O'Reilly and Michael Tushman (2004) of Stanford and Harvard Universities, respectively, proposed the need for *ambidextrous organizations* to deal with this type of problem. They observed:

Some companies have actually been quite successful at both exploiting the present and exploring the future . . . they separate their new, exploratory units from their traditional, exploitive ones, allowing for different processes, structures, and cultures, at the same time they maintain tight links across units at the senior executive level. In other words, they manage organizational separation through a tightly integrated senior team. (pp. 77–78)

O'Reilly and Tushman cited Gannett Corporation, publishers of *USA Today,* and the optometric device manufacturer Ciba-Giegy (Novartis) as examples of companies that have successfully used this ambidextrous approach.

While the ambidextrous approach appears to be a step in the right direction, it falls short of the pragmatic approach to knowledge that we propose in this book. It is a basic principle of pragmatism that innovation will flow from a learning process that links past feedback from experience, knowledge, and reasoning to create new, different knowledge. While much of pragmatic knowledge processing is of a routine nature, yielding only marginal changes in knowledge, it also sets the stage for improvements to knowledge gained through the reasoning processes known as *induction* and *abduction*. Inductions are generalizations from many specific cases of experience that enable us to create new rules for action. On the other hand, abduction enables us to create new explanations for how and why things work as they do in practice. It is the form of reasoning that often provides the most innovative means of creating new knowledge to be found within pragmatism. However, the most powerful approach is to synergistically use all of the major forms of reasoning—deduction, induction, and abduction—to improve or create knowledge.

From the pragmatic perspective, knowledge becomes the fuel that drives innovation forward in sometimes evolutionary (and at other times discontinuous) ways. In pragmatic knowledge-creating companies, innovation is tightly connected with continuous improvement and problem-solving processes that derive from the everyday operational experiences of rank-and-file employees. For example, the Toyota system manages to effectively link ongoing efforts to exploit current businesses with continuous improvement and learning. This system employs what Cavaleri and Fearon (1994) defined as a *concurrent learning system.*

In concurrent learning systems, *the same people* do the work of exploitation and exploration, because one drives the other in a synergistic manner. Of course, this means that production workers are less productive in meeting output goals, but such productivity goals become meaningless because it is like comparing apples and oranges in two completely different kinds of production systems. In traditional production systems, virtually no new knowledge is created and innovation is rare. Gary Hamel (2000) noted this tradeoff dynamic between efficiency and innovation: "In the years ahead, we must build companies that are as full of radical innovation as they are of diligent optimization. There can be no either/or here, there must be an *and*" (p. 25).

In pragmatic operating systems, the dynamic tension between exploration/exploitation and performance/inquiry are correctly coupled, and they have the potential to drive new KD processes in unprecedented ways. The tendency in most companies is to notice the high productivity of traditional production systems, but completely ignore the ways that such systems hinder knowledge creation and innovation. Where, for example, do knowledge creation and innovation show up on corporate income statements? Tools such as Kaplan and Norton's (1996) Balanced Scorecard and the Skandia Navigator System described by Edvinsson and Malone (1997) are attempts to finally account for such dysfunctional business imbalances.

## THE MISSING LINK: PRAGMATIC KNOWLEDGE

Today, many managers unwittingly fall into the trap of myopically focusing on traditional productivity performance measures that were appropriate for the Machine Age, and ignoring the link between inquiry and performance. Ironically, the managers who overlook this link often regard themselves as pragmatic, by which they mean hard-nosed, bottom-line-oriented people. This is understandable, as they assume that their performance measures are valid—that they provide a true picture of reality. Moreover, these managers are typically under considerable pressure from their superiors to deliver results based on these same "valid" performance measurements. It therefore is a great challenge for managers to see things in a fresh way, one that might lead to greater success for the entire organization—not just their one part of it. As an illustration of this principle, take just a moment to decide which one of the following two management systems would be more valuable to an organization.

1. A system that employs 100 production workers who produce 48,000 units per year?

2. A system that employs 100 production workers who produce 24,000 units per year, reduces costs by 20% annually, raises quality by 2% annually, and retools the system for changes that have the potential to cut production time in half?

Obviously, there are not enough facts available in this example to answer the question definitively. However, it does illustrate our point that reliance on simple, local level metrics may provide incentives for managers to undervalue knowledge-creation activities and trade them off for shorter-term performance.

Going back to our definition of *FAST* KBOs, a company's performance needs to be functional, sustainable, adaptive, and timely. Sometimes, combining KD activities with production activities may not be efficient or *timely*, but it may be *functional* because processes are continually being refined and improved. For example, if the strategic planning process is handled in a conventional way, both learning and knowledge-creation processes are usually regarded only as pleasant afterthoughts. By contrast, in various knowledge-based planning approaches (such as Russell Ackoff's Interactive Planning method or the scenario-based planning methods advocated by Arie DeGeus at Royal Dutch Shell), learning and knowledge are considered to be on a par with the planning process itself.

Similarly, some types of corporate structures facilitate higher levels of interaction among employees and create an environment where sharing knowledge is more likely to occur. Knowledge activities and processes also occur within the context of informal workplace settings, such as communities of practice. There is growing attention being paid, for example, to how an organization's culture significantly influences knowledge-based activities and processes. In one Fortune 500 company for which we consulted, we asked the president why managers did not collaborate better and share knowledge. His answer was that the company's culture was based on intense competition among the various departments. He said, "We are all fighter pilots here who are trying to shoot each other down each day. To the victors go the spoils. That's how we allocate resources here." The notion of collaboration and knowledge sharing was a foreign concept in this company.

Cornell University professor Craig Lundberg (1996) captured the essence of how an organization's culture influences learning when he stated that "Organization culture both fuels and fosters learning in organizations" (p. 507). Researcher, Dvora Yanow proposed that knowledge is inextricably bound to a company's culture because most knowledge gained through experience is contextual, local knowledge that arises from employees performing over time. Yanow and colleague Scott Cook (1993) studied the organizational cultures of three high-quality flute manufacturers in the musical instrument business. They noted that all three flute makers, Wm. S. Haynes, Verne Q. Powell Flutes, and Brannen Brothers, make flutes in slightly different ways that cause them to have a "unique and unambiguously recognizable style." Their research also discovered that even when long-time, highly skilled production workers left one of these companies, its unique style endured. The researchers attributed this enduring quality to the persistent effects of the cultures in these respective companies. According to Richard Seel (2004) of New Paradigm Consulting, strategy and culture often interact in ways that have the following effects:

- A change in strategy is effectively a change in the governing story that an organization tells about itself.
- If the strategy is to be effective, everyone in the organization needs to be retelling that story, adapting it to their own circumstances.
- If people are to tell different stories, they need to be able to have different conversations.
- Since culture is what we call the emergent result of all the conversations and stories that take place in an organization, the culture will inevitably change if new stories and conversations take place.
- Most attempts to change strategy founder because there is no "space," "permission," or "capability" for new stories and conversations to take place.

Yanow and Cook (1993) also studied how technology influences knowledge processing by forcing employees to degrade the richness of the local knowledge they had gained via experience into unnatural forms that were mandated to fit the requirements of their company's KM technologies. They wrote:

The design and development of electronic technologies, for example, often result in products that are not (or not easily) usable in work settings, leading to arguments for collaborative or participatory design processes that would incorporate end users' local knowledge of work practices relevant to the technology in question. Designers are typically not managers, and yet they exhibit the same disinclination to draw on local knowledge as the managers in the three case stories. Neither managerial pride nor an aversion to story-telling appear to explain well the attitudes of engineers in such situations. (p. 394)

Such technocratic myopia stems from several sources: (1) expedi-ency, (2) an ignorance of the potentially degrading effects technolo-gies can have on knowledge, and (3) the tendency among system designers to define knowledge from an information-based perspec-tive. This should not be a surprising result, as most KM system designers are trained to deal with knowledge as an extension of infor-mation systems. They are not social scientists or managers who view knowledge as being experiential, situated in communities of practice, and culturally anchored. Clearly, knowledge processes and learning occur within the context of a larger management system, and both KM systems and KD processes are embedded in this milieu. What is the role of knowledge leadership, when so much of what passes for knowledge in organizations is adulterated, engineered, controlled, and changed to force-fit it within the limitations of KM technology?

## PUTTING KNOWLEDGE LEADERSHIP AT THE CENTER

Paradoxically, in such tightly designed systems, knowledge leader-ship must move to the center of both general management systems and KM systems. The rationale for our placing knowledge leadership at the nexus of these systems is simple: successful businesses depend on pragmatic knowledge to reliably take effective action. Pragmatic knowledge is the bedrock that will serve as the foundation for inno-vation, problem solving, and performance-improvement initiatives. Since pragmatic knowledge is the product of relatively sophisticated continuous human processes of experiencing and experimenting, it cannot be easily synthesized or put into a routine process and thus requires leadership to assure its nurturance in the face of competing business needs.

Knowledge leadership has a dual role that incorporates the two distinctly different threads that characterize leadership theory in general. The first role is that *leadership is a process of influencing people toward a goal or ideal future vision.* When it comes to knowl-edge, leadership often means reframing the meaning of human experience. As Max DePree (1989), former CEO of furniture manu-facturer Herman Miller, wrote: "The first responsibility of a leader is to define reality" (p. 11). Similarly, Dr. Martin Luther King, Jr. (1963) said:

Just as Socrates felt that it was necessary to create a tension in the mind, so that individuals could rise from the bondage of half truths . . . so must we . . . create the kind of tension in society that will help men rise from the dark depths of prejudice and racism. (p. 3)

Often, visionary leaders such as these have attained a high level of personal mastery that enables them to formulate a compelling personal and organizational vision for the future. Steve Jobs, the CEO of Apple Computer, is an example of a business leader who has successfully led his company through several major transitions by creating a sense of possibility for overcoming obstacles and achieving greatness.

The second major role of leaders is voiced by systems theorists such as MIT's Jay Forrester (1987) and Peter Senge. They voice a second and equally compelling view of leadership—that of the *leader as system designer*. Senge (1990b) wrote:

In a learning organization, leaders are designers, stewards, and teachers. They are responsible for building organizations where people continually expand their capacities to understand complexity, clarify vision, and improve shared mental models—that is, they are responsible for learning. (p. 340)

Here we can see that leadership is inextricably linked to the process of designing systems for helping employees learn from experience. Forrester and Senge call leaders to be visionaries who influence the behavior of employees toward a more ideal form of performance by designing systems, reframing situations, and facilitating learning processes.

These two different definitions of leadership cause us to revisit the Yogi and Commissar once again. One of the most important lessons of these two colorful leaders is that when it comes to knowledge creation in organizations, there is always both an interpersonal and a structural dimension that require integration by knowledge leaders. This same theme is found in *The New Knowledge Management* (2003) by Mark McElroy. McElroy argued for a hybrid knowledge-creation system that "allows" for self-organizing social systems such as communities of practice. In addition, he called for leaders to redesign the knowledge environment of their companies by reengineering ("reverse-engineering") policies to be more supportive of systemic knowledge and innovation processes. While it is possible to accomplish great feats through leadership and management, it is rarely sufficient to drive sustainable knowledge creation and innovation. McElroy pointed out that many obstacles to knowledge creation in organizations lie in the structures and systems that hinder employee learning and knowledge creation.

In fact, McElroy argued that a company's policies should ideally be aligned with the knowledge-creating behaviors it desires. He proposed a solution known as the *Policy Synchronization Method* (PSM), an organizational reengineering process that deliberately refocuses the company's policies on promoting knowledge-creating behavior. The PSM process requires leaders to understand how employee knowledge and behavior result directly from an organization's structure and policies. It offers a dynamic theory of how performance emerges from the underlying patterns embedded within the management system. The theoretical underpinnings of PSM can be traced to the system dynamics approach for solving *policy-resistant* problems.

## KNOWLEDGE LEADERSHIP: BEYOND EXECUTIVE AUTHORITY

The work of knowledge leaders is not limited to executives; it involves anyone in the organization whose personal vision can influence the process of how people create, share, and use knowledge for performance and innovation. The knowledge leader's role is at the center of the KM system, in that such systems should be defined by individuals or a team with a strategic view of how KM and KD can be integrated. While knowledge leaders are not usually experts on the design of KM systems, they are the people who can integrate the often-opposing perspectives of KM and KD into a unified whole. Since every organization is composed of layers of KM systems, knowledge leaders are needed at every level of the organization. Even at the lowest operational levels, knowledge leaders can work to maintain the balance between knowledge structures, technologies, systems, processes, and emergent social knowledge-creating forces. Unless operational knowledge leadership is present, organizations are at risk for becoming dominated by low-grade knowledge that is further processed into mush by KM technology systems. This effect can spiral downward to the point where critical local knowledge is lost or can no longer be used effectively. To achieve a holistic view of knowledge in organizations, it is necessary for leaders to develop a deeper understanding of the basic dynamics that result from the operation of KM systems.

To achieve this deeper understanding, let us start by discussing the basic concept of a management system. A major principle of systems theory is that a system's elements interact to influence the performance of that system. Despite a relatively sizable body of research to support this point of view, there has been virtually no supporting research regarding *management systems* as a specific case of this principle. To reiterate, we define *a management system* as consisting of interconnected and interactive management tools, functions, and processes that collectively have the effect of influencing performance as if they were acting as a single entity. Viewing management systems through the lens of systems theory enables managers to operate these systems in a more holistic way.

Management systems can also be defined as the set of methods by which a management team plans, operates, and controls its activities through the application of resources (such as money, people, equipment, materials, and information) to achieve a defined ideal future. Traditionally, management systems have been operated in a highly controlled, mechanical way. However, despite the strongest managerial control efforts, management systems are still capable of evolving in unanticipated ways that produce the very dynamics and behavior they are intended to minimize. We will now examine the essential pieces of management systems to see how they are related in ways that are of interest to knowledge leaders.

## The Elements of Management Systems

Cavaleri and Obloj (1993) identified the basic elements of a management system as being composed of several essential managerial tools found in any business, including: culture, leadership, infrastructure (rules and procedures), strategy, and structure. Clearly, there are many more elements that compose this system, but for purposes of illustration we will use these five elements. If the potential interactions among these elements are considered from a dynamic perspective, it becomes possible to envision that unintended outcomes could result. The reasons for nondeterministic, self-organizing behavior are transparent when we realize that none of these five managerial elements is ever completely controllable. While structure and technology are relatively more controllable than, say, leadership or culture, there are different causes that can introduce variability into these subsystems. For example, formal corporate structures do not always reflect the actual patterns of interaction among people in a company. Likewise, many forms of KM technology have limits on reliability or ability to interface with other technologies or human systems.

In fact, the dynamics engendered by management systems are generally not well understood, but it is possible to identify several fundamental systemic forces that influence the interactions and alignments that evolve within management systems. From this perspective, organizational performance is a function of the extent to which alignment can be achieved between the elements of a management system. Such emergent interconnections within or between a system and its environment are known as *structural couplings*. Biologists Maturana and Varela (1987) have defined structural coupling as "a history of recurrent interactions leading to the structural congruence of two (or more) systems" (p. 75). By recognizing these patterns of interaction within a management system, knowledge leaders will have a stronger foundation for developing integrative processes that link desired knowledge activities to management systems.

## A MANAGEMENT SYSTEMS MODEL

It is critical for knowledge leaders to understand how management systems and knowledge-based activities are related to and influence each other. The primary function of any management system is to achieve greater control of organizational processes and behavior. This fact alone indicates that management systems are capable of dampening the effects of any learning-oriented or experimental activities in companies. Management systems are specifically designed to control the balance between an organization and its environment, and between the social and technical aspects of the company. There is, therefore, a natural tension in businesses between the variability and predictability of social systems and the requirements of technical systems. This is one reason policies, procedures, and structures are designed—to reduce the variability within social systems so as to mold human tendencies to comply with task and operating systems.

Management systems include a number of offsetting and compensating interdependencies that make them complex for managers to use; these interdependencies also increase the probability of producing unintended consequences. For example, Figure 14.4 illustrates that there is tension between social and technical systems, as well as between the forces that open and close a system to its environment. If a management system is configured in a way that enables a high degree of self-organization among employees, human behavior is less controlled by structure and technology, but it may be more controlled by leadership and culture. Even so, it will be less predictable on a daily basis. On the other hand, designing a management system to emphasize its technical aspects may achieve greater efficiency and predictability—along with less knowledge and innovation by employees. Certainly, technology can be used to support employees in creating knowledge, but the conventional wisdom is that there are significant tradeoffs between the social and technical aspects of organizations.

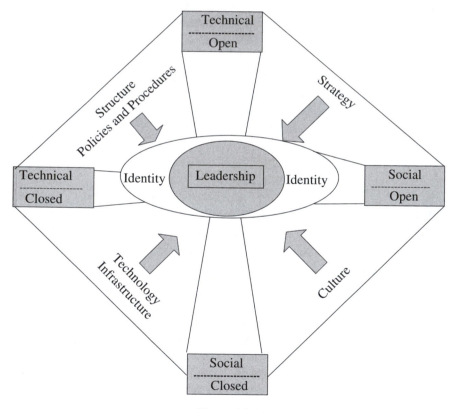

**Figure 14.4**
*Management Systems Model*

There is a long history of more than a half-century of research, dating back to the Tavistock Institute, on sociotechnical systems and optimization. Even though it seems that most companies are still structured so that such tradeoffs prevail, elite innovative companies are challenging the conventional wisdom. KM expert, Karl Erik Sveiby (2001) reports that at 3M Corporation he found that with "60,000 products of their own innovation process, this company has an organisation that balances between creativity and conservatism. 3M's values encourage learning and risk taking, but managers are required to link continuous learning to revenues" (p. 2).

In a similar manner, there is often tension between an organization and its environment. While organizations try to control the amount of information flowing in from the environment so as to create knowledge about customers, markets, and competitors, they also try to limit information so as to not exceed their processing capacity or create a state of overload. Thus, there is a necessary regulatory process of controlling the extent to which an organization is "open" or "closed." If an organization remains too closed to its environment, it will lose touch with customers and miss information about competitors. *Openness* exists when there is a relatively free exchange of resources and information between a company and its environment. Traditionally, when organizations increase their degree of openness to environmental forces, it is often viewed as antithetical to achieving a balanced equilibrium. Most businesses rely on preserving internal equilibrium to assure a steady flow of products and services. They attempt to achieve this reduced environmental influence by restricting their relations with the external environment. Conversely, greater openness affords the potential to develop new external relationships with customers, partners, and suppliers that often places greater pressure on internal operating systems.

A similar sort of compensating feedback relationship exists between the social and technical dimensions of organizations. There is an uneasy tension between these two dimensions because of an underlying compensating feedback loop. The technical system is engineered precisely, by applying the principles of *technical rationality* to organizations (Checkland, 1985; Miser, 1989). Technical rationality is based on the concept of economic optimization: it involves finding the most efficient point where the greatest output can be achieved for the least input.

## FUNCTIONS PERFORMED BY MANAGEMENT SYSTEMS

Management systems perform five major functions in their organizations: (1) regulating, (2) compensating, (3) buffering, (4) opening, and (5) driving.

1. *Regulatory functions*, including tools such as policies, procedures, and structure, are designed to reduce the amount of variety in a system by controlling degrees of latitude in decision making, job task responsibilities, and business processes—all in advance of any action taken.

2. *Compensating functions* seek to stabilize an organization by counteracting those effects that disturb equilibrium. Procedures can serve a compensating role, as can culture. In fact, they may serve as substitute systemic tools for each other, in that they both can achieve the same outcome through different means. Hospitals, universities, nonprofits, and religious organizations are examples where strong cultures and high degrees of professionalism (rather than high salaries) exert controlling effects over employees.

3. *Buffering (closing) functions* protect the equilibrium of a company, or its subunits, from destabilizing influences. Just-in-time inventory strategies can buffer an organization from environmental turbulence by adding variety to supplier-organization relationships and lessening the influence of this potential environmental instability. Culture can also buffer an organization by requiring its members to adjust their behavior in response to unexpected changes.

4. *Opening forces* involve engaging new outside entities or increasing the intensity of relationships with existing customers, partners, or suppliers. Strategy is the main process used to enable the flow of opening forces.

5. *Driving forces* are pattern-breaking initiatives that set the stage for innovations. They often result from reframing perspectives and developing new meaning from past experiences. Culture functions as the main driving force by focusing the attention of corporate members on interpreting their experience in a particular way.

Returning to our discussion of Yogis and Commissars, we can see that in those systems that are designed by Commissar leaders, there is likely to be high compliance and little openness present. On the other hand, Yogi leaders traditionally call for both types of openness: participative and reflective. Peter Senge (1990a) pointed out the difference between the two kinds of openness: participative openness is the freedom to speak one's mind, whereas reflective openness leads people to looking inward. He observed, "Reflective openness starts with the willingness to challenge our own thinking, to recognize that any certainty we ever have is, at best, a hypothesis about the world" (p. 277). Over time, a culture of openness can develop where employees feel free to voice their opinions. Corporate culture can either reinforce or counteract the effects of formal strategies, procedures, controls, or structures.

Alignment between similar management systems tools reinforces existing patterns of behavior. For example, the U.S. Forest Service publishes a regularly scheduled magazine in which employees who dissent with the service's management team can air their opinions in print. A growing number of management theorists are calling for greater openness in organizations. In fact, Firestone and McElroy (2003) have argued that openness should be a defining characteristic of companies that are seeking to improve the quality of their knowledge-processing initiatives (what we call *knowledge quality improvement processes,* or KQIPs). They refer to such an organization as an *open enterprise,* and define it as being:

. . . a normative model for knowledge processing and knowledge management designed to achieve innovation and transparency in management. (p. 317)

Knowledge leaders of the future will be called on to define the degree of openness in their organization, division, or unit. Knowledge leadership involves dedicating time and resources to less predictable, inner-directed, knowledge-creating activities that cannot be simply structured or easily measured. Many executives may feel uncomfortable, especially at first, making room in their management systems for knowledge leadership and knowledge-creating processes. However, the longer they delay addressing this issue, the more negative the consequences are likely to be for their business.

## KNOWLEDGE LEADERSHIP IN A WORLD OF MANAGEMENT SYSTEMS

Leadership is at the center of management systems, yet it reflects a qualitatively different perspective than strategy, structure, technological infrastructure, or organizational culture. *Leadership is the force that unifies and integrates the other elements of a management system.* By virtue of its distinctive function, leadership is central to all the other elements of a management system.

This also holds true with the relationship between knowledge leadership and KM and KD. Knowledge leadership builds on the lessons of both the Yogi and the Commissar. Successful pragmatic organizations need the distinct kinds of knowledge that both the Yogi and Commissar bring to the table. However, the forces represented by the Yogi and the Commissar are not inclined to reach a peaceful balance through their own accord. Knowledge leaders need to mediate and integrate these opposing forces. If left to their own devices, Commissar leaders will use their position to eradicate all Yogis and the philosophies that they advocate—and Yogi leaders will ignore the Commissar and focus all employees on the path of knowledge development. Both of these strategies are clearly unacceptable.

Knowledge leaders must be pragmatists because this approach shifts the discourse away from these kinds of ungrounded ideologies toward discovering what works reliably well in practice. Knowledge leadership, then, is a triadic process that engages three important parts of an organization. These include the following:

- Developing a vision for knowledge processing, performance improvement, and problem solving that influences the knowledge development of employees
- Designing processes and systems for processing, creating, sharing, and validating knowledge that builds on both KM and KD systems
- Serving as a knowledge source for the organization's leaders so as to improve the leadership process itself

A primary challenge for knowledge leaders is to exist in a synergistic way with KM systems. This becomes easier when you realize that KM is essentially a human social process of forming knowledge claims, using knowledge for action, and validating the efficacy of this knowledge in reliably producing the expected results. KM may also involve using technology, or adapting organizational structures and systems to improve the knowledge processes. A major function of knowledge leaders, then, is to set a vision for how KM and KD may be used to improve performance, increase adaptability, and encourage innovation in organizations.

Knowledge leadership enables organizations to be effective in employing various KM systems for improved performance and innovations. Most business executives are not experts on knowledge. They need to rely on the opinions of knowledge leaders to determine a balanced direction for future knowledge-based activities. The era of investing in nonproductive KM technologies and systems appears to be drawing to a close. Corporations can no longer afford to invest large sums of funds to achieve only modest incremental gains in performance when competitors are largely doing the same. Simply, no net gains can be achieved by this strategy.

Sustainable competitive advantage has always been derived from doing those things well (1) that add value and (2) that your competitors have difficulty doing as well. For companies seeking to travel this road, the jumping-off point begins with knowledge leadership—and the development and management of high-quality knowledge. One of the first steps to attaining this goal is for top executives to define their CKO position in a way that connects it directly to the organization's operations. While information technology (IT) or management information systems (MIS) departments can support the KM agenda in an organization, the CKO should be appointed to a position that has stronger ties to the main value-creating, operational aspects of the organization.

Moreover, every department in the company should have knowledge leaders to coach, mentor, and teach other employees about the processes of inside-out pragmatic knowledge development. These departmental knowledge leaders can also help employees build their capacity for using KM systems and technologies so that the new wealth of knowledge they generate is captured for the whole organization. It is important to note that virtually anyone in a business can be a knowledge leader of some type. Knowledge leadership begins with developing pragmatic knowledge that is of benefit to oneself and others. The benefit to others lies in sharing both the knowledge you have gained from experience and the pragmatic process you used to create and improve the quality of your own knowledge.

In the next chapter of *Knowledge Leadership*, we will discuss how knowledge leaders can develop infrastructures in their organizations that will support the management and development of pragmatic knowledge.

## REFERENCES

Cavaleri, S., and Fearon. D. (1994). "Systems Integration through Concurrent Learning." *Industrial Management,* vol. 36, 27–30.

Cavaleri, S., and Obloj, K. (1993). *Management Systems: A Global Perspective.* Belmont, CA: Wadsworth.

Checkland, P. (1985). "From Optimizing to Learning: A Development of Soft Systems Thinking for the 1990s." *Journal of the Operational Research Society*, vol. 36, 757–767.

Cook, S. D. N., and Yanow, D., (1993). "Culture and Organizational Learning." *Journal of Management Inquiry*, vol. 2, 373–390.

DePree, M. (1989). *Leadership Is an Art*. New York: Dell.

Edvinsson, L., and Malone, M. (1997). *Intellectual Capital*. New York: Harper-Collins.

Fearon, D., and Cavaleri, S. (2005). *Inside Knowledge*. Milwaukee, WI: Quality Press.

Firestone, J., and McElroy, M. (2003). *Key Issues in the New Knowledge Management*. Burlington, MA: KMCI Press, Butterworth-Heinemann.

Forrester, J. (1987). "Lessons from System Dynamics Modeling." *System Dynamics Review*, vol. 3, no. 2.

Hamel, G. (2000). *Leading the Revolution*. Cambridge, MA: Harvard Business School Press.

Kaplan, R. and Norton, D. (1996). *The Balanced Scorecard*. Cambridge, MA: Harvard Business School Press.

King, M. L. (1963). Letter for Birmingham Jail, April 16, 1963 published in: King, M. L. (1963). *Why We Can't Wait*. New York: Harper & Row.

Lundberg, C. (1996). "Managing in a Culture That Values Learning." In Cavaleri, S., and Fearon, D., *Managing in Organizations That Learn*. Cambridge, MA: Blackwell.

McElroy, M. (2003). *The New Knowledge Management*. Burlington, MA: KMCI Press, Butterworth-Heinemann.

Miser, H. (1989). "The Easy Chair: What Did Those Pioneers Have Uppermost in Their Mind, Model Building or Problem Solving?" *Interfaces*, vol. 19, no. 4, 69–74.

O'Reilly, C., and Tushman, M. (2004, April). "The Ambidextrous Organization." *Harvard Business Review*, 74–81.

Seel, R. (2004). Retrieved from www.new-paradigm.co.uk/articles.htm.

Senge, P. (1990a). *The Fifth Discipline*. New York: Doubleday/Currency.

Senge, P. (1990b, Fall). "The Leader's New Work: Building Learning Organizations." *Sloan Management Review*, vol. 32, no.1.

Sveiby, K. E. (2001).*What is Knowledge Management?* http://www.sveiby.com/articles/KnowledgeManagement.html.

# 15

# CONSTRUCTING EFFECTIVE KNOWLEDGE INFRASTRUCTURES

## Executive Summary

Decades ago, the founders of the *quality* movement argued that workers should do more than simply produce or assemble products—they could also inspect them, ensure their quality, and continuously improve the processes used to create them. Managers who resisted taking workers away from "production" overlooked the point that employees could actually make production systems *more* effective by removing waste and rework at its source, thereby reducing costs—and increasing the quality and reliability of products and services. Many of the KBOs we see today are the same organizations that embraced *total quality management* (TQM) principles early on and used them to develop *knowledge infrastructures* (processes, tasks, and systems that support knowledge processing). To sustain optimal knowledge-based activity, leaders must make deliberate efforts to design effective knowledge infrastructures that are tailored to their company's knowledge needs. The shift away from mass-production systems toward Japanese-style *lean production* systems is a favorable movement for knowledge leadership because it "bakes" learning, knowledge creation, continuous experimentation, and quality improvement right into the system. In this chapter we argue that *the prime function of an organization is to develop actionable and pragmatic knowledge* that increases its capacity to function reliably well in practice. Many of today's leading organizations are knowledge-creating systems that direct their efforts toward developing pragmatic knowledge. One of the emerging applications of pragmatic knowledge is as

*Continued*

a driving force for *operational innovation*. In KBOs, innovation applies to everything, including operations, and these companies have action-learning or experimentation processes integrated into their continuous improvement processes. Knowledge infrastructure systems contain *structures*, *processes*, and *technologies*. Before designing a knowledge infrastructure, knowledge leaders must know what kind of knowledge is needed for what purpose. The chapter concludes by describing the advantages and shortcomings of three major kinds of knowledge strategies.

At the end of the day, human intent—not technology—governs an organization's effectiveness in creating value through knowledge-based activities. Creating new knowledge is not the only result of purposeful human activity. Another powerful result is that people feel engaged in their work in a more meaningful way. Achieving a high degree of engagement is not strictly the result of KM or KD initiatives, as there are much broader organizational considerations at play here. For optimal knowledge-based activity to be sustainable, leaders must make deliberate efforts to design *knowledge infrastructures*: processes, tasks, and systems that support knowledge processing.

Several decades ago, founders of the quality movement, such as W. Edwards Deming and Joseph Juran, proposed that quality was not just an objective measurement of a property that defines a product. They argued that quality was in the eyes of the beholder—the customer. They also envisioned workplaces where employees, instead of quality control specialists or managers, measured quality. This revolutionary notion was based on the premise that workers could do more than simply produce the products—they could also inspect them, ensure their quality, and continuously improve them. At the time, management resistance to this idea was founded on the assumption that anything that takes workers away from full utilization of their productive capacity is a waste of time, inefficient, and needlessly raises costs. Traditional managers who objected to TQM completely overlooked the point that it could actually make the system *more* efficient and sustainable by removing waste and rework at its source.

Work that is designed with a primary focus on efficiency is the legacy of Frederick Taylor's "scientific management" influence. This impetus toward efficiency, without considering the degree of employee engagement and opportunity for knowledge processing, limits the potential for knowledge sharing and creation. In companies where operational employees are expected to devote 100% of their energies to output-driven production activities, work processes are rigidly structured, and competition is valued more than collaboration, the odds of creating a sustainable knowledge-creating organization are very slim indeed. The shift away from mass-production systems toward *lean production* systems is a favorable movement for knowledge leadership. The lean production system, first developed by Taiichi Ohno (1998) at Toyota, is a management approach that "bakes" learning, knowledge creation, continuous experimentation, and quality improvement right into the system. The lean production system has been used successfully in Honda and in American manufacturing companies such as Wiremold Corporation—as described by Emiliani and colleagues (2003) in their book, *Better Thinking, Better Results*. The principles for lean production provide a framework for designing organizations that use knowledge to drive quality and innovation.

If a basic principle of system design is that its structure should reflect its function, then we need to ask: What is the prime function of an organization? A commonly accepted answer is that the function of an organization is to serve its stakeholders by delivering value to them in the form of superior products, services, and return on investment. But if we examine the principles behind any strategy that increases an organization's capacity to function reliably well in practice, then we would say that *the prime function of an organization is to develop actionable and pragmatic knowledge.* From this view, many leading organizations are simply knowledge-creating systems that direct their efforts toward developing pragmatic knowledge. Numerous organizations have historically invested resources in training, corporate universities, and management-development programs. While these kinds of knowledge activities are helpful, they are much less likely to be a source of competitive advantage simply because they rarely produce knowledge that is actionable or pragmatic.

Knowledge is the basis for effective action in organizations. Unfortunately, *knowledge* has previously been mistaken as being something that only well-educated people or leaders have in their possession. Knowledge is also sometimes assumed to be a commodity that automatically develops as a result of experience and learning. While most employees have knowledge, a relatively small amount of this knowledge is effectively tapped. Even more significant is that relatively few workers have knowledge that is actionable or pragmatic—that is, knowledge that can be effectively tapped for competitive advantage.

Corporations often try to compensate for this knowledge neglect by supplying employees with large quantities of information that they are expected to somehow (miraculously) translate into highly usable knowledge for action. Indeed, every year companies sink large sums of money into new KM technology to fill their employees with information. We call this the "funnel approach" to knowledge management. As shown in Figure 15.1, it is intended to operate by funneling knowledge and information directly into people's heads.

**Figure 15.1**
*Funnel Approach to Knowledge Management*

The KM funnel approach is very attractive to many businesses because it defines KM in a way that is seductively simple. In this view, technology easily transfers information at the speed of light, and employees require minimal downtime to receive and absorb it. We could also call this approach the *sponge model of knowledge* because it assumes that employees are like sponges who receive information, absorb it, and magically convert it to useful knowledge. Many of the KM strategies that adopt this "funnel" or "sponge" approach are what McElroy terms *first-generation* or *supply-side* KM strategies. While sharing best practices and providing relevant information to employees are worthwhile activities, and may even be the best possible approach for organizations with low knowledge-processing capacity, they cannot create organizations that are *FAST* or pragmatic. So how can knowledge leaders design effective knowledge infrastructures that will help their organizations rise above the performance threshold they need to support their strategic performance needs?

## LEADING FOR OPERATIONAL INNOVATION

Becoming a knowledge leader starts with your becoming a person who has pragmatic knowledge of what works reliably well in your own work and life. (This is why we helped you determine your own knowledge leadership style in Part II of this book.) Knowledge leaders are able to appreciate the potential of different forms of learning and knowledge-based activities because they have experienced them personally and feel sufficiently comfortable to use them where warranted. Unfortunately, most managers rely too heavily on consultants and vendors to educate them about the merits and limitation of various knowledge-based activities and technologies. Although it may appear efficient to "let the experts tell us how to manage our knowledge," this approach rarely generates effective results.

Bob Buckman (2004), chairman and CEO of Buckman Laboratories, described his own personal journey to becoming a knowledge leader as one of leading by example:

When we began this journey at Buckman Labs, we were indeed leading culture change in the organization. As CEO, I figured that if people did not see me on this journey, they wouldn't want to go. So, in an effort to get people to use the new knowledge system we were putting into place, I made a point of finding occasions to use it daily. (p. 46)

Knowledge leaders lead knowledge initiatives by example. Few leaders can earn credibility among employees without modeling the change they wish to inspire in them. Learning from experience and creating knowledge both require an openness to change. This openness comes from believing that such change will be instrumental in achieving a desired state or end. And in an era where employees have come to question the authenticity of leaders, one of the potentially most effective ways for you to exemplify the values and strength of your convictions is to embark on the journey of being a knowledge leader. You will soon find that this journey is its own reward, because the practices of pragmatic knowledge creation can offer great benefits for enhancing your personal and professional effectiveness.

Once you become familiar with the process of creating and using pragmatic knowledge for increasing effectiveness and innovativeness, you will become more capable of applying these processes in various organizational settings. One of the emerging applications of pragmatic knowledge is as a driving force for *operational innovation*. Operational innovation is an approach used by a number of the elite businesses in the world, such as Dell, Progressive Insurance, and Wal-Mart to gain a sustainable competitive advantage. Michael Hammer (2004), father of the field known as *business process reengineering*, stated that:

Operational innovation should not be confused with operational improvement or operational excellence. Those terms refer to achieving high performance via existing modes of operation, ensuring that work is done as it ought to be to reduce errors, costs, and delays but without fundamentally changing how that work gets accomplished. Operational innovation means coming up with entirely new ways of filling orders, developing products, providing customer service, and doing any other activity that an enterprise performs. (p. 86)

Effective operational innovation does not simply improve the current way operational functions are fulfilled. Rather, it is a way of rethinking the base assumptions that determine how products and services are created and produced. In most companies, operations are not a focus of innovation efforts because managers believe that efficiency and predictability are needed in operations more than anywhere else in the business. Innovation is viewed as being potentially disruptive to operations, which traditional managers most want to buffer from the forces of change. In fact, operating and innovating are often considered as being at polar opposite ends of the pragmatic performance-inquiry spectrum (which we described in the prior chapter). Traditional management approaches rely on the analysis of data from past history to pinpoint and solve problems. However, it is less effective for leaders to focus on what is wrong with the system rather than focus on discovering the system's potential capacity for operating differently. Harvard Business School professor Clayton Christensen (2003) noted that leaders cannot rely solely on data-driven analysis, which is essentially retrospective by its very nature. Innovation depends on being able to *look forward* into the future. He observed:

I think the science of management wave already has been upon us for twenty years. I hope that we can figure out how to write and teach in a way that helps people develop an intuition for looking into the future clearly. If you only look into it through the lenses of the past, it's very hard. (p. 1)

Systems expert Jay Forrester would have concurred with Christensen. We once heard Forrester compare this management approach to the futility of trying to drive a car forward by looking in the rear view mirror. The lean production systems, operational innovation processes, and the policy synchronization method all work to balance the drive for efficiency against the need for effectiveness in organizations, as shown in Figure 15.2.

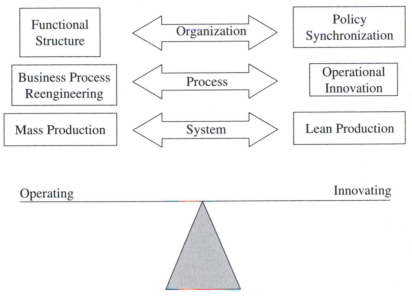

**Figure 15.2**
*Balancing Operating and Innovating*

In companies that employ conventional strategies, the processes of operating and innovating are viewed as repelling each other—in much the same way as Yogis and Commissars do. However, companies that use operational innovation have learned over time that innovation is a continuous process driven by relentless organizational learning. In these companies, innovation applies to everything, including operations. In their new book *Inside Knowledge*, Fearon and Cavaleri (2005) view the process of operational innovation as being driven by pragmatic knowledge. They note:

Pragmatic knowledge-based strategies are the basis for Operational Innovation (OI), but not strategic innovation. Operational Innovation derives from direct experience, whereas strategic innovation is only partially derived from operational experiences. Non–experiential factors, such as opportunities and threats that haven't yet occurred, must also be considered.

Operational innovation positively feeds back upon itself by pragmatically using the gains of prior innovations to further improve innovations. For example, operational innovation at Toyota has resulted in breakthrough insights that have turned conventional wisdom in the auto manufacturing industry upside down. Purposefully idling machines and worker activity as a way to level production is a counterintuitive strategy that most firms would be reluctant to try. However, in these fertile knowledge-creating operational settings, knowledge leaders and pragmatic employees become experts at discovering what works reliably well in practice via a process of continuous experimentation.

The French have a word that means continually tweaking systems and experimenting with cause and effect: *bricolage*, which translates literally as "to tinker." One who tinkers, then, is a *bricoleur*. Although managers often have polished analytical skills, they cannot overlook the importance of tinkering—inquiry and experimentation. Indeed, tinkering can be a significant source of innovation. As if speaking to this point, the American General George S. Patton once recommended, "Never tell people how to do things. Tell them what to do and they will surprise you with their ingenuity."

Balanced knowledge leaders are very different from traditional managers, who typically focus on retaining control. Knowledge leaders know there is a price that comes with control that may be unacceptable, especially when their objective is to elicit knowledge-enhancing behaviors from their front-line people. A low-control approach that frees employees to experiment requires patience, trust, and a willingness to suspend prevalent management theories. For leaders, it is a humbling—but often exhilarating—experience to temporarily suspend judgment about accepted management theories (that explain how things *ought* to work) and instead follow the lead of case-specific insights (based on personal scientific inquiry). But, as Charles Sanders Peirce argued over a century ago, employing the (real) scientific method is the best route to creating new knowledge from experience.

## EMBEDDING KNOWLEDGE IN FUNDAMENTAL PROCESSES

Virtually everything in a company can impact its capacity for creating and sharing knowledge—you name it: staffing, compensation, workflow designs, workplace architecture, accounting systems, quality improvement processes, policies, and technology. In conventionally managed organizations, there are few leaders who have authority over all of these moving parts—much less the clout necessary to align them with the knowledge needs of the system. So how does an organization deliberately embed knowledge-creating and knowledge-sharing activities into its fundamental process? If we look at examples, we see that many of the elite KBOs have an action-learning or experimentation process that is integrated into their continuous improvement processes. For example:

- Royal Dutch Shell—scenario planning, planning as learning
- BP-Amoco—project management
- Toyota—TQM, production management
- UniLever—product development and brand management
- General Electric—operational planning
- Xerox—workplace design
- Buckman Laboratories—new product development
- World Bank—story telling

By using a pragmatic framework, blended with various continuous improvement processes, leaders can integrate various functions and develop knowledge-creating activities that fit the culture and strategic performance needs of the organization.

While some businesses find it advantageous to integrate learning and knowledge-based activities fully throughout the entire system, other organizations may find it beneficial to start on a more limited scale. For example, processes such as project management, planning, or quality improvement can be transformed into knowledge-based functions by adding knowledge-creating features to them, such as action-learning elements (reflection, hypothesizing about cause-effect relations, and experimentation).

## KNOWLEDGE LEADERS AS DESIGNERS AND STEWARDS OF INFRASTRUCTURE

We have described knowledge leaders as being both designers and stewards of knowledge development. But exactly how do knowledge leaders design infrastructure? Obviously, the design challenge facing any knowledge leader depends on several factors: the organization's knowledge needs and objectives, the organization's strategies, and the knowledge leader's level of responsibility. The focus for some knowledge leaders may be as narrow as one unit or a small department. Other knowledge leaders may contribute to changing the infrastructure of an entire organization so that it is more supportive of *FAST* pragmatic knowledge. For knowledge leaders, the starting point of designing a knowledge infrastructure is to surface performance requirements for when the system is fully operational—then envision the ideal and make certain it will work well within the context of the organization's identity, culture, and management systems.

What is an ideal knowledge infrastructure? Let us begin by examining the operation of a city. Most residents of a city can attest to its quality of life. When asked to explain their evaluation of this city's quality of life, people may point to the abundance of recreational activities within close proximity of their homes, or the ease of movement throughout the city via roads, buses, subway, cycling paths, or pedestrian walkways. Typically, a city's infrastructure is thought to include its transportation and educational systems, as well as sewers, water supply, and power. In addition to these physical aspects of a city's infrastructure, there are also services such as support for the arts, police and fire service, and assistance for poor, elderly, and physically or mentally challenged citizens.

Interestingly, a number of cities around the world are investing in the development of knowledge infrastructures so they can become *knowledge cities*. According to Ron Dvir and Edna Pasher (2004) several European cities, including Eindhvoen, The Netherlands, have adopted this innovative and exciting strategy. They quote knowledge leader and former Chief Knowledge Officer of Skandia, Leif Edvinsson who defines a knowledge city as "a city that was purposefully designed to encourage the nurturing of knowledge." They also reference leading knowledge expert, Dr. Javier Carrillo, Director of the Center for Knowledge Systems at the Monterrey Institute of Technology in Mexico, who speaks of cities as being capital systems that serve as stores of social value to regions and countries. Carillo explains that the evolution of cities is progressing at an accelerating pace and that knowledge is playing an increasing critical role in the development of cities. Cities that have adopted explicit knowledge-based strategies for their development include: Calgary, Canada, Barcelona, Spain, Monterrey, Mexico, Melbourne, Australia, and Deflt, The Netherlands (pp. 16–27). Similar to the complex infrastructure of any city, an organization's knowledge infrastructure is composed of many intertwined elements, including structures, technologies, and processes. These intertwined parts of the knowledge infrastructure are also interconnected with the company's general features, such as decision-making styles, hierarchy, culture, identity, preferred communication networks, and many other factors. While, on the surface, the design task of knowledge leaders may appear to be simply an architectural or engineering task, a significant element of creativity is also required. In other words, the design of knowledge infrastructure requires both "art" and "science" from knowledge leaders.

Let us begin our discussion of designing knowledge infrastructures by looking at structures. There are structural elements to knowledge quality improvement processes (KQIPs), organizations as a whole, management systems, KM systems, and KD systems. One of the key questions that arises in the processes of envisioning knowledge infrastructures is whether knowledge systems will be designed on the basis of:

- Top-down "waterfall" flows of knowledge versus bottom-up emergent behaviors
- Outside-in versus inside-out knowledge processes
- Supply-side versus demand-side knowledge processing
- A structural systems approach versus a community-building approach
- A direct functional approach verses an ecological approach
- A brilliant design strategy versus a continuous improvement and redesign approach

One of the great things about knowledge infrastructures is that they are ruled by the principle of *equifinality*. According to systems theory, the principle of equifinality proposes that there are numerous equally effective alternate routes of getting to the same outcome. As it was said in the glory days of the Roman Empire, "All roads lead to Rome." In other words, knowledge infrastructure can be built so that knowledge can be created, shared, and improved by using any one of many different processes. For example, when it comes to KM, energy giant CONOCO focuses on improving the document management capacity available to its employees by building knowledge portals that enable employees to access and interface with its Enterprise Resource Planning platform. CONOCO uses the software produced by SAP Corporation to track and integrate diverse areas of the organization into a unified reporting system. This type of seamless architecture enables employees to search and access SAP content that resides in their document management system directly from the portal. By contrast, competitor BP Amoco focuses on capturing lessons learned at the completion of projects and helping employees who are just starting projects to connect with others who have gained knowledge while working on prior projects. Finally, Seely Brown and Duguid (2000) note that Xerox has tried a more ecological approach at its Palo Alto Research Center. Leaders had the physical space redesigned to facilitate people's natural tendency to create knowledge spontaneously in impromptu meetings in common areas. For example, white boards with colored markers were installed near coffeepots, and stairways were widened to enable people to carry on lengthy conversations without having to move so others could pass by them.

In processed-focused organizations, continuous improvement and innovation all emerge from corporate identity, core values, principles, and guiding philosophies. For example, Liker (2004) stated that Toyota's management foundation rests on a philosophy of long-term thinking, processes focused on eliminating waste, continuous improvement, and relentless organizational learning, coupled with efforts to respect, challenge, and "grow" employees and partners. Toyota has extended its knowledge focus to embrace suppliers, vendors, and partners in a "knowledge network," which is composed of Toyota and all supply-chain partners. The members of this group agree to collaborate in creating and sharing knowledge, and also to keep this knowledge for exclusive use within the network. While many corporations have a process focus when it comes to KM, Toyota employs a process focus *only as a means* to a more pragmatic outcome. That is, it starts out with a simple process of detecting and correcting errors, but this drives much larger performance-driven processes, such as production planning or model revision. The important thing to note about this system is that everything is driven by action and performance improvement.

This is a key principle of knowledge leadership: namely, *knowledge is for performance, and knowledge activities must be anchored in performance improvement*. In other words, KM for its own sake is an expensive, unfocused luxury that few organizations can afford. If knowledge is for performance, in the pragmatic sense, then leaders must know what kind of knowledge is needed for what purpose *before* building a knowledge infrastructure. Pursuing a KM strategy that is not directly tied to performance is ineffective and costly. Unfortunately, that is precisely what a great many companies are doing.

## KNOWLEDGE RESOURCE STRATEGY

In organizations that are more Commissar in style, knowledge-based activities are approached from a *functional* perspective. Here, the emphasis is on well-defined structures for KM functions (such as knowledge sharing) that are designed to raise the general level of knowledge-based activity in the organization. The problem with this approach is that there typically is no particular performance orientation, problem focus, or effort to continuously improve a particular aspect of organizational functioning. We refer to this type of strategy as a *knowledge resource strategy*.

The essence of a knowledge resource (or utilization) strategy is that knowledge is thought of as a virtually untapped economic resource in organizations. This strategy is quite common in American firms. Moreover, Commissars often employ this strategy because it is based on a set of economic principles that are consistent with their fundamental beliefs, which include the following:

1. Employees are a resource in the same way as are the materials used to produce goods and services. This human resource is a cost that must be offset by efficient utilization of the resource.
2. The most efficient use of any resource is to extract or exploit it to the greatest extent possible—indeed, this is the essence of utilization.
3. There are several ways to optimize resource utilization, including increasing the output activity of the resource. This means organizing employees so they spend as much time as possible performing tasks that relate directly to incremental gains in output.
4. Exploiting slack or untapped resources to gain increases in output should be done without incurring significant new expenses or costs in the process. This approach employs *leveraging existing resources* to exploit unused resources.
5. Knowledge is an economic resource. Economists, such as Nelson and Winter, discuss the importance of knowledge resources to organizations. They stress that knowledge is in the form of social capital, which is often difficult to extract.
6. Technology is a very efficient and predictable tool for leveraging knowledge resources in organizations.
7. Knowledge activities should be exploited within the context of existing organizational infrastructure (structures and processes), because knowledge is not a key operational activity but rather the leveraging of an untapped resource.
8. Operational systems must remain distinct from knowledge processes so that these core systems are buffered from any influence that could reduce their efficiency.

The resource-based view of knowledge can be visualized through the metaphor of an integrated petroleum company (such as Exxon/Mobil, Shell, or BP Amoco) bringing its products to market. The first step for a petroleum company is to extract crude petroleum from fossil fuel reserves. Oil-drilling and pumping equipment is required to bring the oil to the surface. The next step is to refine the crude petroleum into oil, gasoline, and other fuels. This processing is very capital intensive: it requires that petroleum products be refined through various stages in large installations called refineries. Next, the petroleum products are transported to storage and distribution facilities where they are held in stock until there is a need for the product at the retail level of operations. Finally, retailers sell or dispense the products, such as automotive motor oil to consumers, railroads, and farmers. With this example, we can see how leaders can use the knowledge resource strategy to mine a supposedly limited resource (knowledge) from employees, then refine, store, and later distribute that knowledge via KM systems to those who will consume it.

## THE KNOWLEDGE SOURCE STRATEGY

The *knowledge source strategy* stands in bold contrast to the resource strategy. *In this strategy, knowledge is regarded as being the source for virtually anything of importance in organizations.* Innovation, new product development, quality improvement, effective action, waste reduction, and superior service are all viewed as being *the effects* of knowledge. In other words, knowledge is seen as being the source of the most significant types of performance that make organizations effective and *FAST*. From this alternative perspective, the economic notion of leveraging knowledge seems to miss the point entirely. Here, knowledge is much more than an untapped resource that can somehow be used in ancillary ways to boost existing processes—it is the source of all existing processes. In the knowledge-source paradigm, the organization places the highest value on creating new knowledge to solve problems, innovate, continuously improve performance, and drive all operational activities.

To the company that practices the economic resource strategy, creating new knowledge is viewed as a bad investment. It is considered a gamble: an unpredictable, ill-defined process that poses unnecessary risks. On the other hand, knowledge source companies have already discerned how to create knowledge for performance in reliable ways, as part of their larger organizational learning and continuous improvement efforts. In such companies, knowledge-creating processes are not an adjunct to routine operational processes; rather *they are instrumental to such processes and run concurrently with them*. Processes such as continuous quality improvement, organizational learning, and strategic planning are viewed as having dual functions—namely, *to create knowledge and improve performance*. These two activities are regarded as being synergistic; they are used as catalysts to set off an upward spiral of improvement (Figure 15.3).

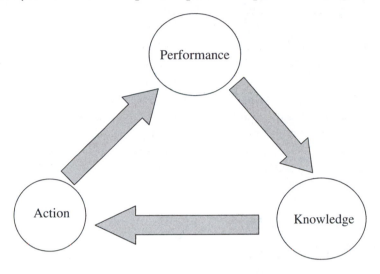

**Figure 15.3**
*Knowledge-Performance Synergy*

Does this mean that every company should become a knowledge source-based organization? Hardly. Some organizations may wish to move in this direction because it reflects their identity and suits their strategic intent. Does it mean that the resource-based knowledge strategy is bad? No, not at all. In fact, the resource-based strategy can help companies shift from a sole focus on hard assets toward taking better advantage of their knowledge capital. The difficulty is that the more entrenched leaders become in the resource-strategy paradigm, the more difficult it is to change. The source-based strategy-represents an intermediate approach to knowledge strategies in that it focuses on driving processes via knowledge. However, obstacles can remain to implementing the source-based approach in conventional organizational structures. Often, these limitations can be addressed by a third knowledge strategy, *the engineered-ecology approach*.

## THE ENGINEERED-ECOLOGY KNOWLEDGE STRATEGY

The *engineered-ecology knowledge strategy* views knowledge as being one of the most, if not the most, critical factor for organizational adaptation and innovation. Innovation is regarded as the wellspring for all sustainable competitive advantage in industry. Due to its intrinsically social nature, knowledge creation is viewed as being an essentially *self-organizing process* that is controlled by certain intrinsic human tendencies. These are the same intrinsic motivations that have governed knowledge creation in human communities since the beginning of civilization. In the engineered-ecology knowledge paradigm, knowledge creation is considered an important evolutionary force in human social systems—indeed the one that drove both innovation and adaptation long before the word *knowledge* was ever coined. This perspective sees knowledge creation as the most critical factor in determining which direction a business will choose while responding to environmental threats and opportunities. Accordingly, if knowledge is so critical to survival, and it has a self-organizing nature, then organizations should make all reasonable efforts to remove any impediments to knowledge creation. *The engineered-ecology organization* is engineered in much the same way as a greenhouse—in order to nurture and support the unfettered development of knowledge. This involves realigning policies to optimize both knowledge-creation processes and operating system productivity.

The policy synchronization method (PSM) developed by McElroy and Cavaleri is designed to achieve alignment between knowledge-creating processes, organization structure, and innovation. McElroy (2003) explained the purpose of the PSM as being.

to establish the conditions within which spontaneous self-organization might occur to produce emergent outcomes. The conditions, I believe, are the policies and programs with the knowledge-processing environment of a firm. *That* is the system of relevance here, and policies and programs are its conditions. (pp. 119–120)

The objective of such a knowledge strategy is to create ideal growing conditions in the "knowledge greenhouse" by (1) allowing self-organizing communities to form freely, (2) encouraging the diversity of knowledge to be easily surfaced and expressed, (3) providing means for inclusiveness in knowledge processing so that competing knowledge claims can be fairly evaluated, and (4) maintaining an environment of openness throughout the organization. This deliberate openness of expression enables knowledge claims to be challenged and evaluated in a scientific manner according to previously established rules, rather than by politics or tradition. While such talk of self-organization and emergent outcomes may strike some as being difficult to translate into everyday business practices, Mirvis, Ayas, and Roth (2003) reported in *To the Desert and Back* that such thinking played an important role in the amazing transformation of European consumer products giant, Unilever,

Understandings about order and chaos, integration and balance can be found throughout this transformation story. [Chairman Tex] Gunning spoke in terms of managing intangibles. (p. 202)

Companies, such as 3M and General Electric (GE), have included some of these features as key elements in their innovation programs. For example, the "10% rule" at 3M is a policy that engenders knowledge creation and innovation by enabling certain employees to spend up to 10% of their work time on creative activities that are not directly tied to their usual work responsibilities. At GE, the "Work Out Program" is a systematic method for assuring that controversial ideas get fairly evaluated and heard, regardless of the person's position in the corporate hierarchy. In one branch of the U.S. Department of Defense with which we worked, officer's improvement ideas were sent up the chain of command by leap-frogging the immediate next level of commanding officers. This policy was intended to give ideas an honest hearing and prevent the possibility of reprisals.

A central principle of the engineered-ecology strategy is that knowledge cannot be effectively managed through conventional management techniques, because these management techniques often rest on assumptions that oppose the very processes needed to create knowledge. Consequently, if companies are knowledge-producing organisms, they should be structured to support the natural knowledge-creating tendencies that are found in all human communities. Firestone and McElroy (2003) have explained many of the principles of the engineered-ecology knowledge strategy in their writings, especially in their vision of the *Open Enterprise.*

Clearly, all three knowledge strategies described here have relevance for knowledge leaders. Viewed metaphorically, all three are useful as principles upon which to lead knowledge processes in organizations. These are as follows:

1. Leverage knowledge and improve its quality whenever possible.
2. Combine knowledge processes with other organizational processes, such as TQM, to focus on performance improvement via knowledge-based activities.

3. Improve your organization's knowledge environment by designing the workplace to enable core knowledge processes to work without undue interference

## AWARDS FOR INNOVATION

We consider it a positive sign that more companies are initiating knowledge efforts and crafting knowledge infrastructure so as to increase knowledge creation and improve innovation. Indeed, the list of companies throughout the world that are becoming known for innovation continues to expand. As one example, Table 15.1 presents the list of finalists for the 2004 American Business Award for Most Innovative Company with more than 2,500 employees.

### Table 15.1
*Most Innovative Companies, 2004*

| Finalist | Acxiom Corp | Little Rock, AR |
|---|---|---|
| Finalist | Humana, Inc. | Louisville, KY |
| Finalist | Memphis Light, Gas and Water | Memphis, TN |
| Finalist | PACCAR, Inc. | Bellevue, WA |
| Award winner | *UPS* | Atlanta, GA |
| Finalist | USEC, Inc. | Bethesda, MD |

From stevieawards.com/aba.

As we move into the emerging Knowledge Age, the knowledge leader's role will become ever more important. The challenge for you as a knowledge leader is to start right where you are now, by envisioning a knowledge strategy, then designing a knowledge infrastructure that effectively fulfills your organization's performance imperatives while simultaneously increasing its capacity to continuously improve both performance and the quality of knowledge.

Elite companies have already demonstrated that steady incremental changes can accumulate over time and enable organizations to move to a level of *FAST* performance that is unimaginable by others. The main question of interest for most knowledge leaders then is this: How do we get from here to there? (Or, perhaps, how do we get our company on this list?)

In our final chapter, we will provide you with a powerful methodology, the *5-Point Dynamic Mapping*® process, to help you chart a pragmatic course to developing and leading a *FAST* KBO.

# REFERENCES

Buckman, R. (2004). *Building Knowledge-Driven Organizations*. New York: McGraw-Hill.

Dvir, R. and Pasher, E. (2004). "Innovation Engines for Knowledge Cities: An Innovation Ecology Perspective", *Journal of Knowledge Management*, Vol. 8, No. 5.

Emiliani, R., Stec, D., Grasso, L., and Stodder, J. (2003). *Better Thinking, Better Results*. Kensington, CT: Clbm Press.

Fearon, D., and Cavaleri, S. (2005). *Inside Knowledge*. Milwaukee, WI: Quality Press.

Firestone, J., and McElroy, M. (2003). *Issues in the New Knowledge Management*. Burlington, MA: Butterworth-Heinemann, KMCI Press.

Hammer, M. (2004, April). "Deep Change." *Harvard Business Review*, 85–93.

Liker, J. (2004). *The Toyota Way*. New York: McGraw-Hill.

McElroy, M. (2003). *The New Knowledge Management*. Burlington, MA: Butterworth-Heinemann, KMCI Press.

Mirvis, P., Ayas, K., and Roth, G. (2003). *To the Desert and Back*. San Francisco: Jossey-Bass.

Ohno, T. (1998). *Toyota Production System*. Portland, OR: Productivity Press.

Seely Brown, J., and Duguid, P. (2000). *The Social Life of Information*. Cambridge, MA: Harvard Business School Press.

# Part VI

# Putting It All Together

# 16

# USING 5-POINT DYNAMIC MAPPING TO LEAD FAST KBOs

## Executive Summary

In this final chapter, we integrate all the major themes developed in this book. We also provide a practical methodology (*5-Point Dynamic Mapping®*) that can help you develop the pragmatic knowledge you need to become a well-balanced knowledge leader and build *FAST* knowledge-based organizations (KBOs). Knowledge leaders can use 5-Point Dynamic Mapping as a flexible meta-framework for ongoing strategic planning or organizational improvement efforts. It provides a highly integrated systems approach that keeps the key components of an organization aligned during ongoing changes. 5-Point Dynamic Mapping allows leaders to assess an organization's strengths and weaknesses, then integrate its identity, vision, mission, interactions, and structure into a high-performing whole system. We also introduce the *Core Learning Spiral* for individual or organizational learning and the creation of pragmatic knowledge, then detail the similarities and differences between the Core Learning Spiral and other standard action-learning cycles. In this chapter, we also provide numerous examples of how we have used 5-Point Dynamic Mapping with organizational clients. We conclude this book by explaining why we consider knowledge leaders to be the future heroes of their organizations.

Our objective in writing this book has been to help you become a well-balanced knowledge leader who is capable of transforming your organization into a *FAST* KBO. Thus far we have provided the following concepts, models, and tools:

- A definition of *knowledge leadership* and an explanation of why it will become increasingly important to the success of organizations.

- A definition of the kind of high-quality knowledge that can provide your company with a significant and sustainable competitive advantage: *pragmatic knowledge* which is defined here as situation-specific knowledge, developed over time, that helps leaders understand what actually works in practice (and also why it works, and under what circumstances).

- The contention that knowledge leaders must use both "science" and "art" to develop the pragmatic knowledge that will enable them to become well-balanced knowledge leaders who can build knowledge-based organizations.

- A description of how your *knowledge leadership style* influences the way you learn, perceive, and lead. On the *Knowledge Bias Profile* (KBP), you rated your degree of preference for two opposing (*Yogi* or *Commissar*) leadership profiles. This self-understanding is important because, from a pragmatic view, knowledge leadership begins with an awareness of your own leadership style.

- An in-depth view of the strengths, weaknesses, and key lessons of Yogi and Commissar leaders plus an explanation of how either of these can impede—or enable—your efforts to become a more effective, balanced knowledge leader.

- A summary of the findings of a major cross-cultural study on the KBP—and an opportunity to compare your KBP results with those of our research participants.

- An explanation of why successful knowledge leadership is a balanced leadership/managerial approach that integrates (1) awareness of knowledge leadership style, (2) creation of an environment that supports knowledge development (KD), and (3) oversight of knowledge management (KM) systems.

- An outline of the roles that knowledge has historically played in commerce and why, in the emerging *Knowledge Era*, knowledge will become even more central to business success.

- A description of common obstacles that prevent learning and knowledge development, and an explanation of how learning can be transformed into useful knowledge.

- A list of the learning components that could potentially compose a *knowledge mix* for your company's *knowledge-based initiatives*.

- An exploration of different kinds of *knowledge strategies* you can implement, depending on your organization's identity, culture, existing management systems, and readiness for change.
- An explanation of why an understanding of organizational identity is essential to the success of knowledge initiatives, and why KD and KM must be aligned with your organization's identity, vision, strategy, and existing management systems if they are to be effective.
- Examples of successful leaders and companies who are already implementing some aspects of the pragmatic knowledge approach.
- A rationale for why *FAST* (*functional, adaptive, sustainable, timely*), KBOs will increasingly have a significant advantage over their competitors.

In this final chapter, we will build on everything you have learned so far by providing you with a strategic knowledge compass and a *FAST* roadmap to move you further forward on your knowledge leadership journey. Specifically, we will describe how you can use the 5-Point Dynamic Mapping process to develop pragmatic knowledge for yourself, your employees, and your organization. First we will examine how you can use 5-Point Dynamic Mapping to transform your company into a *FAST* KBO. Later in this chapter we will examine how you can use a related 5-point process to (1) support learning and knowledge development, (2) create a workplace environment where innovation and knowledge creation can flourish, and (3) retain your most talented employees.

The transformation to becoming a KBO is indeed a leadership challenge that requires much more than mere technical competency. As Karl Wiig (2004) proposed:

Compared to past practices, advanced enterprises have, in effect, reinvented the way they now conduct business. The story does not end there. Significant leadership is required to achieve the desired results." (p. 19)

We believe that the "significant leadership" Wiig alludes to is best exemplified by effective knowledge leaders—who are defined by their self-knowledge, perceptive understanding of other people, and an appreciation of their company's, identity, culture, and operating mechanisms.

# Assessing Your Organization

We will now offer you the opportunity to do a brief assessment of your own organization.[1] After you have your results, we will discuss how to interpret your scores and the potential organizational problems they point to. We will then provide you with examples of how the 5-Point Dynamic Mapping process has worked for some of our organizational clients.

**The 5-Point Balance Sheet (Short Form)**

---

© 2003 Sharon Seivert

Evaluate your company's strengths and weaknesses by assigning a number to each item (from a high of 10 to a low of 1). There are six questions for each of the five categories below, so your scores can range from a low of 6 to a high of 60 in each category. We will help you interpret your scores later in this chapter.

| Step 5. Structure | Total = |
|---|---|

_____ Adequacy of financial capital, cash flow, physical resources, and physical space
_____ Productivity of work processes, procedures, habits
_____ Effectiveness of infrastructures and systems that support the activities of the organization
_____ Efficiency of internal policies, protocols, rules
_____ Degree to which organizational structure facilitates business performance
_____ Quality of the company's products and services that are delivered to customers

| Step 4. Interactions | Total = |
|---|---|

_____ Teamwork; trust; level of cooperation within and between company's departments
_____ Employees feel recognized, are treated respectfully, are loyal to company
_____ Ease of timely access to needed information and feedback systems throughout the organization
_____ Strong connections to customers and vendors; mutually loyal relationships
_____ Business reputation of being a "great place" to work; takes good care of its workers
_____ High level of emotional intelligence in leaders and workers

| Step 3. Mission | Total = |
|---|---|

_____ Clarity of and focus on shared direction throughout company; easy prioritization of tasks
_____ Workers have pride in their work and a sense that what they do matters, their jobs have meaning/context
_____ Everyone is allowed the autonomy to get work done (i.e., not micromanaged)

____ Honest, above-board, rapid management of conflict and mediation of differences

____ Level of activity and action; place is "on fire" to accomplish goals

____ Sense that what company does "makes a difference"

| Step 2. Vision | Total = |
|---|---|

____ Shared beliefs/worldview about what is "reality"; common perceptual filters and paradigms

____ The ratio of hopes to fears throughout the company regarding its future

____ Level of inspiration and optimism in workers and leaders

____ Capacity to think ahead, to plan for best possible future before acting

____ Knowledge "capital"—current expertise; ability to create innovative products/services

____ Willingness to learn (adapt to changing environment); ongoing training and learning

| Step 1. Core Identity | Total = |
|---|---|

____ The core values (real, nonnegotiable) of company; congruence or alignment between who you say you are (stated values) and who you really are (how business is run)

____ The core identity of the business; clarity of "brand"; understanding of why the business exists; answers the questions: "What's the point?" and "What makes us unique?"

____ Sense of having a strong gravitational center that holds things together, a relatively stable reference point from which all corporate actions and decisions are aligned

____ The integrity, ethics, and honesty of leaders and workers in dealings with each other, the company as a whole, customers, stakeholders, vendors, the community at large

____ Leadership actions are congruent with stated values and identity ("walking the talk")

____ A feeling of calm, ease, low stress, of being on the right track; navigate crises with sense of equilibrium

# A POWERFUL TOOL FOR CREATING *FAST* KBOS

*5-Point Dynamic Mapping*® is a process that acts as a combined compass and roadmap to help businesses, work groups, and individuals first chart their own course, then systematically navigate their way to their chosen destination. The power of this methodology is that it enables leaders to progress by following a logical step-by-step formula, where each step builds naturally upon, integrates, and supports the step that precedes it. The effect is cumulative, and the results often constitute a significant evolutionary shift from what would have occurred without this inovative roadmap.

We have chosen to detail this proprietary process in *Knowledge Leadership* because we hope it will support prospective knowledge leaders in their efforts to create *FAST* KBOs. Knowledge leaders can use the "compass" of 5-Point Dynamic Mapping as a flexible meta-framework for their ongoing strategic planning or organizational change efforts. It provides an integrative systems approach that keeps the five major elements of an organization aligned during ongoing changes.

The 5-Point Dynamic Mapping process employs a *FAST* approach because it requires that all organizational decisions begin with, and remain tied to, a clear understanding of the organization's *identity*. An organization cannot successfully do what is outside of its identity. Yet many business leaders set goals that have little relevance to their company's primary function. When the importance of organizational identity goes unrecognized by leaders, there is a tendency to engage in tactical decisions that only further obscure the sense of corporate identity among leaders and employees. For example, if an organization merges with another that has a quite different identity, then, a hidden battle for survival of these two identities can ensue, creating a powerful, "unidentified" undercurrent that can sabotage the system's best efforts. (Later in this chapter we will discuss how you can clarify your organization's identity.) Here is a description of how the four *FAST* criteria and organizational identity support each other.

- The *function* of an organization is an extension of its identity. An insurance company has certain functions that it fulfills to address the needs of its stakeholders. Consulting firms, hospitals, and school systems serve completely different societal functions. Moreover, activities that organizations engage in are only functional if they further fulfill the company's identity.
- Successful *adaptation* requires that an organization express its identity, in a self-referencing way, through the choices it makes as it interacts with its environment. The concept of organizational identity can be a troubling one to leaders who perceive it

as a limitation to potential actions they may choose to take. However, an organization's identity is not genetically predetermined—it has some degree of fluidity and capacity for evolving over time.

- *Sustainability* is also anchored in an organization's identity. Ideally, an organization's sense of its own identity should determine which processes, products, and relationships will receive the necessary attention and resources required to sustain them. All business decisions regarding what to fund or cut should be determined by identity. That is, rather than resources going to department heads with the most political savvy or being distributed "across the board," leaders need to first determine what functions are most important for the business to sustain if it is to retain its unique and distinct identity. Identity also determines what knowledge needs to be developed and maintained to sustain the best features of the business. As Reed and Seivert (1996) noted: As "identity is that which makes something distinct from all others and the surrounding environment" (p. 384).

- Our final *FAST* criterion serves as an indication of *timeliness*. Good timing is determined, indirectly, by an organization's identity. That is, business activities are timely when they are appropriate at that moment to support the functioning, adaptation, and sustainability of the company's identity. As we mentioned earlier, many corporations are better equipped to do the things that are most familiar to them—efficiently—than they are to be innovative and effective. Effectiveness and innovation require knowledge. For example, arriving on time for a meeting may appear efficient, but it is ineffective if we relied on inadequate knowledge and wound up in the wrong building. Timeliness also involves choosing the most appropriate activity for a specific situation at a specific time—for example, it is timely to throw water on a campfire when we want to douse it, but it is bad timing if we are trying to ignite that same campfire on a cold, dark night.

In the face of adversity, it is often a sense of its enduring identity that determines what a company will valve most and determine to most essential to its survival. For example, in the 1990s, Aetna Insurance Company, then a large multi-line company, sold off its property casualty divisions to Travelers Insurance and its pension and personal investments division to ING. After acquiring a large health insurance company, Aetna repositioned itself as primarily being a healthcare company under the name Aetna U.S. Healthcare.

One of the most significant moves that Aetna made to redefine its identity as a healthcare company was to hire a medical doctor, Dr. John Rowe, as its new CEO.

In 2003, Rowe and Aetna U.S. Healthcare were nominated for the Stevie Award as part of the American Business Awards competition. Some of the accomplishments achieved by Rowe and Aetna U.S. Healthcare's employees to redefine the company's identity are detailed in this excerpt from its nomination for the Stevie Award:

Tapping Dr. John W. Rowe as its new leader marked an important step in the company's commitment to improve its strained relationships with physicians and hospitals.... Rowe envisioned a new direction for Aetna: a massive restructuring focusing on profitability as opposed to size.... Key to profitability was controlling the relentless rise of medical costs, a trend plaguing the industry.... Aetna's stock price has hovered near $80 since February 2004, compared to being near $25 in May 2001. Aetna is now seen as the leader in improving physician relations.[2]

When knowledge leaders use the four *FAST* criteria in conjunction with 5-Point Dynamic Mapping, it enables them to develop a clear vision of how their organization can be transformed into a KBO that is capable of fulfilling its core identity and values. An illustration of how identity can shape business decision making is how Toyota adheres to its basic philosophy by not compromising a long-term goal in order to achieve a short-term one.

The 5-Point Dynamic Mapping processes provides knowledge leaders with a solid starting point for creating a *FAST* KBO. Identity becomes the "X" on the map from which a knowledge leader begins the company's knowledge journey. Without a clear sense of identity, organizations tend to lurch expediently from one action to the next or operate like rudderless ships on turbulent seas. Identity provides a reliable self-referencing point for leaders to make vital decisions. Without a strong corporate identity, leaders may propose grand visions of what is possible, but ultimately they discover they cannot propel the ship forward. Moreover, priorities tend to become confused, as virtually everything becomes perceived as *mission critical* and urgent. The long-term effect of ignoring corporate identity is usually a beleaguered, very stressed workforce with high rates of turnover and burnout.

We often see organizations that start with a clear sense of identity, but due to management changes, mergers, and environmental pressures lose their bearings somewhere along the way. So the first step in your development of a *FAST* KBO is to clarify—or redefine—your organization's identity. This is because (1) identity will determine what kind of knowledge is required for your company to meet its goals and (2) having a strong corporate identity will serve as a powerful self-referencing center that holds together all efforts and provides a strong foundation on which to build the future.

## THE 5 POINTS ON THE DYNAMIC MAP

5-Point Dynamic Mapping represents the five key components of an organization that must be integrated to successfully launch, or enduringly change, it. These points constitute the *5 Elements of Success* (Seivert, 2001) that can serve as both a diagnostic and a prognostic tool. That is, you can use this methodology first as a map to see what is—or is not—working well in your company; then you can use it as a compass to stay on course for continuous improvement.

When businesses and work groups are firing on all five of these cylinders, they soar. Typically, however, organizations move forward without the full benefit of these five distinctly different qualities. To evaluate your company, you may transfer your scores from the assessment at the beginning of this chapter to the grid that follows. This inventory can help you flag weak spots in your business that you need to address so they do not sabotage your *FAST* KBO efforts. Please tranfer your scores from pages 308–309 to the grid below.

| Your score: | Workplace symptoms if this point is weak. |
|---|---|
| **1. Identity** <br> _____ | Lack of applied ethics, not walking the talk. Activities/efforts disjointed—not holding together or accumulating in effect. Organization is easily diverted one way or another. Brand is unclear or changing. |
| **2. Vision** <br> _____ | Fears about future. Dysfunctional beliefs. Scattered efforts from pursuing idea "du jour." Lack of innovative thinking or new product design. |
| **3. Mission** <br> _____ | Confused priorities/goals. Hidden agendas, internal competition and conflict. Unfocused efforts. Lack of autonomy and pride in work. Micromanagement. |

| 4. Interactions | Poor communication between key parties. Lack of connection or loyalty. Decreased morale. Low emotional intelligence ("EQ") among leaders. Disrespectful behavior. Inadequate feedback. |
| --- | --- |
| 5. Structure | Poor stewarding of physical resources and finances. Ineffective policies, processes, and procedures. Inefficient, unproductive work habits. Counterproductive rewards. |

Each one of the 5 points of the dynamic map are critical to an organization's success—much as with a baseball diamond, where you must touch all the bases to score a home run. We will now describe the distinctly different qualities of each one of these points so that you can use this roadmap to create a healthier organization. If you have rated your company as weak in any one of these areas, the following descriptions may provide you with some ideas about how to remedy the situation.

## Identity

To reiterate, organizational improvement of any kind (including becoming a *FAST* KBO) begins with clarification of a company's identity. The identity of an organization is the reason for its existence. It provides the answer to why it is in business. What is its *function* in society? What makes it unique, different, one of a kind? How would you describe its culture? What does the organization most value or consider most important, and how do these core values evidence themselves in the organization's culture and its ways of conducting business? The identity of a business is what it really *is*—not what anyone *says* it is or should be. Identity is the organization's "essence," what is most *essential* to this system—that is, what must be *sustained* during any *adaptation*.

During change efforts, including knowledge initiatives, leaders must be careful to safeguard and sustain these essential parts of the organization while simultaneously letting go of what is not essential to it. This understanding is vital. It allows leaders to remain clear about what can, what cannot, and what should be removed from the system to allow it to become optimally effective. Identity serves as the self-referencing center that makes sense of a company's activities. Without a strong identity to intergrate their behavior, organizations can act inefficiently, ineffectively—and sometimes in questionable or unethical ways. We have noticed that this is particularly true if leaders believe that "making money" is the purpose for the company's existence—then, of course, anything goes. Except for financial institutions, the notion that *we are defined as an organization by our ability and need to earn a profit* is of little utility in helping a company become a KBO. This is similar to saying that your purpose in life is to breathe, drink, and eat, because these things are required for your survival.

## Vision

The second point on the 5-Point Dynamic Map is the organization's vision. The difference between this point in our mapping process and most business "visioning" is that here vision arises organically from the organization's identity. For example, it may be an exciting vision to have the top office in a 50-story building, but if your business depends on active street traffic, this vision does not fit with your business identity. An organization's identity serves as the touchstone for a vision that projects the best of the organization into the future. In other words, in this mapping process, leaders use identity as a driver behind the wheel to help them see more clearly where the company is right now and where they want it to arrive in an ideal future.

Another issue to be addressed in vision is the current ratio of hopes to fears within your company. The organization's members are already moving your business toward the shared vision they have imagined. Leaders need to realize that if employees are feeling nervous, then this collective sensation of fear provides the perceptual framework for the vision they are already busy creating in their imaginations. One of the reasons knowledge leaders need to be inspiring is so they can shift the balance in the whole system's perception of what reality exists right now and also its vision of the future—from fear to hope, from confusion to clarity. This will create a heightened level of cooperative excitement that will result in learning, creativity, knowledge development, and innovation. Here is where knowledge leaders *show the bees the way out of the jar so that they can fly again*—and start "buzzing" around to "cross-pollinate" knowledge activities (much as Oscar Wilde described in *Her Voice*):

The wild Bee reels from bough to bough with his furry coast and his gauzy wing,
   Now in a lily cup, and now setting jacinth bell a-swing, in his wandering.

## Mission

The third point on the 5-Point Dynamic Map is mission. This element provides an organization's members with a good reason to accomplish their goals, a strong sense of direction, and clarified priorities. It can generate excitement, energy, focus, and a sense of pride for everyone. When the organization's identity and vision are clear, more people are likely to feel on track. Employees understand where their job fits within the context of the whole picture. They believe that their work really matters; they have a stake in the success of the business; they feel personally invested in doing whatever needs to be done. Moreover, they will become more interested in learning and working with colleagues to develop knowledge. When people have a clear direction, the organization's performance is likely to move ever closer to narrowing the gap between its current state and its ideal future. Mission can align and unify employees' efforts, provide fuel to lift their efforts off the launching pad, and propel the company toward its ideal future.

## Interactions

Now that the organization's direction has been clarified and all efforts aligned, it is time to change *Interactions* in ways that enable various communities of practice within the company to do what they do best—that is, create knowledge. This is a good time for knowledge leaders to initiate dialogue and conversation or to support the self-organizing launch of various learning communities that are focused on inquiry and practice. Giving people greater autonomy is not terribly risky at this point in the 5-Point Dynamic Mapping process. Now that the organization's mission, vision, and identity are clear, workers are likely to act in self-policing and congruent ways. Because they have a clear role to play in the organization's future, employees are also more likely to abide by professional norms and accepted community standards of behavior.

## Structure

The fifth point on the 5-Point Dynamic Map is *structure*. An organization's structure includes its policies, processes, procedures, workplace architecture, information technology (IT), management information system (MIS), KM, and reward systems. All aspects of organizational structure need to be designed to most effectively house the organization's interpersonal interactions, mission, vision, and identity. Part of a knowledge leader's challenge is to custom-design the organization's structure so that it is optimally: (1) *functional,* that is, built to further the organization's identity, vision, mission, and most fruitful interactions, (2) sufficiently strong and flexible so the organization can *adapt* quickly and appropriately to changing circumstances while supporting the organization's efforts to stay on track, (3) *sustaining* and supportive of the most essential organizational behaviors, and (4) *timely,* that is, designed to provide feedback that allows managers and workers to respond in appropriate and timely ways to internal and external organizational needs.

Structure is the point on the 5-Point Dynamic Map where leaders can finally harvest honey from the hive. Now managers can see and measure the improvements to outputs, the quality of products and services, and the number of innovations. Because leaders can taste, touch, see, and feel this physical component of an organization, structure traditionally has been the point on the 5-Point Dynamic Map that receives the most attention. But knowledge leaders know that a great deal lies beneath this surface body of the organization. Indeed, the other four (often ignored) points are vital to the long-term financial and systemic health of a business.

In summary, the 5-Point Dynamic Map consists of five distinctly different elements of an organization. All of these elements are necessary, much as an automobile needs its chassis, transmission, and four wheels to drive down the road. If any of the tires is flat, the going will be slow indeed, and will delay—or prevent—the car's arrival at its destination. A knowledge leader can use the 5-Point Dynamic Mapping process to notice any points that need immediate attention, thereby helping leaders deal with organizational troubles before they result in obvious and inescapable difficulties.

## FINDING THE ROOT CAUSE OF A PROBLEM

Another issue to keep in mind with this 5-point analysis is that organizational troubles surfacing in one place may have their roots elsewhere. *Root cause* is a powerful concept popularized in the total quality management (TQM) movement. It encourages leaders to trace organizational problems to their root, where they can be fixed more permanently. Otherwise, the unresolved issue is likely to surface again, perhaps in another place. In the case of the 5-Point Dynamic Map, once you identify the point where the symptoms have surfaced, you can use this map to help you trace the problem to its root cause.

Root causes typically lie upstream in this 5-point spiral map. For example, if people in your department are fighting, you could (1) ignore the issue, (2) treat the problem where it surfaced (by having communication training or firing the people involved in the conflict), or (3) trace the conflict to its root. In this case, the root cause might be "confused priorities" at the mission level or "fear about the future" at the vision level. Moreover, because all these five elements are highly integrated with each other, you may also need to test further to see if this problem originated elsewhere in the five points. For example, perhaps your people are fighting because their work-spaces are too cramped, or noisy, or they have inadequate supplies to share. In this case, an adjustment in structure might significantly alleviate this interactions difficulty. In any case, if you treat the issue at its root cause, the dilemma will be resolved in a significantly more enduring way.

Once you eradicate one potential root cause, you will be able to observe whether it has the desired effect of reducing the problem. Sometimes symptoms have multiple, complex, intertwining causes. But if you scientifically explore, then systematically eliminate, one root cause at a time—as part of pragmatic knowledge development—you will chip away at the problem until you have arrived at an effective solution. Treating the root cause takes inquiry and a little scientific investigation, but it is well worth the effort because it will increase both the effectiveness and efficiency of your organization over time. It will help you find lasting solutions so that the same costly issues do not surface time and again.

## IDENTITY BLINDNESS, OR THE CASE OF THE SWALLOWED PORCUPINE

Of all the points in the 5 Point Dynamic Map, organizational identity tends to be the most frequently overlooked organizational component. This is understandable because it is the most subtle (yet fundamental) aspect of an organization. Not having a clear corporate identity is a bit like being one of those amnesia victims on the daytime soap operas who vaguely understands that he has a name and came from somewhere but just can't remember where or when.

Not understanding the power of identity can bring previously successful organizations to their knees. We have seen it countless times in the failure of mergers or acquisitions. According to an article in the *Harvard Business Review* (1998), "a study ... of 300 major mergers conducted over a ten-year period ... found that, in 57% of these merged companies, return to shareholders lagged behind the average for their industries." And according to the international consulting firm Bain & Company, more than half of acquisitions actually destroy shareholder value instead of achieving cost or revenue benefits. As is described in the healthcare industry example that follows, we believe that many disappointing results from mergers can be attributed to *identity blindness*.

Over the past decade, hospital mergers have been frequent and numerous. Although it might have looked good to the leaders and directors to merge "Bentley Hospital" and "Daniels Hospital", it was evident even to casual observers that these two institutions were very different. Bentley Hospital was the larger institution, and stronger financially. Its leaders believed that it was not going to be too much trouble to merge with (that is, take over) the smaller Daniels Hospital. However, the cultures of these two institutions were very dissimilar: Bentley Hospital prided itself on being a teaching hospital, while Daniels Hospital was a neighborhood-based hospital. Bentley Hospital was run by one religion-affiliated sponsor, while Daniels Hospital was aligned with another. Daniels Hospital was in serious financial trouble, so Bentley Hospital agreed to assume Daniels Hospital's financial burden upon merger. The executives of Bentley Hospital were confident that it could absorb Daniels Hospital and, subsequently, turn it around.

Unfortunately, there was no coherent plan for integrating the two hospital cultures after the merger. Departments were thrown together and left to figure things out for themselves. As a result, there was tremendous political jockeying and infighting, and plenty of "bloodletting" in the name of cleaning house. In this new organizational jungle, those who manage to survive were the "fittest" politically, while many of the most talented employees left for jobs in other organizations. Not long afterward, the board changed executive leadership after the merged organization began to lose millions of dollars. Major cutbacks ensued as the hospital's managers tried to stop the internal bleeding. Hundreds of workers were summarily laid off as part of a larger cost-cutting effort.

## Possible Organizational Lesson: "Sometimes It's Not Wise to Swallow a Porcupine"

A senior executive from Bentley Hospital, upon learning the 5-Point Dynamic Mapping process, exclaimed: "This is amazingly on target. In fact, I can tell you the *dates* after the merger when Bentley lost a clear sense of its identity. Then, fear overtook us and we lost our vision. Not long after that our mission became unclear, our priorities confused. Then, our formerly good interactions went haywire, and the in-fighting started. It got really ugly. After that, our financial problems started to surface—and we responded with layoffs and restructuring. And then the reporters descended and our scandal was out in the open. It was a nightmare." As this healthcare manager realized upon reflection, Bentley Hospital's problems had started years before—with an ill-designed merger that did not account for the separate organizational identities of the two hospitals. If the leaders of these organizations had taken identity into consideration, they could have brokered the best of their two different worlds. The merger would then have turned out quite differently—as a thoughtfully considered marriage.

## USING THE CORE LEARNING SPIRAL FOR PRAGMATIC KNOWLEDGE DEVELOPMENT

Not only can you use the 5-Point Dynamic Map as a tool to assess your organization's readiness as a KBO, you can also use it as a *Core Learning Spiral* (Seivert, 1998, 2001) for the development of corporate (or individual) pragmatic knowledge. There are two fundamental differences between the Core Learning Spiral (Figure 16.1) and other standard action-learning cycles. First, with 5 points the Core Learning model becomes a spiral rather than a 4-point cycle. Second, the additional point at the center of the spiral represents identity, which forms the self-referencing starting point for learning and knowledge development. The 4 points on the outside ring of the Core Learning Spiral correspond directly to the plan-do-check-act (PDCA) cycle (also called the Deming or Shewart cycle) that is commonly used in TQM efforts. These four points also correspond to the standard action-learning cycle by Kolb, Rubin and McIntyre but with two of the steps in inverted order (Figure 16.2).

The first step in using the Core Learning Spiral for knowledge creation is to discover, clarify, or redefine the organization's identity.

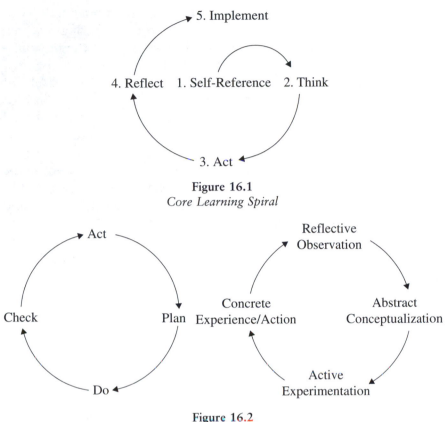

**Figure 16.1**
*Core Learning Spiral*

**Figure 16.2**
*The PDCA and Action Learning Cycles*

This is a fundamental step, without which the organization's *FAST* knowledge efforts will founder. At each step in this 5-point process, you must determine if these knowledge efforts are furthering the identity of your company. This self-referencing center assures congruence and integrity in all corporate action. It increases effectiveness by helping you keep your business on track to reach its goals, making certain its actions are aligned with its core values, and ensuring that it will not drift off course into mediocrity.

The second step in this knowledge-creating process is to envision or *think* (plan/analyzing and conceptualizing) about where the company is right now and where you want it to go. This step focuses on uncovering perceptual biases, mental models, and beliefs. Here you deliberately experience the *irritation of doubt* so you can remove any dysfunctional perceptual blinders. This step asks a knowledge leader to be completely candid: How aligned with the principles of *FAST* are the shared beliefs in the company? How have these beliefs supported or harmed us? Knowledge leaders need to candidly evaluate the results of the organization's work to date. During this step you will also need to envision the kind of knowledge the organization needs to bring it into the future you desire for it.

This is a necessary pragmatic step. If you do not like the results of your prior actions, you need to think about why something has (or has not) worked, how, and under what circumstances. You will need to ask: What gap exists between our current reality and our ideal? Where do we have recurrent problems? If we don't like where we are now and want to wind up in a different place, this is the point in the process where we need to be completely honest with ourselves. Otherwise, we will be like insane people who do the same thing over and over—all the while expecting different results.

The third step in the Core Learning Spiral is to determine what *action* (do/active experimentation) you will take to close the gap between where your business is right now and where you wish it to be. It requires leaders to focus, prioritize, then carefully choose their next actions. In pragmatic terms, it requires taking small steps in the service of science. You may launch a pilot project to test the waters, trying things out on a small scale. You may pilot a change at this point to determine if you want to proceed in that direction. Here you take a small experimental action, in a scientific way—suspending judgment, to see how an action works in practice to produce the results you want. In the creation of a KBO, this is also the point at which you will need to determine a knowledge strategy that will best fit your company's identity and help it attain its ideal vision.

The fourth point in the Core Learning Spiral is to see whether or not (plus how, why, when, and under what circumstances) the action you initiated is working. In pragmatic knowledge terminology: Is your action effective in producing your expected results? By receiving feedback from your actions, you are able to *reflect* (check/reflective observation). Then you tinker. You adjust. You work with others—for example, by dialoguing in a community of learners or meeting with the senior management team—to fit together the jigsaw puzzle of collective learning and develop new knowledge. You receive feedback from the front line. With these collective insights and feedback about the effectiveness of your actions, you will be able to make your action even more effective. These interactions will keep you on course to bring the organization's identity, vision, and mission to fruition. Then, when all signals are go. . . .

You move into the fifth stage of the Core Learning Spiral, which is *implementation* of that change (act to implement/concrete experience/action). You put the action that has proven effective into practice throughout your division or entire organization. This is also the point at which you can build more effective KM systems that capture, measure, and store the new, high-quality knowledge that has been developed.

In summary, then, you can use this 5-Point Dynamic Map as a strategic planning tool or as a model for knowledge development. In addition, knowledge leaders can use these same 5 points as a knowledge checklist to make certain they have considered all the vital knowledge aspects necessary to create a *FAST* KBO. (Note that there is a natural logic to the order in this checklist. That is, knowledge initiatives will probably work best if they follow the steps as outlined in Figure 16.3.)

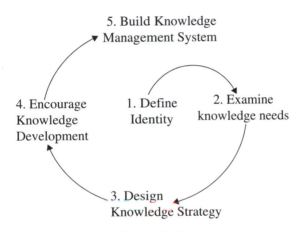

**Figure 16.3**
*Touching All the Bases: A Systemic Approach to Creating FAST KBOs*

## THE KNOWLEDGE ROOTS OF THE 5-POINT DYNAMIC MAP: THE ORIGINAL SYSTEMS APPROACH

This 5-point formula (whether Dynamic Map, Core Learning Spiral, or knowledge initiative checklist) is powerful in its effect because it is based on a cross-cultural systems template for balance, wholeness, and healing. This model is derived from the rich, cross-cultural metaphor of the classical five elements, which have been used for millennia to describe the building blocks that are vital for our well-being. This template is easy to remember and use because people are familiar with its images in diverse cultures across the world. These include compasses (that point us in the right direction and keep us on track), clocks (that chime on the quarter hour), baseball diamonds (where you touch all bases for a home run), Native American medicine wheels (with their center and four directions), the "X" that marks the spot (where treasure lies), the alchemists' squared circle (to make gold), and spirals in nature.

In *The Balancing Act: Mastering the 5 Elements of Success in Life, Relationships, and Work*, Sharon Seivert (2001) details how each one of these five elements contribute to individual and organizational success. Taken together, these fundamental components constitute a whole system, whether that system is your organization or yourself. The grid in Table 16.1 shows how well this comprehensive classical systems approach describes the five parts of an organization, five steps in knowledge creation, and 5 points in a knowledge initiative checklist.

Table 16.1
*The 5-Point Dynamic Systems Approach*

| 5-Point strategic map | Core learning spiral | KBO checklist | Metaphor of five classical elements |
|---|---|---|---|
| 1. Identity | Self-reference identity (+) | Define organizational identity | Soul/"Essence"/center |
| 2. Vision | Think (plan) | Examine mental models and envision knowledge needs | Mind/"Air" |
| 3. Mission | Act (do) | Design knowledge strategy | Will/"Fire" |
| 4. Interactions | Reflect (check) | Encourage KD | Emotions/"Water" |
| 5. Structure | Implement (act) | Build KM systems | Body/"Earth" |

For knowledge leaders who hope to transform their companies into KBOs or launch knowledge initiatives, the 5-Point Dynamic Map demonstrates how the act of creation actually works—that is, it always moves from abstract possibilities to concrete realities. Here is an example:

1. You are an architect. (Identity)
2. You have a great idea for a new building. (Vision)
3. You draw up the blueprint for this building. (Mission)
4. You connect with all the people who will make it a reality: colleagues in your firm, financers, laborers, real estate brokers, attorneys, government agencies for building permits. (Interactions)
5. The building is constructed over a 2-year period; it eventually becomes part of the city skyline. (Structure)

## PUTTING 5-POINT DYNAMIC MAPPING TO WORK

The beauty of 5-Point Dynamic Mapping is that—because it is a natural template and a logical formula—it is very easy for leaders and workers to learn, remember, and put to work (Seivert, 2005). As a compass or checklist in the hands of knowledge leaders, it dramatically increases organizational *resilience* by charting a more pragmatic path to effectiveness (Seivert, 2005a). This 5-point compass helps companies and workgroups stay on their chosen course despite obstacles and inevitable setbacks. Moreover, you and other leaders in your organization can use this tool again and again to adapt to—and safely find your way through—constantly changing circumstances. In our experience, leaders have described insights that "hit like lightening." Work groups comment: "Of course. It's so obvious now that I see it in front of me." Executives report that the formula is "very useful" on a day-to-day basis, helping them to "roll with the punches." Senior management teams relay that it has helped them "keep the best of the business intact" while adjusting intelligently to the industry challenges confronting them. Here are some more examples.

## THE CASE OF THE RELUCTANT LAW FIRM

We worked with a large law firm that, according to the new CEO, was having growing pains. Within the first hour of an annual planning session with the firm's senior partners, it became obvious to us that their former corporate identity was no longer relevant to their current interests and concerns. One aspect of this shift is that this group had grown into an international law firm, yet their managing partners still acted as if they were a regional firm. With the use of the dynamic mapping process, the group quickly named the subtle-but-pervasive root of the problem. They were then able to articulate, and start steps to narrow, the gap between their old and updated definitions of the firm. They established task forces to revise their non-inclusive (region-based) policies and decision-making processes. The outcome was to redefine the firm's identity from the inside out. The senior partners were rather startled by the revelation initially, but moved quickly to remedy the situation once they saw the disparity between the organization's old and new self. As one of the senior partners from another region commented to us afterward: "The guys back at the office are going to think I'm some kind of hero when I tell them that we're finally going to be listened to."

## The Case of Crossing the Chasm at a Social Service Organization

An American nonprofit social services organization had been undergoing tremendous change. Its founder was a charismatic leader, a leading expert in her field, and a principal lightning rod for governmental funding. We were called in to the organization to help separate the somewhat merged identities of the leader and the organization as part of a succession plan to ensure this nonprofit's long-term success. The staff members of this organization were intensely committed to its cause—but they all had different ideas about priorities and what was most effective to do. They were a passionate and hard-working group, but not particularly well aligned in their efforts. Over the course of a few weeks, the entire group was brought into the same room, where they began by hotly debating the question of their identity.

These animated conversations verified our suspicion that the organization was at a major crossroads and that a careful decision needed to be made before it took a next step. After assuring that everyone had an opportunity to speak, we asked the group to let the issue settle over the course of a week. When we returned, the group members were able to craft an identity statement with which they were very pleased. Next, they were able to move on to the second step of visioning. Nearly 90% of the participants drew a stunningly similar picture of their vision of the future. After that, the group revised its vision and mission statements with the ease of child's play. The group had successfully redefined itself and determined a new future—one that all the group members (and not just the organization's founder) would be carrying forward. The leader referred to the new level of energy, productivity, and creativity as being "nothing short of miraculous."

## The Knowledge Leader's Primary Task: Releasing the Genie from the Bottle

In *FAST* KBOs, knowledge leaders do not have to carry the full burden of success on their shoulders. This is typically a great relief to them, because they realize that their organization's future wealth will be increased if they encourage and support knowledge leadership at all levels of the organization. This more "democratic" knowledge approach solves the workplace dilemma defined by Studs Terkel (1972) in *Working* when he concluded that "Jobs are not big enough for people" (p. xxix).

If you have inherited a traditionally managed organization or unit, the task before you will be: "How do I get the bees to fly out of the jar after I have removed the lid?" In many cases, the first task of the knowledge leader in encouraging employees to join knowledge initiatives will be to drive out fear. Indeed, this command was one of W. Edward Deming's famous Fourteen Principles. As we stated in *Managing in Organizations That Learn* (Seivert et al., 1996):

Fear is the first obstacle to the adventure of learning, keeping the individual from even stepping onto the path. And there's more. Fear is toxic: it can pollute an entire system, adversely affecting everyone. Interestingly, when we ask workers the characteristics of their worst and best bosses . . . one issue that surfaces every time is fear. The worst bosses are described as inspiring fear or being afraid—sometimes both. . . . The best bosses . . . take risks, encourage their employees to grow, are supportive . . . in short, they have taken responsibility for their own actions. (pp. 356–357)

We believe that knowledge leaders help evolve the quality of knowledge in the organization, over time, from "good" to "great" by establishing a work environment where others can learn, process knowledge, and create pragmatic knowledge. Specifically, knowledge leaders can do this by (1) modeling awareness of knowledge leadership styles so others know that it is safe to experiment and learn in new ways, (2) clearly defining lines of authority and areas of autonomy, (3) establishing systems that support learning and knowledge development, and (4) understanding how learning and knowledge are developed in organizations.

There is one more way the 5-Point Dynamic Mapping process can help knowledge leaders. The ideal in KBOs is that all employees function as potential developers of knowledge within a community experiment strategy where processes, operations, and products are constantly tinkered with and improved by workers. Unfortunately, there is a common belief in Western business that there are only a few stars or MVPs in their companies. As Margaret Butteriss and Bill Roiter (2004) noted in *Corporate MVPs: Managing Your Company's Most Valuable Performers*, most CEOs identify only 5% of their workforce in this elite category. A knowledge-based approach turns that paradigm on its head by using a *community experiment* strategy to create workplace conditions where there is an opportunity for all employees to be knowledge developers—inventors, tinkerers, improvers of processes, and generators of new corporate wealth. Rather than treating employees like students where only 5% can receive top grades, we suggest shifting the entire bell-shaped curve over to new ground—that is, to deliberately foster excellent performance company wide.

A tool to help knowledge leaders develop their workers is the career application of the 5-Point Dynamic Mapping process—which can help employees define and reach their own goals within the context of their work group's goals. (See Appendix C for a description of *5-Point Dynamic Mapping* for retention and development of corporate talent.) Indeed, we have found that previously disenfranchised workers became more self-directed and engaged in creating their own futures—and more cooperative with their supervisors and coworkers. If you help your employees define their own career goals so that their talents find an optimum fit within the organization's goals, you will certainly release the creative genie from the bottle.

## THE KNOWLEDGE LEADER AS HERO

It has been our intention in *Knowledge Leadership* to serve as guides for you as you journey into a new territory. As George Roth indicated in the Foreword, accomplishing a heroic task—such as becoming a knowledge leader and creating a knowledge-based organization—sometimes requires having no choice. We concur that, for many organizations, there is no viable path back to the old way of doing business. We hope that we have provided you with the concepts and tools you will need to lead your organization forward into better days. We sincerely hope that you have found this book to be a helpful roadmap thus far, and we applaud your "heroism" in proceeding into this unknown territory.

We hope that *Knowledge Leadership* has provided you with many ideas about how to envision and develop a workplace where *FAST* pragmatic knowledge can drive innovation. We end *Knowledge Leadership* by refocusing your attention on the pragmatic learning process of the knowledge leader. We believe that taking a pragmatic knowledge path will require some courage and determination on your part. We will even go so far as to say that this is the choice of a heroic leader. Don't count on being thanked for your efforts. You may even experience some backlash from entrenched managers who do not understand what you are talking about or who feel threatened by the changes you propose. Because we are not in favor of political suicide missions, we ask that you proceed intelligently, pragmatically—testing the waters, receiving feedback, and seeing the results of your actions as you proceed.

The heroic path of pragmatic knowledge is "selfishly altruistic" or "altruistically selfish." as defined by biologists Humberto Maturana and Francisco Varela (1987). In *The Tree of Knowledge,* they stated that species survival often depends on members of the group taking risks that appear altruistic—but that it clearly benifits the individual if the group survives. (Much as it benefits you if your department and organization do well.) The good news is that by taking such risks, nothing is lost. That is, the individual learns—even if the group does not.

One of the first steps on the journey to becoming a knowledge leader is to learn more about how you see opportunities, solve problems, and view your own abilities as leader or manager. To that end, we have introduced you to your knowledge leadership style. We encourage you to continue your self-knowledge development. For example, you may choose to engage an executive coach from whom you can receive reliable ongoing feedback and dispassionately discuss the results of actions. Indeed, some executive coaching/mentoring firms claim a 10-to-1 return on corporate investment in such coaching services. We have seen that, although many managers are cautious or resistant at first, they soon find it exhilarating to reverse dysfunctional behavior of which they were unaware. Independent reports and self-reports indicate that the managerial skills and effectiveness of leaders can dramatically improve when they address emotional intelligence issues that have heretofore handicapped their careers.

Starting change efforts by increasing self-knowledge may not be the most comfortable for business leaders, but it is where knowledge leaders have to begin—and we think it will be a differentiating trait between good and great leaders in the future. In *Managing in Organizations That Learn* (Seivert et al., 1996), we stated that:

Learning is, first and foremost, an adventure of self-discovery . . . the leadership needed to develop learning organizations requires a different form of risk taking than has been encouraged in the past. Instead of tough-minded executives who focus externally on wiping out the competition or internally on directing activity and maintaining control, we will need individuals who have the courage to face and deal with their own issues, including their and others' fears about a tumultuous present and an uncertain future. (pp. 352–353)

So if knowledge leadership requires heroism, we have a tried-and-true roadmap from cultures from around the world that outlines a path for those with the right stuff to become knowledge leaders. The encoded story goes a bit like this:

In ancient days, strong and handsome knights—or beautiful and courageous maidens—could not become rulers of the kingdom until they had journeyed into the deep dark woods (of their inner selves),

Slain dragons (faced their own weaknesses; dealt with detractors),

Claimed the treasure (discovered their own identity),

Rescued the kidnapped princess or prince (integrated all opposing parts of themselves [remember the Yogi and Commissar!]), and

Brought their newfound heroism, treasure, and princess or prince (the knowledge gained).

Back to rejuvenate the wasteland kingdom so it will bloom/be fertile (innovative, competitive, wealth generating) again.

While knowledge leaders may in fact be heroes who are in service to a worthy cause, they are also individuals who are becoming increasingly capable of achieving the results they desire from both work and life. Throughout history, leaders have usually been cast as a small percentage of individuals who were "born to lead" or who were transformed into great leaders through an external force, such as having a great mentor or studying with learned scholars in an elite MBA program.

We contend that leaders are created on the ground, not in the classroom. Knowledge leaders do not need anyone to empower them. They are self-reliant in creating the knowledge they need by treating their experience as a source of insight into how things really work in practice. That's why we consider them to be the "heroes" who are blazing new trails into the business world of the future.

So now we will leave you, the aspiring knowledge leader, with a benediction from Henry David Thoreau to send you on your way:

Go confidently in the direction of your dreams. Live the life you have imagined.

We wish you the very best in your efforts.

## REFERENCES

Butteriss, M., and Roiter, B. (2004). *Corporate MBPs: Managing Your Company's Most Valuable Performers.* Canada: Etobicoke, Ontario: John Wiley and Sons Canada LTD.

*Harvard Business Review.* (1998, January/February). "Making the Deal Real."

Maturana, H., and Varela, F. (1987). *The Tree of Knowledge: The Biological Roots of Human Understanding.* Boston, MA: Shambala.

Reed, F., and Seivert, S. (1996). "The Implications of Autonomy for Learning in Organizations." In Cavaleri and Fearon (Eds.), *Managing in Organizations That Learn*. Cambridge, MA: Blackwell Business Books.

Seivert, S. (1998). *Working from Your Core: Personal and Corporate Mastery in a World of Change*. Burlington, MA: Butterworth-Heinemann.

Seivert, S. (2001). *The Balancing Act: Mastering the 5 Elements of Success in Life, Relationships, and Work*. Rochester, VT: Inner Traditions.

Seivert, S. (2005). *5-Point Dynamic Mapping for Leaders*. Cambridge, MA: The Coreporate Press.

Seivert, S. (2005a). *5-Point Dynamic Mapping for Organizations*. Cambridge, MA: The Coreporate Press.

Seivert, S., Pattakos, A., Reed, F., and Cavaleri, S. (1996). "Learning from the Core: The Heroic Leader and the Conscious Organization." In Cavaleri and Fearon D. (Eds.), *Managing in Organizations that Learn*. Cambridge, MA: Blackwell Business Books.

Terkel, S. (1972). *Working*. New York: Avon Books.

## Notes

1. This instrument is an abbreviated version of *The Organizational Balance Sheet* from *The Balancing Act*, Seivert (2001).
2. www.stevieawards.com/pubs/awards/70_1438_8436.cfm.

# Appendix A

## Development and Use of the Knowledge Bias Profile

### Use of the Knowledge Bias Profile

If you would like to know more about the complete Knowledge Bias Profile and how this instrument might be used in your organization, contact the authors of *Knowledge Leadership* at www.thecoreporation.com.

### Development of the Knowledge Bias Profile (KBP)

The KBP was designed and tested in four separate parts. The items in the questionnaire were designed to clearly differentiate between the two distinct worldviews of the Yogi and Commissar archetypes. We focused on measuring constructs that we felt were vital to understanding knowledge leaders including their (1) worldview, (2) values, (3) beliefs about change (its nature, how it originates, and how it should be focused), and (4) ways of reasoning.

Part A of the KBP was a 42-item survey instrument that contained 21 questions each about the worldviews of the two types of leaders. This is the instrument we tested in the first part of our four-part study. Our research indicates that the items we crafted had a high degree of validity for measuring each of the two respective worldviews. That is, the statements within each worldview had strongly significant positive relationships to each other and strongly negative relationships to statements in the opposing worldview.

Next we developed Part B of the KBP, which is a 40-item behavioral scale. This part of the KBP measures whether these two different worldviews would result in different types of leading, looking (perceptual), and learning behaviors. Research on Part B of the KBP became the second part of the four parts within our overall study.

We were pleased to find very strong correlations between worldview and behaviors.

We then developed Part C of the KBP, which consists of two short narrative descriptions that depict some of the core characteristics of the Yogi and Commissar, respectively. Two studies were conducted using these narratives. The third part of our study of the KBP used this narrative to ask American management students and managers which of the two leadership styles they believed would be more effective.

The fourth part of the KBP study was a cross-cultural testing of Part C. Here we presented two groups of Chinese managers with translated narratives and asked them three questions—that is, which of the two styles best described (1) their self-image, (2) the business leader they would prefer, and (3) who would make a better leader of their country.

In the research we conducted on the KBP, we used a 5-point Likert scale rather than a forced-choice method. We deliberately chose the 5-point scale because we hypothesized that people were likely to have a mix of these two archetypal leadership styles. Our belief was based on observations of many leaders as well as our reflections about our own work styles. We assumed, therefore, that a 5-point scale would present a more "true" picture for leaders. Interestingly, even on a scale with complete freedom of choice, the results we obtained were highly significant. A forced choice questionnaire—where the moderate ("neutral") option was eliminated—would likely have generated an even more significant match.

# Appendix B

## ESSENTIALS OF CREATING PRAGMATIC KNOWLEDGE

BY STEVEN A. CAVALERI AND FREDERICK REED,
CHIEF TECHNOLOGY OFFICER OF
AS IT IS CORPORATION

### INTRODUCTION

Charles Sanders Peirce first outlined the science of creating pragmatic knowledge over a century ago. Peirce was the leading philosopher and scientist in the United States at the turn of the 20th century. Peirce believed that high-quality knowledge could be created by applying the scientific method of experimentation to the knowledge-creating process itself. Among other things, Peirce was an accomplished logician and emphasized the importance of reasoning in the creation of knowledge. His basic idea was that knowledge is composed of elements known as *acts*. In turn, each act is composed of a case, a rule for action, and an expected result. Peirce believed that if a person knew any two elements of an act, he or she could then employ reasoning to arrive at the third element. For example, if you know the problem (case) and you know the ideal outcome (result), you can then infer which rule for action you should employ to attain it. This is called a *triadic system* because it contains three elements. Knowledge leaders can be trained in the simple use of this method and the principles of experimental design, and they will be ready to start using the fundamentals of Peirce's approach. The remainder of this appendix provides an extended example of how the pragmatic method might be used in practice.

## ESSENTIALS OF PRAGMATIC ORGANIZATIONAL KNOWLEDGE CREATION

In practice, every act of knowing is intertwined with an act of doing. Every act is purposeful and depends on the recognized set of circumstances. For example, a leader would lead employees differently if the goal is to increase quality in a company that is straining with orders above its production capacity versus a case where the goal is to increase productivity in an organization where employees are chronically underpaid.

From the perspective of pragmatic knowledge creation, an act is always defined as being based on a perceived situation in which rules for action are employed to reach a goal or desired state affairs. Thus, we propose that *an act is a triadic (three-way) relation between a (1) case, (2) rule, and (3) result* (Figure APPB.1).

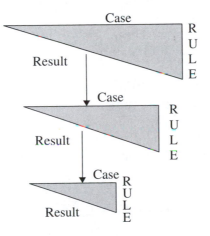

**Figure APPB.1**
*A Cascading Hierarchy of Acts*

- A *case* is the perceived situation that enables the act to be performed. For example, in order to grab a piece of cheese from the refrigerator, it must first be within reach.
- The *rule* names the law governing the performance of the act. This law can be thought of as a general principle that relates the case and result, such as the "law of addition" relating

*Continued*

numbers and a mathematical sign (1 + 1) to 2. It is considered a law because it is a generality that covers an inexhaustible set of actual instances. This law also governs a class of possible physical actions at some level of abstraction. For example, at some level, "Grab the cheese" is an act that can be specifically accomplished in an infinite number of ways at greater levels of detail (e.g., different starting positions of the hands).

- The *result* expresses the anticipated consequences of having acted.

In pragmatic knowledge-creating processes, the case and result of any potential act express possible *sets of conditions* that a person or system can later recognize as actually being present. These sets of conditions define the rules for action or *acts* that can also be recognized by their respective potential *knowledge acts*. The result of this triadic process is that there is an overall layering of the effects of potential knowledge acts. These acts within the cache of knowledge in a person or organization emerges or surfaces to greater levels of awareness in a self-organizing way. This cascading process begins with the most elementary knowledge acts and ends with the most abstract ones at the top of the collection of potentially usable acts that we call our knowledge. Those acts that are of a more general or abstract nature tend to build on, in their cases and results, the rules of more elementary acts that have been previously established.

## PRAGMATIC LOGIC

According to Peirce, three types of reasoning can be applied to acts: (1) deduction, (2) induction, and (3) abduction. These three forms of inference work together both to apply existing knowledge and to create new knowledge. *Deduction* is a process of reasoning that flows from the case and the rule toward the anticipated result. In the process of deduction, the case is an existing fact that has already been experienced. Given this fact and the law named by the rule of the act under consideration, deduction infers a future or consequential fact, the result of the act. For example, one can deduce from the fact (2 + 2) and the law of addition a consequential fact "4." Because the antecedents of deduction are a fact and a law, the inferred results, then, necessarily follow. In other words, if both the case and result are true, the consequent result obtained by deduction must also necessarily be true. Of the three forms of inference, deduction is the only one having this character. It is also probably the best known form of inference, and is usually what comes to mind when the term *logical* is invoked.

*Induction* is inference from a case and result, both appearing as facts in experience, to the rule of a potential act in knowledge. Notice that induction works entirely in the past, seeking to explain actual experience in terms of existing knowledge. Unlike deduction, induction is only possible rather than necessary. Even if the case and result are true, there is no guarantee that an inferred rule is the correct one. For example, if the case is a *buzzing fly* and the result is a *dead fly*, the rule might be *swat the fly*, but it also might be *old age*. Abduction is a logical process that creates or modifies knowledge on the basis of "logical" observations arising from applying induction to experience. The observations are logical because they are observations of the *process* of induction rather than the *content* to which induction was applied. Such observations include estimates of the relative frequency of the application of potential acts and their relative rates of success. Induction may also come across surprising facts that cannot be explained using knowledge presently available. When this happens, the logical observations note the circumstances under which this surprise occurred.

From those observations that resulted from inductive reasoning (a result) and the policies we follow that are relevant to how knowledge *ought to be* (a rule) comes the third type of reasoning that we might want to use at some point. *Abduction* enables us to infer what specific problem must have existed in knowledge so as to produce those logical observations (i.e., the case). The effect of abduction is then used to revise knowledge by incorporating new potential acts in knowledge or modifying existing potential acts. Abduction is not a commonly used form of reasoning as it used mainly to create new explanations for how things work and is used in a more speculative way than either deduction or induction.

If a system embodies adequate knowledge for its present environment, then knowledge-creating activities and modifications made through abduction are no longer necessary for the present. Under such circumstances, induction and deduction iteratively operate in a cycle we call the *knowledge performance loop*. The process of induction, operating on past experience, infers (but not with certainty) what acts and rules were operant during that period of experience. The consequential rule arising from induction then becomes the case for a deduction of a contemplated act. The process of reasoning we call deduction works by inferring any number of possible anticipated results that can be obtained at any given time from employing any potential acts, in knowledge, given the particular induced case in question. With satisfactory knowledge, results will actually be attained, thus meeting the ultimate objective of increasing our capacity for reliable action (i.e., action that produces the anticipated result).

On the other hand, when the system's knowledge is inadequate, either from lack of learning or because the environment has changed, the anticipated results are not reliably obtained. In this case, induction and abduction will be called on to iteratively operate in a cycle we call the *inquiry loop*. In actuality, a system may shift back and forth between inquiry and performance loops. In a pure inquiry mode, a leader may sit quietly and contemplate past experience in order to better understand it. But under high stress and rapidly evolving conditions, a leader may just "go with what I have" without taking the time to consider how to do things better. This would be essentially a pure performance mode. In most circumstances, however, there would be a constant shifting between the two.

## A CASE OF CREATING KNOWLEDGE FOR INVENTORY CONTROL

Jayne Smyth works as a production control manager in the manufacturing company known as Blue Sky Widgets, Inc., and is charged with planning monthly and annual production targets. She is currently working on planning for the month of October. As part of the planning process, Jayne previously checked production numbers for last September and found that it was slightly above her projected target. Later, she checks the current finished goods inventory and finds that it is below normal. This sequence of experienced observations present the following element in Jayne's thoughts as she reflects: the case (higher production) and the result (low inventory), from which several simple rules may be induced (see example below). Presently, Jayne has several potential thought-acts in knowledge that she can induce, for example:

| Case | Result | Possible Rule |
|------|--------|---------------|
| High production | Low inventory | Theft has caused a reduction in inventory |
| High production | Low inventory | Increasing demand caused by increasing rates of orders |

This time, Jayne induces that her customer base has bought more product than the average historical demand and that this has resulted in the lowered inventory. This situation (case) has now been abstracted to a more general rule present in her mind (increasing demand). From this case and the potential act in knowledge, she makes the following rule with which to proceed:

| Case | Result | New Rule |
|------|--------|----------|
| Increasing demand | Normal inventory | Increase production to accommodate more orders |

Jayne deduces that if she acts to set a production target for October at a level equal to the average monthly demand, plus the current inventory deficit, plus an extra margin to account for increased demand (rule), she expects to have her inventory back to normal levels by the end of October (result). Jayne sets that target and waits a month to see if her act/target-order produced the result. At the end of October, she checks and sees that inventory is now *above* the normal level by an amount essentially equal to the extra margin she included in last month's target. In other words, this act did not produce the anticipated result. She induces from this new observed fact that production was on target (case) and that the inventory was above normal (result), another potential act currently in knowledge:

| Case | Result | Rule |
|------|--------|------|
| On-target production | High inventory | Decreasing demand |

Demand is now going down. This, in turn, leads to another deduction based on the potential act in knowledge:

| Case | Result | Rule |
|------|--------|------|
| Decreasing demand | Normal inventory | Decrease production |

This time, Jayne sets a reduced monthly target, anticipating that her inventory will finally return to normal. At the end of November, she is dismayed to find that she has again failed to return inventory levels to normal. Notice that this manager has been operating in performance mode, iterating between inductive and deductive inferences.

In response to these surprises, Jayne shifts to inquiry mode and gathers her production and inventory records for the past several years. She again performs induction on these facts and finds that inventory levels and predicted demand have been unreliable, but in a pattern that suggests a new idea—perhaps the demand naturally varies from month to month in a predictable way because customers buy more or less product depending on whether the month contains a major holiday. As a result, she creates (abduction) a new act/rule in her knowledge that includes the holiday factor.

Taking the present inventory level, as well as next month's calendar into account as the case for this act of setting a target, Jayne returns to performance mode and deduces that she will finally get inventory under control. As it turns out, she is successful this time and for most months afterward. These future inductions again provide relevant facts for a future abduction, one that eliminates from knowledge those target-setting acts that do not account for monthly variations in demand, since these have proven significantly less reliable than those that do account for variations in demand.

## SUMMARY

This example of how pragmatic knowledge is created demonstrates that pragmatic knowledge is relentlessly focused on improving performance through the application of reasoning to the process of experimentation. In actual practice, knowledge leaders need not be as formal as Jayne was in the example provided in order to gain benefits or create pragmatic knowledge. Essentially, pragmatic knowledge is created from one's experience—and there are many possible ways to refine the quality of this knowledge through the use of logical inference.

## ADDITIONAL SOURCES

Cavaleri, S., and Reed, F. (2000). "Designing Knowledge-Generating Processes." *Knowledge and Innovation Journal*, vol. I, no. 1. Retrieved from www.kmci.org/media/cavaleridesigningkcprocess.pdf.

Reed, F., and Cavaleri, S. (2001). "Organizational Inquiry: The Search for Effective Knowledge." *Knowledge and Innovation Journal*, vol. I, no. 3. Retrieved from www.kmci.org/media/cavalerireedkiv1n3.pdf.

# Appendix C

## 5-Point Dynamic Mapping for Talent Retention and Development

The *5-Point Dynamic Mapping*® process can also be used as a career compass that helps leaders "release the bees from the jar" by assisting employees in tailoring a career roadmap that is rooted in their innate gifts and that leads to a more satisfying—and productive—work experience. When coordinated with organizational or workgroup 5-Point Dynamic Mapping, this process also increases organizational fit and retention. Moreover, it creates a workplace environment that supports learning and knowledge development.

Consultants in *The Coreporation*, Inc. uses this highly innovative career mapping process to help talented professionals "connect the dots" for success. This methodology helps individuals build their careers in a logical way, each step building naturally upon, integrating, and supporting the step that precedes it. The effect of this process is accumulative—and often is a dramatic departure from where individuals would have arrived without this powerful guide. Here's what executives have said about the results they experienced:

I would recommend this to virtually anyone. . . . There is no one who walks the earth who would not benefit from learning this material. . . . Thought provoking . . . very useful for career, life, and work situations. . . . I have spent the first half of my life wasting much valuable time and energy. The second half of my life will be much improved because of the wisdom I have gained. . . . I would recommend this to anyone whose life has been out of balance and/or is in transition. . . . Perfect for anyone in a transition point in life. . . . Excellent! Excellent! I will continue to use it in my work, relationships, and day-to-day activities . . . a wonderful guide for reevaluating your career, interpersonal relationships, and future goals . . . a great experience. . . . It has taught me about myself and how my habits enhance or sabotage my efforts.

341

This dynamic mapping tool moves with professionals to increase their career *resilience*—that is, it helps them stay the course despite difficulties and also more intelligently adjust their course when necessary. This learned resilience significantly reduces the odds of good workers getting lost along the way—that is, giving up, leaving the company, or settling for unhappy, unproductive careers. When professionals employ the five distinctly different qualities listed in the table, they are able to create better balanced and more successful careers and lives.

| 5-Point Career Mapping | The career gifts of this point |
|---|---|
| 1. Discover Your Core (identity and values) | Strong self-esteem, awareness, and confidence; sense of calmness, well-being, and balance; strong ethics (application); activities hold together |
| 2. Clarify Your Vision (the future you want to create) | Focus on hopes rather than fears about future; observation of thoughts and control of mind; develop more functional beliefs; creative thinking |
| 3. Determine Mission (choose path to focus on) | Clear sense of direction; focused efforts; pride in what you do; ability to set priorities, keep on schedule, and work autonomously |
| 4. Improve Interactions (link with those who help you) | Good communication and presentation skills; high emotional intelligence; respectful interactions; sense of connection and ability to develop helpful community |
| 5. Build Structure (form habits to make you successful) | Careful stewarding of money, work space, living space, and other physical resources; develop more functional life and work habits; take good care of own body |

Both *5-Point Dynamic Mapping* processes (Strategic Mapping and Career Mapping) are based on the cross-cultural template of the five classic elements that have been used for ages to describe the building blocks vital to our well-being. This template is easy to remember and use in career planning because people are already familiar with its image in compasses (that point us in the right direction and keep us on track), clocks (that chime on the quarter hour), baseball diamonds (where you touch all bases for a home run), the Native American medicine wheel (with its center and four directions), the "X" that marks the spot where you start on a map (and where treasure lies), the alchemists' squared circle (to make gold), and spirals in nature.

Steven Alan
Cavaleri

**Steven Cavaleri** is an author, educator, and consultant in the areas of knowledge systems and organizational learning. He is the Editor of the Learning Organization Journal, and Senior Executive Vice President of KMCI (www.kmci.org), a Washington, D.C. based think tank specializing in issues relating to knowledge and innovation. Steven has also worked in several marketing positions in the food and publishing industries. He has served as a consultant to various Fortune 500 companies, including Dow-Jones and IBM. Dr. Cavaleri has written a number of books on the topic of using knowledge, learning, and systems thinking to improve business performance. He is co-author, with Krzysztof Obloj of the University of Warsaw, of the award-winning book *Management Systems*. His most recent book, *Inside Knowledge*, with co-author David Fearon, is a fictional tale that illustrates how pragmatic knowledge can be created to improve business performance.

Dr. Cavaleri has been a Visiting Scholar in the System Dynamics Group at MIT's Sloan School of Management. He holds a Ph.D. from Rensselaer Polytechnic Institute and is a Certified Systems Integrator in the Institute of Industrial Engineers. Steven is a co-developer of the patent-pending Policy Synchronization Method for using knowl-edge to drive innovation in organizations. Steven has over twenty-five years of university teaching experience in the area of business strategy, and currently teaches at Central Connecticut State Univer-sity. He is also an avid golfer and practitioner of Tai Chi.

Sharon Seivert

**Sharon Seivert** serves concurrently as President of The Corepora-tion, Inc. (an international business consulting, training, and testing firm [visit www.thecoreporation.com for more information]) and its non-profit affiliate, Core Learning Services, Inc. (an educational ser-vices organization). She is the author of *5-Point Dynamic Mapping for Leaders* (2005), *The Balancing Act* (2001), and *Working from Your Core* (1998), and also co-author of *Magic at Work* (1995).

Sharon's business background includes having served as the CEO of a ground-breaking Group Health Plan, VP of an innovative think-tank, Executive Director of a regional health center, Manager of political campaigns, a TQM and OD consultant, and an Executive Coach. Her clients range from large and small corporations in diverse industries (financial services, high tech, bio-tech/pharmaceutical, retail, professional service firms, and manufacturing) to organizations in the non-profit sector (federal and state governments, healthcare, research or service organizations, and universities), to entrepreneur-ial start-ups, to private executive clients. Sharon, who lives in Cam-bridge, Massachusetts, is also an accomplished musician who has written hundreds of songs and recorded numerous discs.

# INDEX

Page numbers with "t" denote tables; those with "f" denote figures